Mt. Ararat
CASPIAN SEA
Here lay
ME
where some of th
(The Ten Tribes) were driven
in 722 B.C and later los
Nineveh
Halah
Asshur
Here some of the Israelites were held captive after 722 B.C.
gion came to be called
POTAMIA
tween the Rivers
This is the great River Tigris
ver Euphrates
This region was called
ELAM
Shushan
where Esther was queen
Babylon
CHALDEA or BABYLONIA
RT
Here the Jews were held captive from 586-536 B.C.
Ur
where Abraham was born
This is now dry land
10 0 20 40 60 80 100
Statute Miles
Here lies
PERSIA
PERSIAN GULF
ient World
the
criptures
Rothkowitz
Browne

Samuel Choo

THE GRAPHIC BIBLE

THE GRAPHIC BIBLE

By LEWIS BROWNE

In "The Graphic Bible," Lewis Browne presents the story of the Old and New Testaments, from Abraham to Paul, in a swift and unusually interesting style. The text is accompanied by nearly one hundred "animated maps," to show at a glance not only when but just where the great events of the Bible took place.

This book is printed in large, readable type, contains a handy index to text and maps, and the end papers are maps of the ancient world of the Scriptures.

"The Graphic Bible" is fascinating reading and most helpful to every Bible reader, student and teacher.

LEWIS BROWNE

Lewis Browne, the noted writer, is author of "This Believing World," "Stranger than Fiction," and many other books. He was born in London, England and did post-graduate work at Yale. Since 1926 he has devoted his time to writing.

By LEWIS BROWNE

STRANGER THAN FICTION:
A Short History of the Jews

THIS BELIEVING WORLD:
An Account of the Religions of Mankind

THAT MAN HEINE:
A Biography

THE ADVENTURES OF ANCIENT ISRAEL:
From Abraham to the Dispersion in Maps and Charts

THE GRAPHIC BIBLE:
Genesis to Revelation in Maps and Charts

The Graphic Bible

FROM GENESIS TO REVELATION
IN ANIMATED MAPS & CHARTS

BY

Lewis Browne

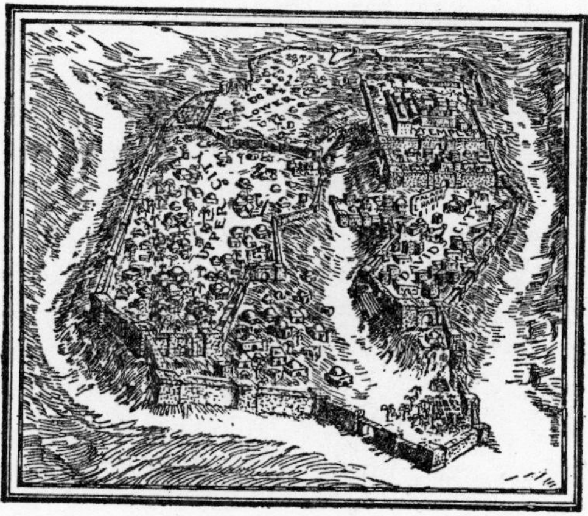

New York · The Macmillan Company · 1944

Set up and electrotyped.
Published, August, 1928.
Reprinted, October, 1928.
Reprinted, January, 1929.
Reissued April, 1932.
Reissued October, 1935.
Reissued June, 1937.
Reprinted August, 1938.
Reprinted March, 1939.
Reprinted December, 1939.
Reprinted March, 1941.
Reprinted January, 1942.
Reprinted December, 1942.
Reprinted April, 1944.

Printed in the United States of America by
THE CORNWALL PRESS, INC.

TO MY FATHER

The first artist I ever knew;

AND TO MY MOTHER

The first historian.

CONTENTS

THE GRAPHIC BIBLE

BY WAY OF INTRODUCTION

"BUT," cried little Pauline, "it's all *so* mixed up! I simply can't make head or tail of it."

"Yes," agreed her cousin, Bess, "it's—it's all a pudding of funny names sprinkled with 'begats'." The others chuckled, and Bess smiled at her own brightness.

"That's just what I think too," chimed in Blanche. "Our Sunday-school teacher says the Bible's all true; but just the same, none of it seems *real!*"

That rather perplexed me, and I asked the little girl to explain herself.

"Well, Uncle, it's this way: every time—" But just then the motor-car horn was heard honking outside, and, knowing they were already almost late for Sunday-school, the children hurriedly gathered up their hats and Bibles and scampered off to the waiting machine.

But later in the day we returned to the discussion so abruptly interrupted that morning. The children still felt that the Bible was dull and all mixed up, and, since I was only their uncle, they took no pains to conceal their feeling. Indeed, one or two of them grew even vehement on the subject. I tried to reason with them. I tried to tell them that if the Bible seemed dull, it was not the Bible's fault but their own or their teacher's. Indeed, I went so far as to say that to my mind the Bible was the most exciting story-book I had ever read. But that was too much for them.

"Whew, Uncle!" jeered Arnold almost rudely. "You ought to read 'Treasure Island'!"

"But I *have* read it," I replied. "Tell me, Arnold, why do you find 'Treasure Island' more exciting? Do you think it is truer than the Bible?"

"No, not exactly truer, Uncle. But somehow it seems more real."

"Why?" I asked. "Doesn't it tell about a place quite as foreign to you as Palestine?"

"No," the lad replied with assurance.

"But why?"

"Well, I suppose it's because I know my way around on Treasure Island. You see, Uncle, *there's a map inside the cover of the book!*"

2

The idea for this "Graphic Bible" did not first come to me as a result of that remark of my nephew. I rather think it came to me much earlier, and as a result not of a single bright remark but of a series of trying experiences. It came to me when I myself was a Sunday-school teacher and had to contend week after week with a roomful of children who did not even pretend to be interested in what I sought to teach them. They were frankly bored, and seemed able to keep awake only by dint of incessant fidgetting, giggling, or passing of notes. For a whole year the torment continued, and

Sundays became to me days of unspeakable dread. No matter what tricks I tried, what games I played, somehow I could not arouse in those children any sustained interest in the Bible tales.

And then, almost by accident, I hit on the idea of drawing crude maps on the blackboard. They were exceedingly crude, especially in the beginning. I used to scrawl them hurriedly while I talked to the class, cluttering them up with little hills and trees and forts and ricocheting arrows as the lesson progressed. But their grotesque inaccuracy seemed to make them only the more interesting to the children. At times I did not use the board at all, but instead made a sort of relief map on the floor. The desk over here became Mt. Gilboa, the chairs over there represented the hills on which the Philistines were encamped, and the chasm in between we called the Valley of Jezreel. The radiator across the room was the cauldron of the Witch of Endor, and the bookcase in the corner became the fortress of Beth-Shean. And with the topography thus indicated, the class and I proceeded to fight out the battle between Saul and the enemy.

This book is in a measure the outgrowth of that happy discovery made ten years ago. It is an attempt to make the Bible story vivid and actual by depicting it in terms of space as well as time. I can well understand my young nephew's feeling that the presence of a map in his edition of "Treasure Island" made the whole romance real to him. A map does give one a sense of reality—that is, if it is the right sort of map. Those modern colored things with names printed all over them in differences sizes of type—they're almost useless. They are neat and proper and accurate, but somehow they don't live. They tell everything but say very little. And the little they do say is often misleading. A friend of mine assures me that once, while flying from Constantinople to Bucharest, he heard a little girl in the cabin cry out above the muffled roar of the engine: "But no, Mama; that *can't* be Bulgaria down there! See, it's quite green—and on the map Bulgaria is always yellow!"

No, the ordinary modern map with its regular type and flat coloring is hardly calculated to give one a sense of reality. For that purpose the old-fashioned map is far superior. With its dolphins and mountains and galleons and trees it may be absurdly inaccurate—but at least it is not dead. That is why in this book I have strained quite consciously after the technique of the ancient cartographers. The maps—with one obvious exception—are all drawn to scale, and coast-lines and rivers have been traced with approximate accuracy. Of course, a navigator would have a perilous time if he attempted to steer his course by no better charts than those in this book; but a reader may quite safely guide his ideas by them. Aside from the more or less careful tracing of the outlines, however, no sustained effort at accuracy has been so much as attempted. The little fortresses like the great ships, the sporting dolphins like the drooping palms, are obviously all out of proportion. But that, I am sure, must only heighten the effectiveness of the maps.

What is needed is living actuality rather than dead accuracy in our lay study of the Bible. If our Sunday-school sessions are to be more than recurrent hours of boredom, we must come to realize that most of the Bible tells of real men who lived in real places. Jerusalem, the Jordan, Mt. Carmel, Nazareth—these must therefore be made more than mere names to us. The whole of Palestine must become as real to us as the county in which we live. But it is not easy to bring that about. Not until one has actually been in the Land of Israel can one quite realize that such a region actually exists. At least, so it was with me.

3

I can still quite vividly remember my emotions the morning I first set eyes on Palestine. All through the night the train had rattled and screeched its way across the Wilderness—the very Wilderness through which the ancient Hebrews dragged their way full forty years. But when the dawn came we were already there—there in the Land of Israel. And I wondered if it was not all a fantasy—wondered if those palms and olive-groves and little flat-roofed houses were not mere daubs on a canvas drop. The sun climbed up behind the rolling weathered hills, raining fierce heat on our caravan. Out of the carriage windows we could see bedraggled Arabs ploughing in the fields with oxen, or guiding strings of camels along the roads, or wandering with flocks of sheep and goats. We stopped at wayside stations half-covered with wind-swept sand; we passed through palm-groves, over dry river-beds, around high sand-dunes, by thronged villages. Through Gaza, Ashdod, Jabneh, Lydda—through all those ancient towns we careered on raucously: but still it seemed a fantasy. And then at last we reached our journey's end: Jerusalem. High on top of the hills it stood, a wondrous thing of yellow walls and grim gray towers and cluttered domes and minarets. And that seemed most unreal of all. For years I had read of Jerusalem; for centuries my people had mourned its fall and wept for its redemption. Yet now that my eyes were filled with it, I could not believe it to be there. Not until I stood in the very shadow of its walls, and ran my fingers over the crumbling boulders, could I believe a real city to be there. And then a gasp almost of incredulity left me. "It is true!" I cried. *"It is all real!"*

Perhaps a complete conviction of the realness of the Bible scene is only possible when one has thus actually laid eyes on it. But only the rare Bible student can be expected to make a pilgrimage to Palestine. The others must seek the conviction solely through imagination, and that is no easy task. We dwell in lands far distant and different from those of the orient—indeed, we are almost in another world. Our imagination must be sharply stimulated if we are ever to be able to picture the Bible scene from afar. And it is in the hope of providing a little of that stimulation that I have drawn this book of maps.

4

When I originally planned this work I thought it would contain no text whatsoever. I hoped the maps would prove self-explanatory. But before I had drawn many of them I saw they were inadequate, for they quite failed to reveal the flow of the Bible story. That is why I have added so extensive a written text. Nothing is more moving to me than the fine dramatic flow of the whole Bible narrative. The Scriptures are not a mere "pudding of funny names sprinkled with 'begats'," and if they impress many people as such, it is probably because they have been told to believe the Scriptures rather than made to understand them. There is a grand swing to the Bible, a majestic surge. It is more than a collection of chapters and verses, more than a disjointed list of names and places; essentially it is a coherent epic. When read intelligently the Bible reveals itself as the immortal epic of a people's confused, faltering, but indomitable struggle after a nobler life in a happier world.

The main incidents in that epic are recounted in the text in this book, and they are recounted quite without debate as to their historical truth. I have sought to follow the Scriptures quite literally, and have purposely avoided being either apologist or critic. For in this book I am attempting not to justify but to simplify the Bible. Those who care to believe the whole story, may believe; and those who are moved to doubt it, may doubt; but all should at least know the story.

5

Help in the preparation of this book came from many sources. First there were the atlases I consulted, of which the most valuable was the "Atlas of the Historical Geography of the Holy Land" (London, 1915), by the great Bible scholar, Dr. George Adam Smith, and the royal cartographer, Dr. J. G. Bartholomew. I found Townsend MacCoun's "Bible Atlas" (New York, 1912), to be handier and more informative, but far less dependable. Hermann Guthe's "Bibelatlas" (2nd edition, Leipzig, 1926), the most recent German work on the subject, was most accurate of all, but also least stimulating.

After the atlases the most generous sources of information were certain geographies, chief among them: Smith's "Historical Geography of the Holy Land;" Kent's "Biblical Geography and History;" Paton's "Jerusalem in Bible Times;" Stapfer's "Palestine in the Time of Christ;" and Ramsay's "The Cities of Saint Paul."

But for aid in the execution of this work I am indebted not alone to books but even more to people. Of these I must mention first my friend Dr. Hendrik Willem Van Loon, in whose studio at Westport I first tried my hand at illustration. More immediately I am grateful to Mr. Marcus Rothkowitz for assistance in the execution of the maps in this volume, to Miss Ruth Kayton for aid in the preparation of the manuscript, to Mr. Max Maccoby for correcting the proofs. Finally my profound thanks are due to a number of friends versed in Bible lore, who have generously gone over parts of the manuscript and have helped to free it of those many little errors which almost inevitably creep into a work of this character.

THE JEWISH SCRIPTURES

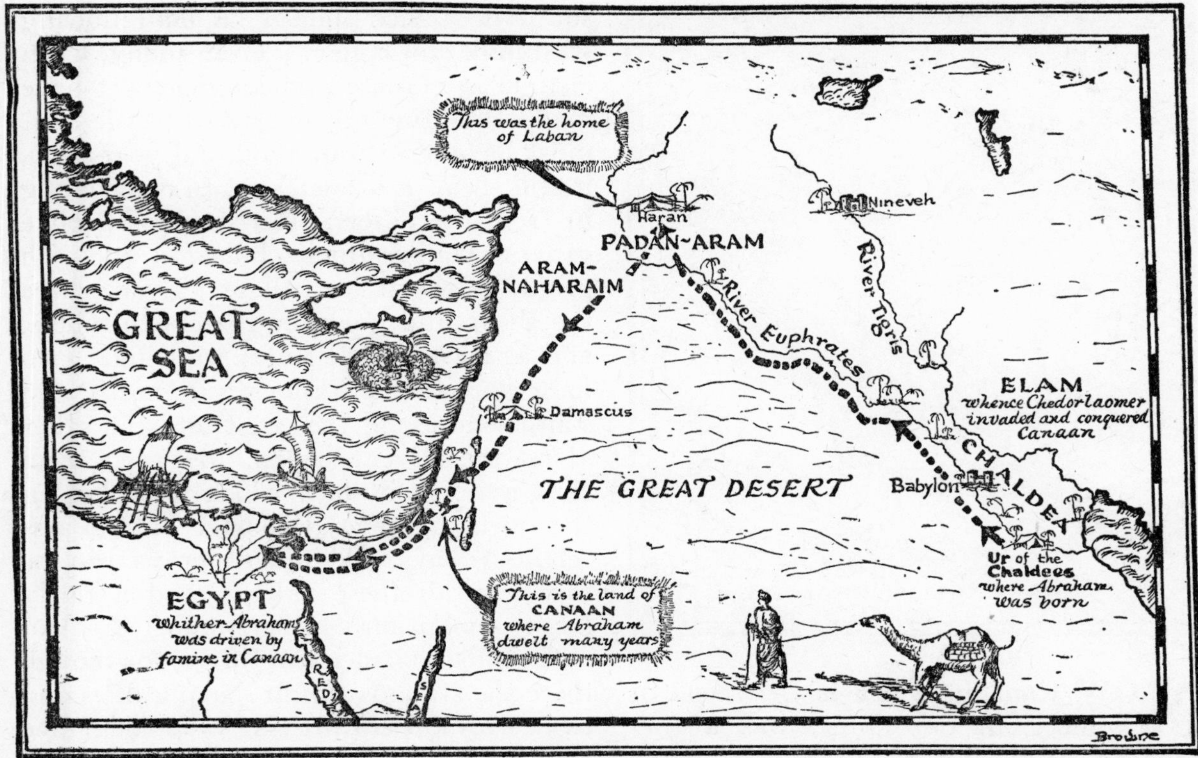

"IN the beginning God created the heaven and earth." With that event the Bible story opens, and with that event, too, this atlas of the Bible should commence. But how is one to draw a map showing just where in space the heaven and earth were formed? Indeed, how is one to draw maps showing where *any* of the events in the first chapters of Genesis occurred? Where, for instance, was the Garden of Eden situated, or the Land of Nod, or the Tower of Babel? That is why this atlas begins not with the first but with the eleventh chapter of Genesis, wherein are recorded the first wanderings of Abram.

Abram—later named Abraham—was the father of the Chosen People. He came of one of the many tribes of half-savage bedouins who once roved on the fringe of the fertile river-lands which stretch like a huge crescent across the north of the Arabian Desert. His original home seems to have been Ur of the Chaldees, which lay at the extreme eastern end of this "Fertile Crescent;" but when grown to manhood he trekked with the rest of his tribe hundreds of miles up the River Euphrates to Haran, in Padan-Aram (which today is in the region of Aleppo). There the tribe settled down and lived in the manner of all the other pastoral folk of the time. But after a few years, Abram, at the command of God, struck off with his own household and settled far south in Canaan. For God had told him that Canaan would be the homeland of his descendants.

NOW Canaan, which is the scene of almost all our story, was a tiny country. Indeed, it was little more than a strip of grassland on the edge of the desert. Even when we think of it as Palestine, or the Holy Land, and add to it the hill-country east of the River Jordan, the whole area is still not even one-sixth that of England and Wales, as can be seen by the map above. In America the entire land could be tucked away in the little State of Vermont. From north to south it measures little more than 150 miles, and from the Mediterranean on the west to the desert across the Jordan on the east it is never more than 100 miles wide. In a motor-car you can go from end to end of the country today between breakfast and tea!

Yet though small, Canaan was greatly coveted because it was moist and fruitful. Compared with the desert on the east and south it seemed indeed "a land flowing with milk and honey." Even today, when change in climate and long neglect have made Palestine not nearly so fertile as it must have been four thousand years ago, it still seems a blessed spot to one coming in from the desert. Vineyards and olive groves clamber up its hillsides, and rich grain grows in its valleys. Everywhere the sheep and goats find grass to nibble, and at least a little water to drink. Two long and fertile valleys run north and south, one along the coast and the other along the River Jordan. Between them rises a range of hills which is broken in the north by several shorter but no less fertile valleys. Abundant crops can be raised in all these valleys, and a fairly large population can be supported. And in the hills, too, men can thrive, for though there the streams run in sharp gullies and extensive agriculture is impossible, the limestone knolls provide excellent pasturage for sheep. To us, who dwell in broad lands filled with plenty, Palestine may seem no larger than a county, and of but little allure. We must remember, however, that human standards have altered tremendously during the past four thousand years, especially here in the western part of the world. Life in the ancient Orient was far harder than it is among us. Men there were glad to have a bare crust to eat; they went delirious at the sight of clear water to drink. When Abram came to Canaan he was no magnificent rajah traveling in the luxury of a conducted tour. To him that stretch of green 'twixt the Jordan and the Great Sea must have seemed immensely desirable, and more than worthy of being his seed's Promised Land.

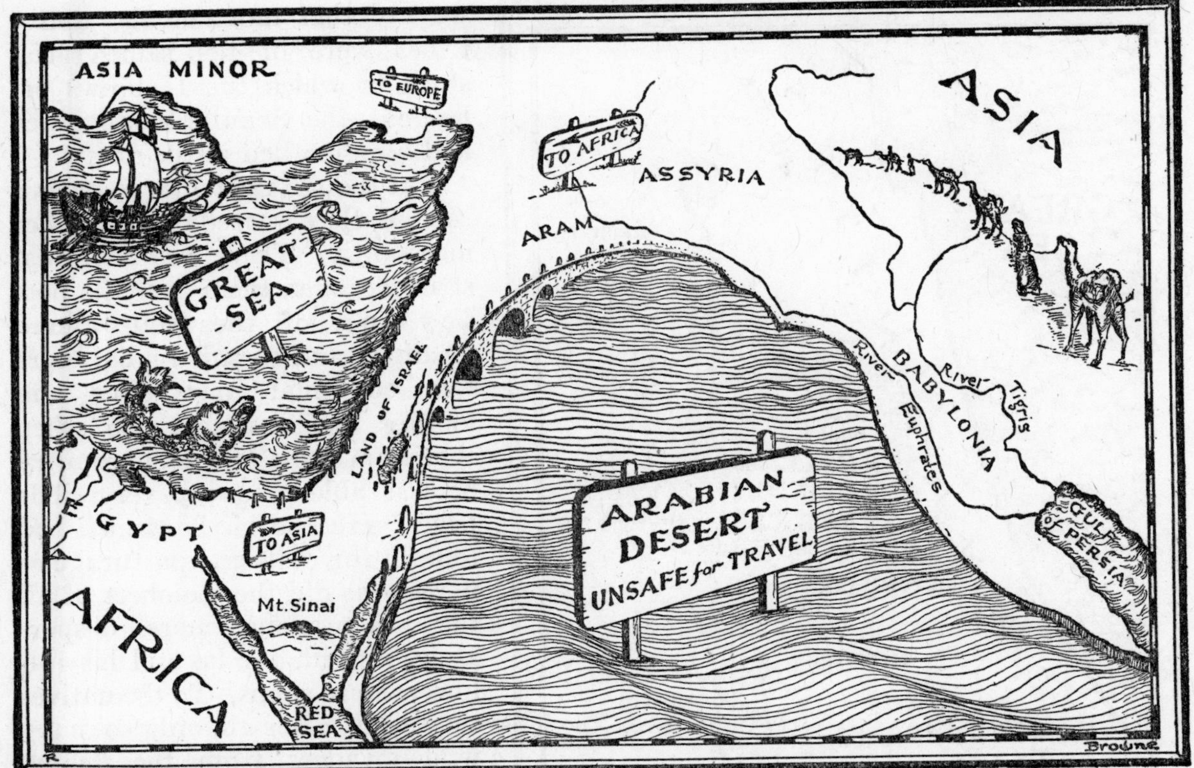

TO Abraham the chief physical attraction of Canaan may have been its fertility; but later the region was found to possess quite another and greater virtue. It was so situated as to become in later years the very center of the ancient world. The great empires of olden times grew up either in Africa on the banks of the Nile, or in Asia on the banks of the Tigris and the Euphrates, or in Europe on the Mediterranean coast; and the only firm and open highway between these three regions ran through Palestine. The little land lay like a bridge between the continents, for on one side of it was the Great Sea, and on the other there stretched the Great Desert. Therefore Palestine could not help but become the most vital bit of territory in the ancient world. Every trading prince and conquering king had to pass through it at some time or another, and the country never ceased to ring with the tramp of caravans and armies. And thus is explained a good deal that the descendants of Abraham were destined to learn and suffer in Palestine. Settled on the hills overlooking the highway from Egypt to Mesopotamia, they could watch the pageant of the Gentile nations as it streamed by incessantly, for the world was forever in their midst. But that had its grave disadvantages, for it meant that the children of Israel were never left alone. It was as impossible for them to live in peace in Palestine as it would be to have a picnic in the middle of Broadway.

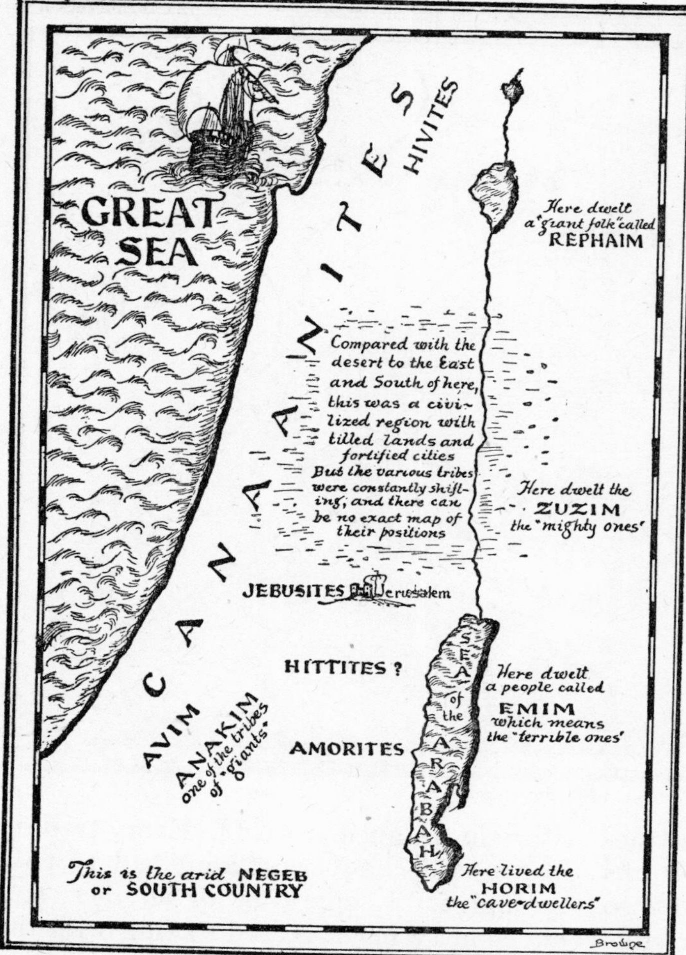

CANAAN, because of its fertility, was already a well-settled land when Abraham came there. Many of its valleys were tilled, and not a few of its hilltops were crowned with walled villages. We do not know for certain whence its earlier inhabitants came, but in all probability it was from the great Arabian Desert. The names of some of the tribes—for instance, the *Emim,* which means "Terrible Ones," or the *Anakim,* "Giants"—tell us about the appearance of the tribesmen, not their origin. We are fairly safe, however, when we say that most of the native tribes were of the same racial stock to which the Hebrews belonged—the Semitic stock which had been cradled in the desert.

Yet though the tribes were thus related, they warred on each other incessantly. There was continual strife between them over the possession of the well-watered meadows and fortified hills; there was continual marauding and looting and carnage. So when Abraham came into their country he was able to enjoy very little peace. He and his herdsmen had to fight for wells and pasturage as fiercely as did the members of all the other clans—more desperately, indeed, for he and his followers were aliens. To the natives they were, after all, only so many wild invaders from the desert. The land was already too small to support even those who dwelt in it by right of birth; there seemed to be no room for newcomers.

But this did not halt the Hebrews. They were doughty warriors, and Abraham, their chieftain, knew he was the chosen of the Lord. This little land, he believed, was his by right of divine election. So, room or no room, he would not budge. Once he was driven by famine to take refuge in Egypt, where the River Nile gave water to thousands of miles of meadow-land. But he did not remain for long in Egypt. No, as soon as conditions made it possible, he trekked back to Canaan and there he remained all the rest of his days.

THE Hebrews remained in Canaan, living off their flocks and herds like the rest of the pastoral tribes in the land. But they refused to merge with these other tribes despite that they were so like them. When their chieftain's son, Isaac, was ready to take a wife, his father sent all the way to Padan-Aram—about 450 miles!—to get a Hebrew maiden for him. And, years later, Isaac was in turn exceedingly anxious that his own son, Jacob, should also seek his wife in Padan-Aram. Intermarriage with the Canaanites was counted altogether a crime.

Abraham died full of years, and Isaac succeeded him as chieftain of the Hebrews in Canaan. He and his followers dwelt in what was called the South Country, a sandy region on the edge of the desert. Perhaps they were unable to penetrate farther north, where the soil was much more fertile, because the Canaanites there were better able to keep newcomers out. Even in the South Country, which was a sort of No-Man's Land, the Hebrews had their fierce battles to fight. Genesis 26:19-20 reports what may have been a common incident in their daily life: "And Isaac's servants digged in the valley, and found there a well of springing water. And the herdsmen of Gerar did strive with Isaac's herdsmen, saying, The water is ours." There must have been much of such "striving" until finally Isaac made treaties with certain of the neighboring sheikhs. (The word "sheikh"—which is pronounced *sheych*—is the Arabic for chieftain. It does not even remotely connote the handsome, impetuous lover in desert garb who is so popular a figure in our cinemas.) Thereafter Isaac dwelt in peace at an oasis named Beer-Sheba, and not until he was near death did he move again. He went then to Hebron, which had been the central camp of the Hebrews during Abraham's time. There, in the Cave of Machpelah, Abraham and his wife, Sarah, lay buried. And when Isaac died, he too was buried there.

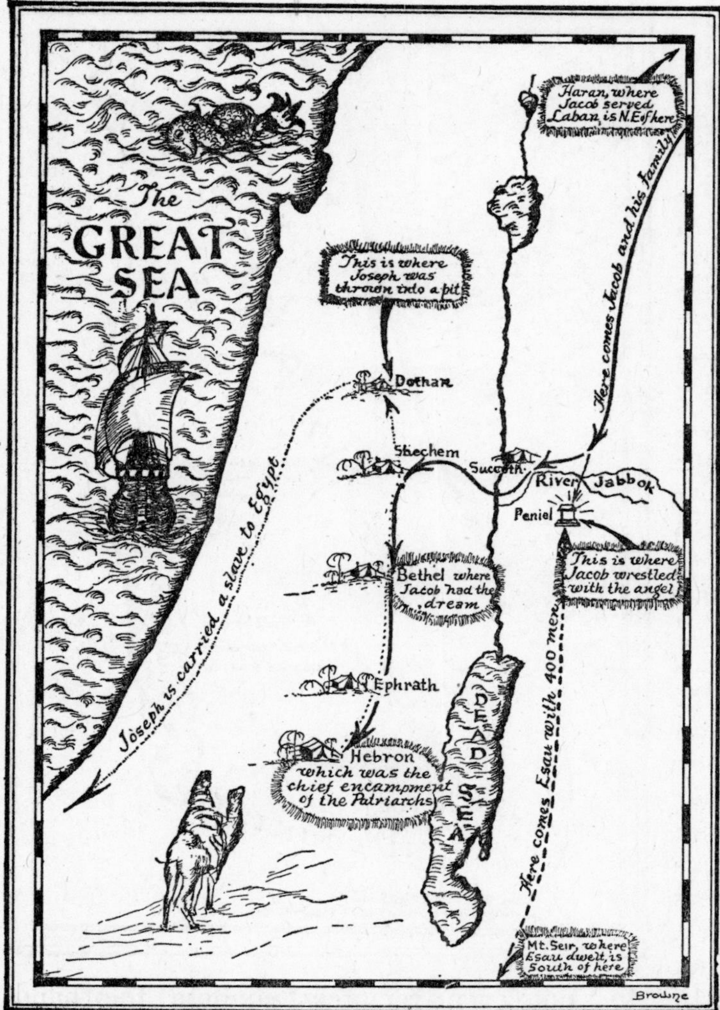

JACOB, although he was the younger son of Isaac, became the chieftain of the Hebrews when his father died. His elder brother, Esau, was a wild fellow who took native women for his wives and became the father of a race of marauders down in the wilderness of Mt. Seir. Jacob managed to trick Esau out of the blessing which belonged to the first-born, and then fled north to Haran, his mother's native land. There he joined the clan of his uncle, Laban, and with his labor bought two of Laban's daughters as his wives. And with the aid of God, Jacob so prospered that soon he had a clan of his own. He then returned to Canaan, for that was, after all, his real homeland. On the way back he was met by Esau, who had marched up from Seir with 400 of his followers; but there were no hostilities, for Esau had forgiven his brother.

Jacob led his clan across the Jordan and settled near Shechem; but before long an unpleasantness with the natives forced him to seek new pasturage for his flocks. He moved south, stopping at Bethel, which was a holy place to him because there he had had a wondrous vision when on his flight to Haran. (It was still an important shrine many centuries later, as we shall learn farther on in this book.) At Bethel Jacob renewed his covenant with Jehovah, and then moved on to Ephrath, where he buried his beloved wife Rachel. Finally he got as far south as Hebron, where he laid eyes once more on his aged father, Isaac. And in Hebron he stayed many years, ruling there, after his father died, as chieftain of the whole Hebrew clan, and prospering all the time. Perhaps he would have remained in Hebron till his death had it not been for his son Joseph. But for that part of the story we must go to the next page.

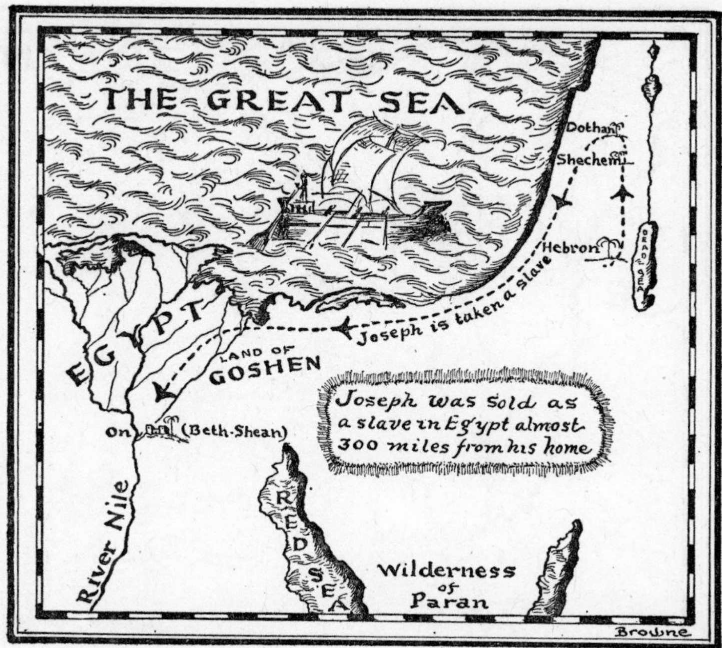

JACOB had many sons, but of them all his most favored was the young one, Joseph. Joseph was unlike his brethren, for he was a dreamer and an ambitious youth, while they were stolid, hard-headed fellows content to be mere herdsmen. And therefore they all distrusted and envied Joseph. Now it came to pass that one day his father sent the boy to see how his brothers were faring, for they had gone off to the north with the tribal flocks. The Hebrew herdsmen evidently found it necessary at times to wander far from the tribal encampment at Hebron in order to find fresh pasturage. In this particular instance they were reported to have gone to Shechem, which must have been at least a two- or three-days' journey away. Joseph followed them thither, only to learn, however, that they had wandered still farther north. So he followed after them and found them at Dothan. But when his brethren saw him coming, instead of welcoming him, they took him prisoner and sold him to a caravan of Ishmaelite or Midianite traders going to Egypt. By these traders he was in turn sold as a slave to an Egyptian official named Potiphar, and bitter were the experiences which Joseph then encountered. False accusation was brought against him by Potiphar's wife, and Joseph was flung into prison. But through the intervention of Jehovah he won his release after a time, and then actually rose to be viceroy of all Egypt. He forewarned the king—or pharaoh, as each king was called in Egypt—that a famine was coming, and urged him to store up grain in advance. And when ensuing events proved the value of Joseph's counsel, he was given the highest honors in the land.

Now the famine came also to Canaan, and old Jacob, hearing there was grain stored up in Egypt, sent his sons to buy some there. And thus were the brethren brought face to face with Joseph once more. But they had long repented of their crime, and Joseph took the sweetest revenge by returning good for evil. He obtained royal permission for all of them to settle in the fertile meadows of Egypt. Jacob, still the chieftain of the Hebrews, did not hesitate to join in the long trek through the desert, even though he was a very old man by now. He settled in a region called Goshen, and there his descendants continued to live for generations.

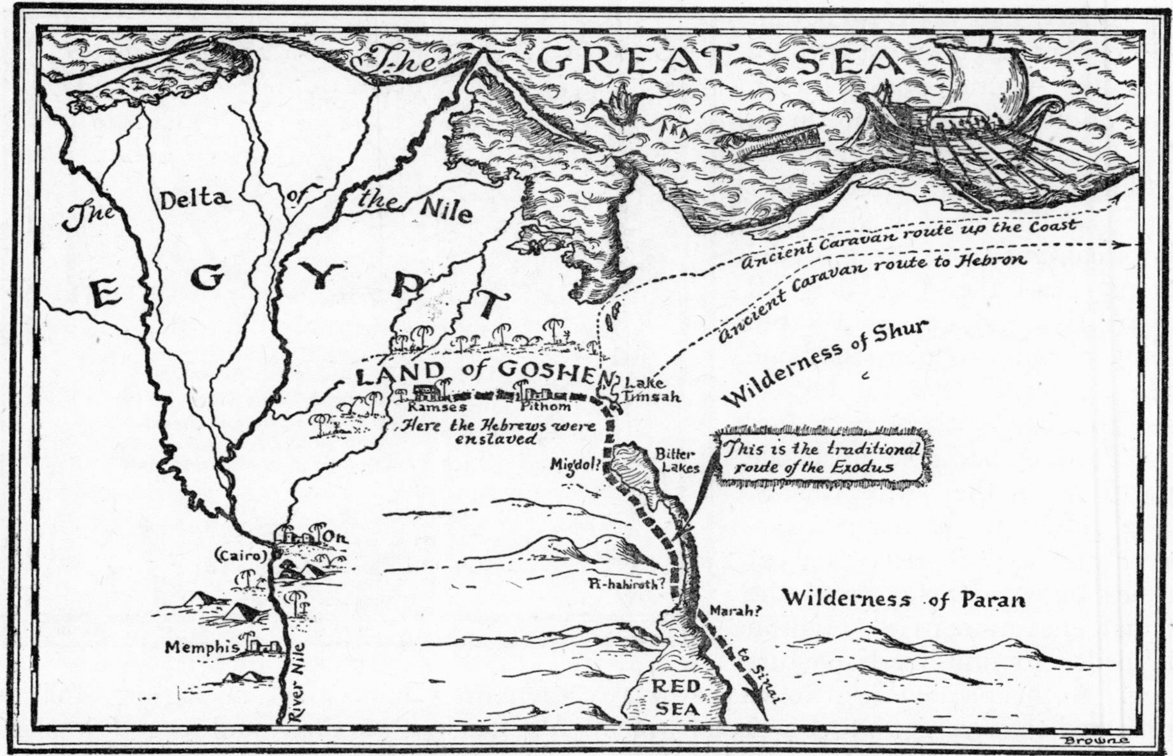

SO long as Joseph was still alive, the Hebrews were left at peace in Goshen. Dwelling in the generous delta of the River Nile, they prospered exceedingly and multiplied until "the land was filled with them." But when Joseph died, and his service to the country was forgotten, the Egyptians turned on the alien folk and made them slaves. Taskmasters lashed them to work on those huge buildings, the ruins of which are still to be seen in Egypt. They built "treasure-houses," that is, fortresses or garrisons, for the ruling Pharaoh. (The ruins of two of these "treasure-houses," Pithom and Ramses, have been located in modern times, and are indicated on the map above.) Bitter indeed was the travail of the Hebrews, for their masters were without mercy.

But then Jehovah had mercy on His people and sent them a leader named Moses to deliver them from bondage. The story of that deliverance is recounted in the Book of Exodus, and it is a story full of wonders. Moses had to bring down ten fell plagues upon the Egyptians before at last Pharaoh would let the Hebrews go. Even then the tyrant was not sufficiently humbled, for immediately after the slaves departed he gathered his army and set out to recapture them. The runaways, heavily laden with the booty they had taken from their former masters, had not been able to travel fast; indeed they were still no farther than the Bitter Lakes when Pharaoh was almost on them. And they were in despair for, as can be seen on the map, the Red Sea barred their one way of escape. But Jehovah came to their aid and miraculously parted the sea for them. The waters were swept away so that the Hebrews could cross over on the dry sea-bottom. But when the Egyptian army with all its chariots and horses tried to follow, the waters rushed back to their place and the whole host was drowned. And thus were the children of Israel delivered from bondage.

The course of the runaways can be followed on the map on the next page. In a slow, tortuous procession they pushed on toward Mt. Sinai, which was one of a little range of volcanic mountains almost 200 miles southeast of Goshen. It was a gruelling journey, for the Hebrews were not accustomed to desert travel. Food gave out; there was no water; the desert tribes attacked them. Very soon the runaways began to wish they had never left Egypt, where they had always had at least enough food to eat. But Jehovah was with them, and by Moses' hand He performed miracles which enabled the wanderers to reach Mt. Sinai. At this holy spot Jehovah entered into an agreement with the people, promising to care for them and prosper them on condition that they kept His commandments. The Israelites remained at Sinai about a year, and then, led by Moses, they set out for Canaan, their Promised Land. They straggled along in a northerly direction across the desert until they reached an oasis named Kadesh-Barnea, and there they encamped while awaiting the report of the spies they had sent in advance to Canaan. But when at last the report came, the Israelites were terrified. Of the twelve spies only two, Joshua and Caleb, brought back an encouraging story. The rest declared Canaan to be a land of mighty fortresses inhabited by tribes of giants!

One can well understand the reason for so exaggerated a report. The Canaanites, living in a fertile land, were well-nourished and rather advanced in the art of war. To the half-starved bedouins they must indeed have appeared a fearsome folk.

The Israelites utterly lacked the courage to attempt an invasion and whined with chagrin that they had ever left Egypt. Whereupon Jehovah was wroth and swore that none of that generation save the heroic Joshua and Caleb would be privileged ever to enter Canaan. The Israelites had to return to the terrible Wilderness of Paran and wander there thirty-eight years. Apparently they became merely another of the many wretched bedouin peoples roving about in that wasteland.

But at last, when the next generation grew to manhood, the aimless wandering ceased. The young Hebrews, born and reared in the fierce want and wild freedom of the desert, had the courage of desperadoes. They were sick of the Wilderness with its blistering heat by day and freezing winds at night. So, led by the aged Moses, they struck out anew toward Canaan. They tried to enter the land directly through the South Country, but discovered their way barred by the native tribes roving in that region. There was nothing left for them, therefore, save to make a wide detour to Elath, then around Mt. Hor, and thus on through Moab to the River Jordan. It was a long journey, and hostile tribes infested every mile of the way. But the Hebrews had by now become a hardy and desperate people. No matter how heavy the odds against them, they could not be stayed.

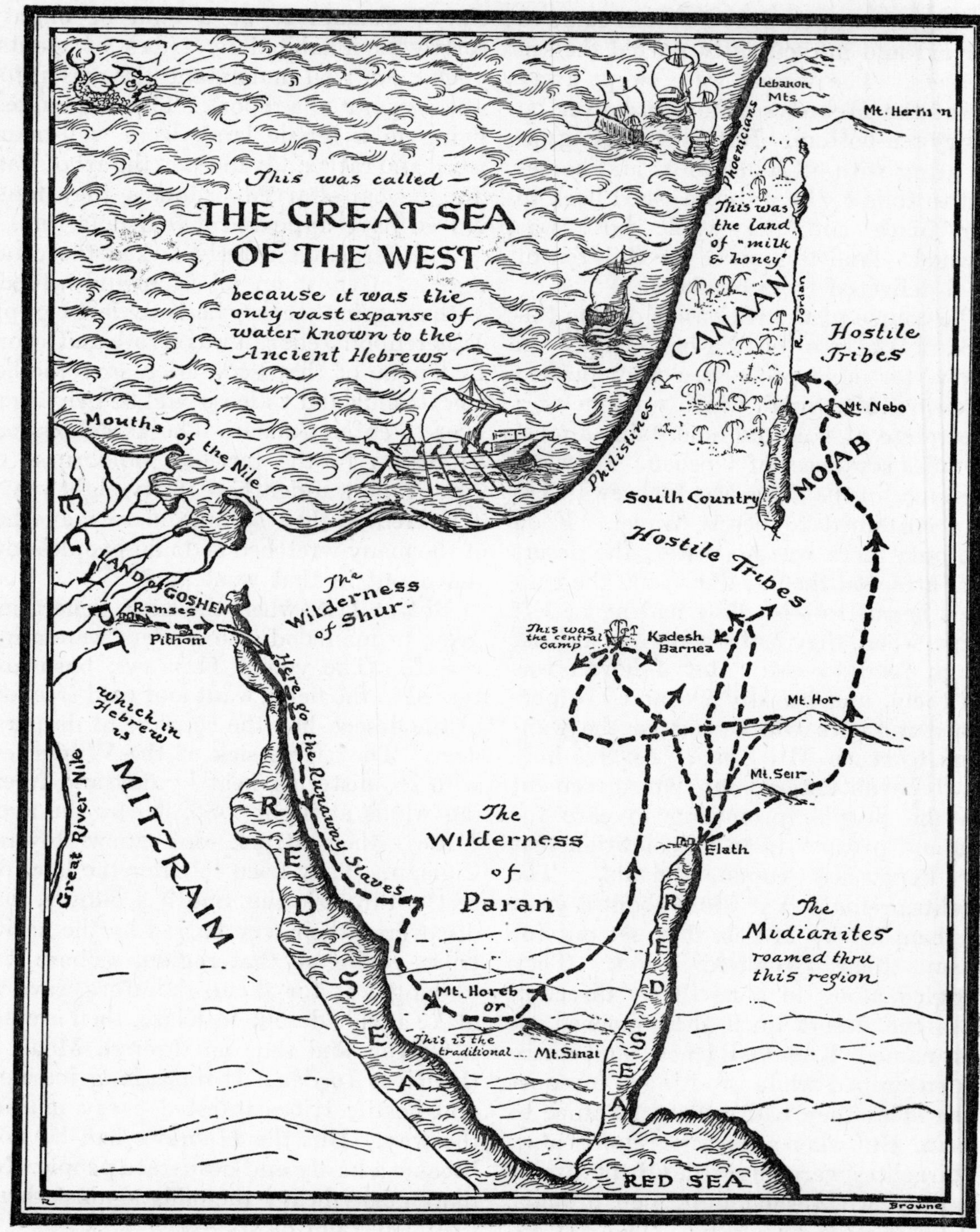
This was called —
THE GREAT SEA
OF THE WEST
because it was the only vast expanse of water known to the Ancient Hebrews
Lebanon Mts.
Mt. Hermon
Phoenicians
This was the land of "milk & honey"
CANAAN
R. Jordan
Hostile Tribes
Mt. Nebo
Philistines
MOAB
South Country
Hostile Tribes
Mouths of the Nile
EGYPT
LAND of GOSHEN
Ramses
Pithom
The Wilderness of Shur
This was the central camp
Kadesh Barnea
Mt. Hor
Mt. Seir
which in Hebrew is
MITZRAIM
Great River Nile
Here go the Runaway Slaves
RED SEA
The Wilderness of Paran
Elath
The Midianites roamed thru this region
Mt. Horeb or
This is the traditional ... Mt. Sinai
RED SEA
RED SEA
Browne

THE Moabites, who at the time were a weakened nation, did not dare resist the wild Hebrews as they came plunging up from the desert. But the Amorites, who had but recently conquered the region north of the River Arnon, were less docile. The Amorites had two kings, Sihon and Og. Sihon ruled over the southern kingdom, Gilead, but he did not wait for the Hebrews to invade his realm. He went out to meet them at Jahaz, on Moabite soil, and was utterly defeated. The victorious Hebrews then swept up north and forthwith invaded the rich pasture-land of Bashan, which was ruled by Og. At Edrei they met Og's army, defeated it, and slew the king. And then the Hebrews were virtually the masters of all the region north of the Arnon and east of the Jordan. The Moabites and Midianites, in a belated effort to resist the invaders, employed a magician named Balaam to curse the Hebrews; but Jehovah turned his words to blessings, and the conspiring races were severely punished. And then Moses, who had led the Hebrews all this time, went up on Mt. Nebo to gaze across the Jordan at the land which his people was about to conquer. It was not his lot to enter that land. There on Mt. Nebo he breathed his last and was buried no one knows where. For his great work was done: Israel stood on the threshold of Canaan.

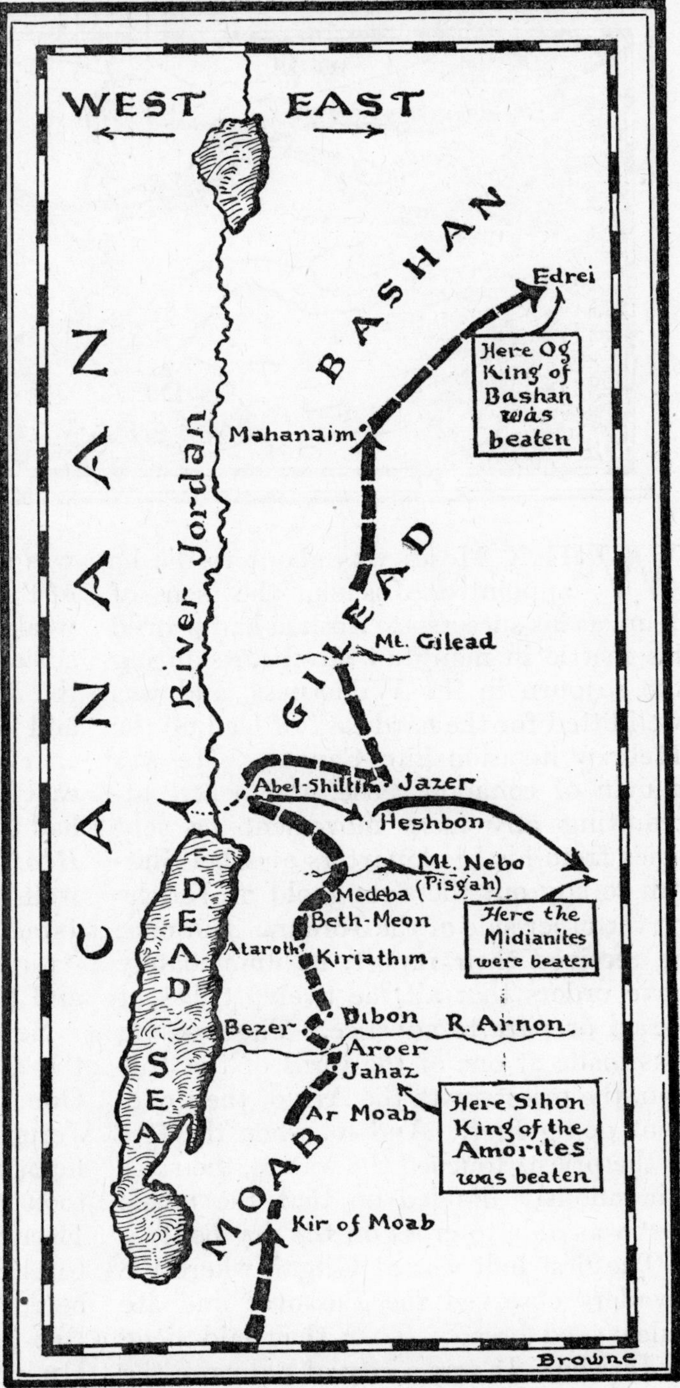

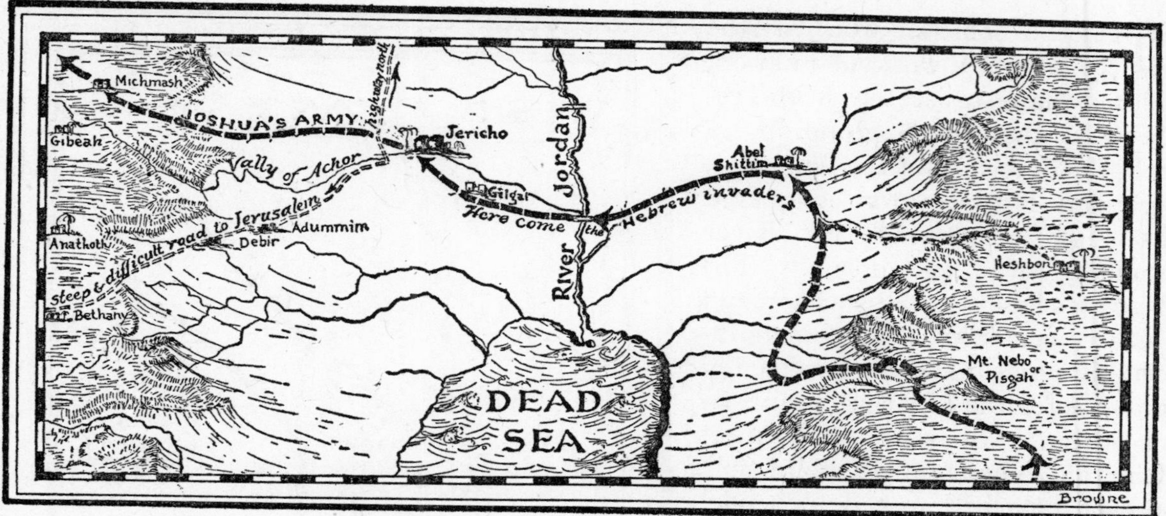

WHEN Moses was about to die he appointed Joshua, the son of Nun, as his successor. Joshua had proved his mettle in many an adventure during the sojourn in the Wilderness, and was well fitted for the hard task of leading the Hebrew invasion into Canaan. He was a man of common sense, and before attempting any mass movement he sent spies from his headquarters at Abel-Shittim to spy out the stronghold of Jericho on the other side of the Jordan. But once he received their report, he immediately gave orders that all the twelve tribes of Israel prepare to advance. The crossing was made at one of the fords of the Jordan, the priests with the Ark of the Covenant going first. And lo, when the feet of the priests touched the waters, the river miraculously divided so that the whole host was able to cross on the dry bed!

The first halt was at Gilgal, where the invaders observed the Passover and ate unleavened bread. Then they laid siege to Jericho. It was a city of palms in the midst of gardens of balsam trees, and it was rich because of the luxuriant fertility of the soil. But they that dwelt in it were weak—as have been all its occupants ever since. Jericho lies deep in the valley of the Jordan, full 800 feet below sea-level, and the climate there is hot and humid and enervating. The city has always fallen an easy prey to an invader. Joshua's army had to do little more than shout one lusty *Boo!* and by the grace of Jehovah "the wall fell down flat." Whereupon the Israelites rushed in, pillaged the city, slew its inhabitants in proper military fashion, and then burnt the place to the ground.

Several roads led up from Jericho to the Canaanite strongholds in the hills. One led to the city of Jebus, later called Jerusalem, but this was too steep and difficult to attempt. So instead the invaders took the trail which led to Michmash. Even this was by no means an easy pass to climb, especially for an army encumbered with women, children, and flocks. But the Israelites were not to be stayed. Up, up they clambered, until at last they were on the very top of the plateau.

JOSHUA'S aim in taking the road through Michmash was to capture the stronghold of Ai, which was important because it was the key to the mountains west of Jericho. His whole army went up—the distance from Jericho was only about 15 miles—took Ai by a stratagem, and forthwith laid it waste. The quick victory struck terror in the hearts of the inhabitants of the neighboring towns, and without waiting to be attacked they fled or else made terms with the invaders. Joshua, now master of the central portion of the land, marched rapidly to Shechem, and there had the Holy Law, with its blessings and curses, read from Mt. Ebal and Mt. Gerizim to the assembled Israelites. Then he rushed back to give aid to the natives of Gibeon, who were being attacked by other Canaanite tribes for having become allies of the Hebrews. Joshua swept down through the valley of Ajalon as far as Makkedah, commanding the sun and moon to stand still so that he could finish the slaughter of the routed Canaanites. And thus the passes toward the south fell into his hands. In rapid succession he took Libnah, Lachish, Eglon, Hebron, Debir, laying each city utterly waste. Apparently Joshua went even farther, conquering all the South Country as far as Kadesh-Barnea, and the coastal plain even to Gaza. The Canaanite kings of the north, terrified at Joshua's advance, joined in a league and made ready for war. But Joshua, at the command of God, did not wait to be attacked. By a forced march he rushed his army to the Waters of Merom—almost 100 miles north of Gilgal, his headquarters—and there pounced upon the Canaanite host. Once more he was completely victorious, and when he was done pursuing his enemies as far as Misrephoth-Maim he turned back to Hazor, where the league had been formed, and reduced the city to ashes.

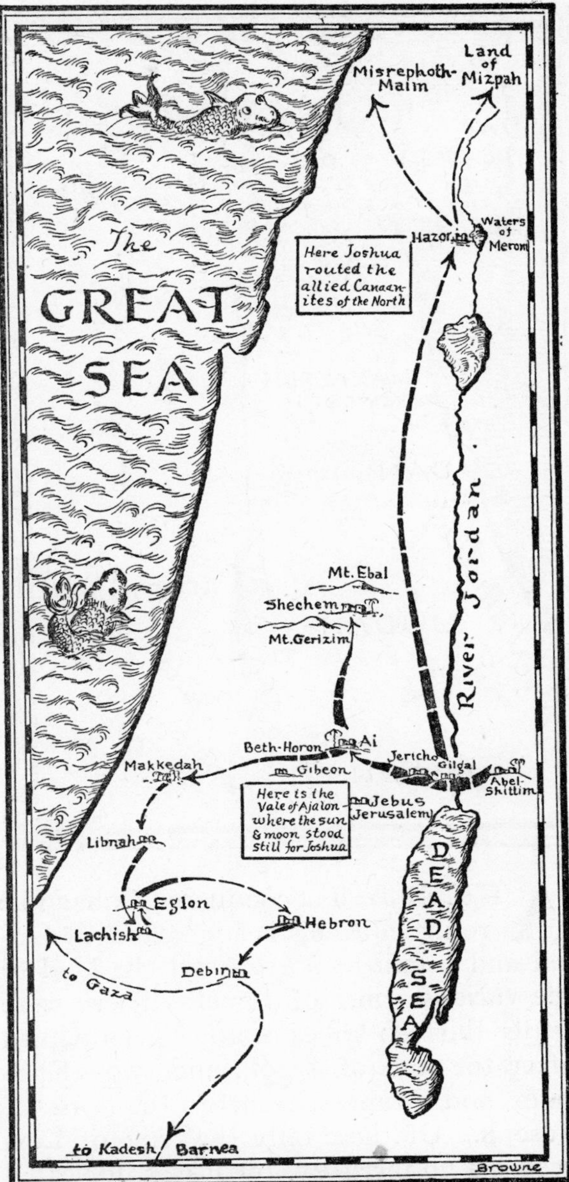

And thus did Joshua conquer the whole land of Canaan.

AFTER Joshua conquered Canaan he returned to his headquarters at Gilgal and began to portion out the land to the various tribes of Israel. There were really thirteen tribes in all; eleven named after the sons of Jacob, and two—Ephraim and Manasseh—after the sons of Joseph. Of these only the tribe of Levi received no territory, for it was dedicated to the religious service of Jehovah and was therefore scattered throughout the whole land. Reuben, Gad, and half the tribe of Manasseh, had already been awarded their territories by Moses when the Israelites were still east of the Jordan. The other nine and a half tribes were settled west of the river. Judah, Ephraim, and the second half of the tribe of Manasseh, were the first to be giver their portions. The remaining seven tribes had to draw lots for their heritages. The tribe of Benjamin, which was small but exceedingly warlike, received a bit of the hill-country in central Canaan. Simeon went far to the south, on the edge of the desert. Asher, Zebulun, Issachar, and Naphtali inherited the north, the region later called Galilee.

The extent of these various regions is given—but very approximately—in the diagram on this page. The smallness of the portions can best be seen when one compares them with the areas of mere cities in our world. The whole heritage of Benjamin was not as large as New York proper, and not half as large as the metropolitan area of "Greater London." But though so small, wondrous things were destined to occur in those tribal lands of Israel.

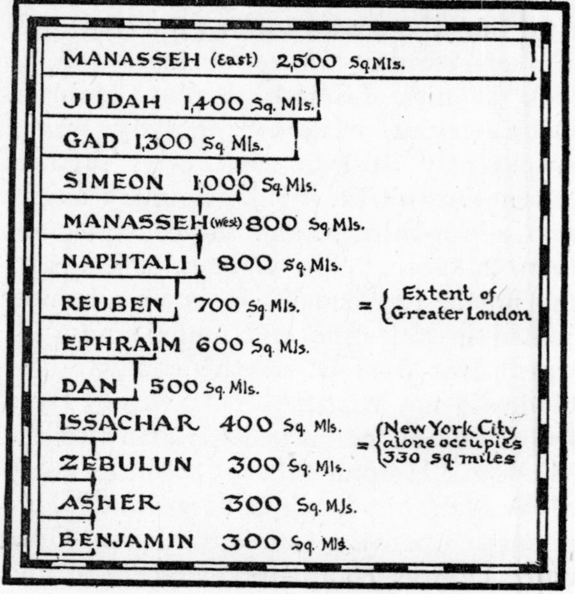

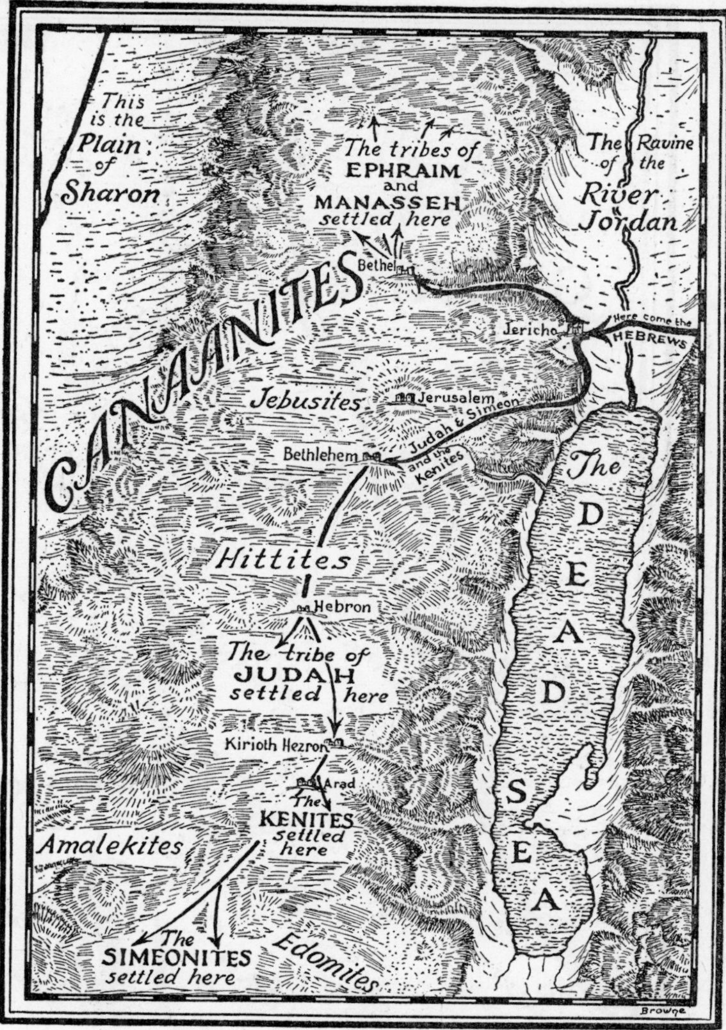

BUT apparently the conquest of Canaan was not at all completed under Joshua. In the opening verses of the Book of Judges we read how after Joshua was already dead and buried the children of Israel were still asking the Lord, "Who shall go up for us against the Canaanites first, to fight against them?" It would seem that the conquest had to be accomplished all over again, and this time not swiftly by all Israel under one leader, but slowly by the separate tribes. Judah and Simeon, with their allies the Kenites, struck out toward the south, while Ephraim and Manasseh invaded the north. And fierce was the struggle that ensued. The Canaanites were not an easy people to conquer, for they dwelt in walled cities and were well armed. They had chariots and cavalry, whereas the Hebrews were all on foot and possessed only the most primitive weapons. In the broad valleys the Canaanites were always more than a match for the invaders, and only in guerilla warfare up in the hills could the latter be victorious. As we read in Judges 1:19, "And the Lord was with Judah, and he drove out the inhabitants of the mountain; but could not drive out the inhabitants of the valley, because they had chariots of iron."

The Hebrews intrenched themselves at two points; in the south in the heights of Judah, and in the north in the highlands of what came to be called Samaria. Only gradually and with limited success did they later manage to spread down into the lowlands. For generations they remained penned up in the hills, each tribe, or group of tribes, separated from the rest by lines of Canaanite strongholds. Turn to the large map on the next page, and you will be able to see quite clearly how straitened was the position of the children of Israel.

The GREAT SEA
Phoenicians
Hittites
DAN
ASHER
NAPHTALI
ZEBULUN
Arameans
ISSACHAR
MACHIR
Son of Manasseh
Dor
Megiddo
Canaanites
Beth-Shean
Teanach
GILEAD
MANASSEH
Canaanites
EPHRAIM
The DESERT
BENJAMIN
GAD
Ekron
Gezer
Gibeon
Ajalon
Jebus
Ammonites
Ashdod
Gath
Askelon
REUBEN
Philistines
Gaza
JUDAH
SIMEON
Edomites
Moabites
This is the "howling wilderness" whence the Hebrews escaped
N
W
E
S
ELEVATION of the LAND
sea level
Jerusalem
Mt. Gilead
Mt. Nebo
Plain east of Jordan
Dead Sea
Browne

All the richest portions of the land were still in the hands of the enemies of Israel. The fertile coastal plain remained the undisputed possession of the Philistines, Canaanites, and Phoenicians; and the major valleys running east and west bristled with fortresses still occupied by the natives. Two such valleys in particular ran like blunt wedges into the side of the Hebrew domains, and though they were finally conquered they remained for centuries the centers of Canaanite life. There is reason to believe that even in the highlands the Canaanites remained numerous and were not utterly vanquished. Indeed, in one way it was the Hebrews who were vanquished, for though they conquered the Canaanite soil they almost lost their own Hebrew religion. They became attracted to the native gods —the Baalim, as they were called—for these gods demanded less of them than did Jehovah. The Baalim were worshiped with magic practices and rites that were little better than debauches. Little wonder, therefore, that the Hebrews, being mere flesh and blood, soon began to forsake their own far stricter and more exacting Jehovah.

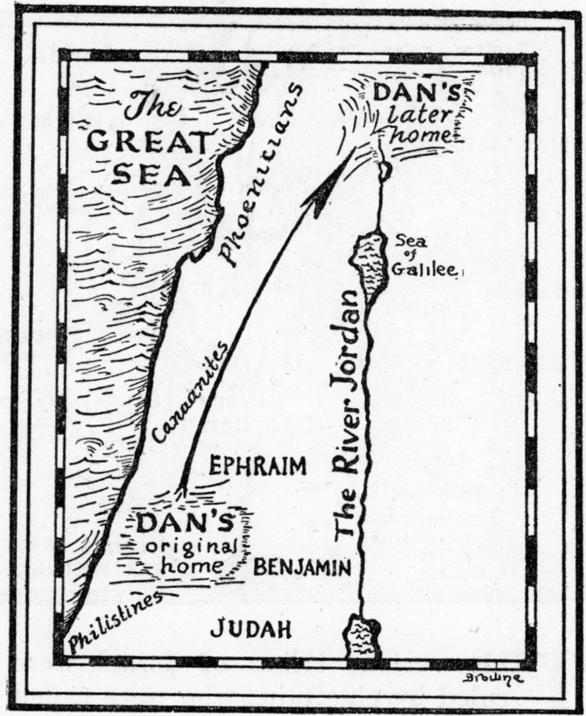

Nor was this the only way in which the Hebrews sinned. They accepted not only the Canaanite gods, but also the Canaanites themselves. They took native women for their wives, and gave their daughters to native men. Especially did this happen among the tribes in the extreme north and south. Asher grew friendly with the Phoenicians and became a seafaring people; and Simeon became intimate with the Edomites and became almost completely a desert tribe.

Anarchy reigned, for "every man did that which was right in his own eyes." Each tribe fought to conquer a bit of land for itself and fought sometimes not only against the Canaanites but even against the other Hebrew tribes. The conduct of the tribe of Dan is an instance of this. Originally the Danites had settled at the foot of the Judahite hills, but finding themselves at the mercy of the Philistines there, they soon began to look about for a more favorable dwelling-place. They found such a place far to the north, in a broad valley at the headwaters of the Jordan. Thither the Danites migrated, wandering no doubt for many months before they finally reached their goal. The place was captured and the Danites made themselves masters of the countryside. And thus, quite unaided by the rest, did one of the Hebrew tribes carve out its heritage.

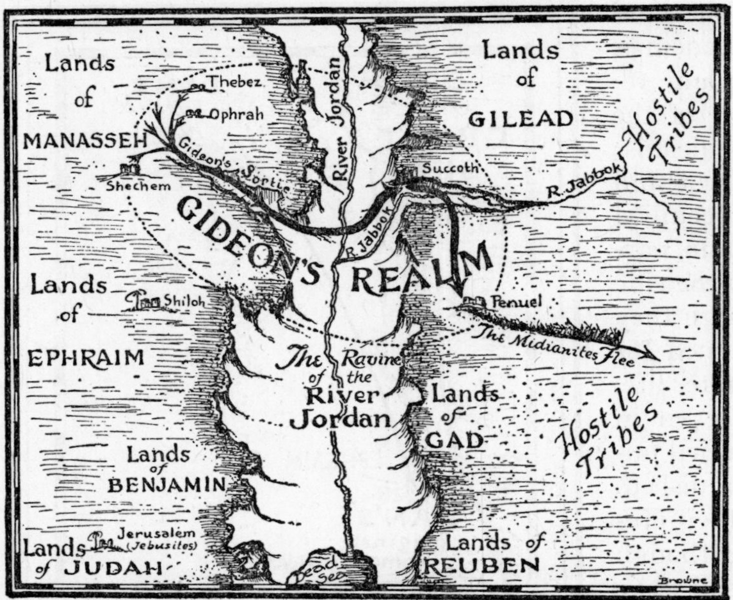

THE various tribes of Israel were ruled by chieftains who were called "judges." These chieftains did not inherit their office, but won it largely through military prowess. When a tribe had to go to war it made its ablest warrior the leader, and usually retained him as the civil ruler after the war was ended. Some of the judges were anything but true men of Jehovah, and their influence on the people was often not altogether righteous. Matters therefore went from bad to worse in Israel. Each tribe fought for itself, and there was no trace of unity among them. Only the even greater lack of unity among the natives made it possible for the newcomers to retain their hold on the hills.

But soon the Hebrews were brought face to face with more redoubtable enemies than the native Canaanites. Just as the Hebrews themselves had invaded Canaan a generation or two earlier, so now other desert tribes sought to invade the land. Among them there came the Moabites, who swept up along the East Jordan lands and terrorized over all Israel. Only after eighteen years were they driven back by Ehud, judge of the tribe of Benjamin. The Ammonites, too, came raiding from the east, and the Amalekites and the Midianites. But these incessant invasions proved a blessing in disguise, for they gradually drove the Hebrew tribes to unite. Judges 6-8 tells a significant story. The Midianites, who for centuries had roamed in the desert far to the southeast of Canaan, had come up, and were spreading terror along all the frontiers of Israel. For seven years they raided and plundered almost without hindrance. But finally there arose a Hebrew farmer named Gideon who, with 300 fighting men picked not alone from his own tribe, Manasseh, but also from Asher, Zebulun, and Naphtali, made a sudden attack on the invaders and drove them back across the ravine of the Jordan. (His line of march is marked on the map.) Once Gideon had the enemy on the run, the warriors from other Hebrew tribes joined in the pursuit, and the Midianites fled for all they were worth. And when Gideon returned in triumph to his native city of Ophrah, his neighbors made him king of the whole countryside. His realm was not extensive—perhaps no more than 25 miles from east to west. But it was significant, for it marked the beginning of unity among at least some of the tribes.

BUT the tribes from the desert were as nothing compared with another invading host, the Philistines. These Philistines were not originally a Semitic folk from Arabia. They came, it seems, from Crete, or the northern coast of the Mediterranean, and they may have reached Canaan first as pirates. Then, shipload by shipload, they began to settle along the southern end of the Canaanite shore.

Already in the time of Joshua the Philistines on the coast had grown so numerous that they were beginning to spread up into the very hills which the Hebrews were trying to conquer. It was inevitable, therefore, that the two peoples should clash. At first the Philistines were easily the victors, for they were better armed than the Hebrews, and far better organized. The kings of their five chief city-states in Philistia—Gaza, Askelon, Ashdod, Gath, and Ekron—were close allies. The Hebrews, who possessed only the most primitive weapons and were totally disorganized, had little chance against them. Under the leadership of a strong man like Samson, they were able to wage guerilla warfare against the Philistines; but when it came to a pitched battle, they were utterly lost. At Aphek the Hebrews went down to a crushing defeat, and the Ark of Jehovah, which had led them all through the Wilderness, was captured by the Philistines. In triumph it was carried over the great highway to Ashdod; but there the Ark caused such misfortune that hastily it was shipped to Gath, to Ekron, to Bethshemesh—finally right back into the hills to Kirjath-Jearim. And there it remained, still a Philistine prize, for many years.

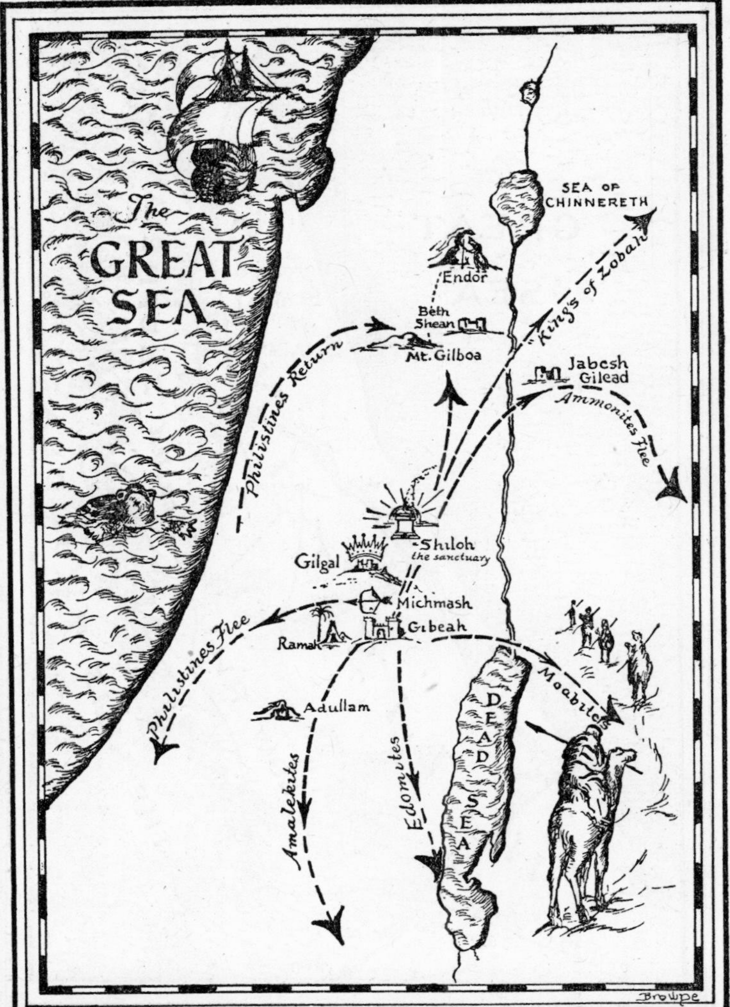

IT was the menace of a united Philistia that drove the Israelites to unite. They could not help but realize that soon they would be utterly destroyed if they remained without a head. Therefore they called on a holy man named Samuel, who dwelt at Ramah, asking him to select a king for Israel. Samuel, guided by Jehovah, chose a stalwart, middle-aged farmer named Saul, and events soon proved how wise was the choice. An old enemy, the Ammonites, had just made a raid on Jabesh in Gilead, demanding that its inhabitants not only pay ransom but also allow their right eyes to be gouged out. The men of Jabesh sent a desperate plea for help to their kinsmen across the Jordan, and Saul immediately responded. With a dire threat of vengeance if they refused, he summoned the braves of all the Hebrew tribes to follow him to the relief of Jabesh. His summons was obeyed, and, with a horde at his heels, Saul swept down and delivered Jabesh.

It was a great victory for Saul, and well established his right to the kingship. With one accord the elders of Israel assembled in the hills at an ancient sanctuary named Gilgal, and there formally crowned Saul their monarch.

The war with the Philistines then took a new turn. At Michmash the tide was turned, and the Hebrews won their first great victory over this enemy. The Philistines were driven back to their coastal plain, and Saul was left free to attend to the other troublers. He organized a standing army of which his own tribe, Benjamin, was the backbone; and with this army he waged untiring war on every frontier.

Never to his dying day did Saul succeed in ridding Israel of its enemies; but succeed he did in at least holding those enemies at bay.

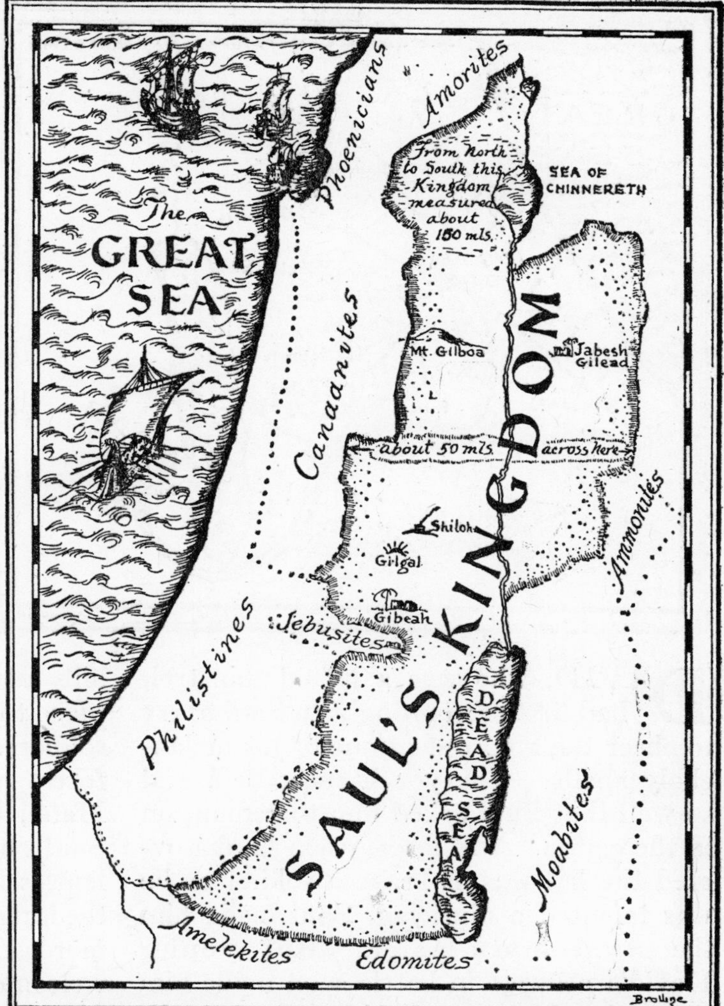

SAUL'S kingdom was no more than a narrow strip of hill-country along the River Jordan. It had no fixed frontiers and was never free from attack. As you can see by the map, the little realm was surrounded by the Philistines, Canaanites, Phoenicians, Amorites, Moabites, Edomites, Ammonites, and Amalekites. And of all these races only the Phoenicians, who were seafaring traders, did not seek to overrun Saul's territory. The most impregnable stronghold in the land, the city later called Jerusalem, was still in the hands of a Canaanitish tribe known as the Jebusites; and the other fortresses, though nominally in the hands of the Hebrews, were still largely inhabited by natives. Saul's capital was his birthplace Gibeah, which seems to have been no more than a poorly fortified village.

But what was perhaps more menacing to Israel was not the hostility outside the nation, but the dissension within. Saul, though an excellent warrior, was a wretched statesman. He was jealous, hot-tempered, and at times quite mad—anything but the sort of man fitted to weld the Hebrew tribes into fast and solid union. As a result he very soon ran into difficulties. He broke with the prophet Samuel, and thus alienated an important element in the population—the prophets. In those days there were to be found throughout Israel many bands of holy men who went up and down the country shouting excitedly about the glories of Jehovah. The Hebrew farmers and shepherds stood in great awe of these prophets, for they were supposed to possess all sorts of magic powers. And Samuel, who was recognized as chief of the prophets, was therefore a person of considerable influence. Nor was Samuel the only important person whom Saul antagonized. In addition there was the gallant warrior, David.

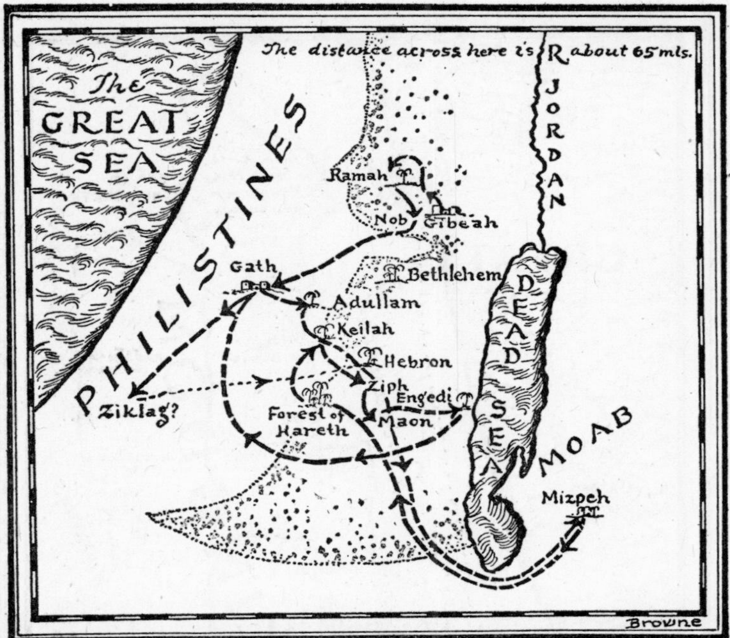

DAVID, who was a gifted minstrel, had first been brought to Saul to try to cheer the king out of one of his melancholy spells. The youth succeeded, and so well that Saul asked him to remain on in the camp. And later, when he discovered the lad was as brave a soldier as he was talented a musician, Saul made him the royal armor-bearer. But young David's prowess in battle soon made him the national hero, and this aroused Saul's jealousy. So David, knowing his life was in danger, fled from the king's presence. From Gibeah, the capital, the young warrior fled to Ramah, where the aged prophet Samuel dwelt. Thence he doubled back to Gibeah, hiding there until he received warning from Jonathan, the king's son, that he must leave. David then escaped by way of Nob to the Philistine stronghold of Gath, thinking that there he would be safe. But, despite that he was fleeing from the Hebrew king, the Philistines were suspicious of David and plotted to do him evil. So once more he fled, this time to Adullam, a hiding-place in the foothills of Judah. Here he was within the territory of his own clan, and therefore was quite secure. A number of his fellow-tribesmen came out and joined him, and he became the chieftain of a small rebel army. For fear his aged parents, who dwelt in Bethlehem, might be persecuted by Saul, he conveyed them out of the country and placed them in the care of the King of Moab at Mizpah. Then he and his band returned to the hills of Judah and dodged about from place to place in order to elude the king's soldiers. They lurked for a while in the forest of Hareth, then at Keilah, Ziph, Maon, Engedi, and again at Maon. But Saul's army continued to pursue them relentlessly, and finally David had to flee the kingdom and take refuge in Gath once more. This time, however, the Philistines welcomed him, for they realized now he was truly a fugitive from Saul. For a while they thought of using him and his followers in a campaign against Israel; but at the last moment they reconsidered and decided to use him on another frontier. They sent him and his band down to Ziklag, on the border of the desert, to hold it against the bedouins who were continually raiding and pillaging that region. And there David remained, a sort of freebooting mercenary, until at last Saul's reign came to an end.

ALTHOUGH the Philistines had been routed by Saul at the beginning of his reign (see page 38), they had remained a powerful and menacing enemy. For some time, however, they contented themselves with minor forays, and with giving aid to the outlaw, David. Only when they learnt that Saul's mad ways had alienated his chief supporters and that the morale of his army was weak, did they attempt to launch a heavy counter-attack. Uniting all their forces they marched up the coast highway and encamped at Shunem, north of Mt. Gilboa. (The route is approximately indicated on the map on page 38.) This method of approach enabled the Philistines to advance with their chariots over broad plains, where opposition was not as easy as in the hills. Saul rallied his forces and took up his position on the slopes of Mt. Gilboa, across the valley from Shunem. This gave him a decided advantage, for from his height he commanded the whole countryside. But he was in despair nevertheless, for many of the Hebrew captains together with their regiments had deserted him. The regular oracles, through which he sought to determine the will of Jehovah, were silent, and he was reduced to consulting a witch to find out what was in store for him. Disguising himself, he stole out across the valley one night, and went to the wretched village of Endor, back of Shunem, where dwelt "a woman with a familiar spirit." There Saul learnt his fate—that he had lost the support of Jehovah and was doomed. Brokenly he staggered out into the night and went back to his army. The spirit was gone from him, and the army, sensing his despair, knew itself defeated even before a blow was struck.

When the Philistine host advanced up the slopes of Mt. Gilboa, the Hebrew ranks crumpled helplessly. The Philistine archers drove them eastward over the crest of the hill and then down the steep slope almost to the Jordan. Within a few hours the contest was at an end. Jonathan and the other two sons of Saul died fighting like lions, and Saul himself, badly wounded, fell upon his sword to escape capture. The army was routed ignominiously.

The next day the Philistines stuck Saul's mutilated body on the walls of the city of Beth-Shean. And thus ended the reign of the first king in Israel.

THE moment David heard of the tragedy on Mt. Gilboa, he took his men and marched quickly up to Hebron, the chief city of Judah, to have himself made the new king. It was not difficult for him to achieve this. The southern tribes had all along been restive under the rule of Saul, who had belonged to the north, and they had no desire now to accept his son as their king. They much preferred David, who was one of their own. David was a valiant warrior, and in addition a man of wealth, for he had married a rich widow named Abigail. He seemed eminently fitted for the throne, and therefore the elders of Judah assembled in Hebron and without further ado anointed him their king.

So now there were two kingdoms in the tiny strip of hill-country belonging to the Hebrews. The northern tribes took a son of Saul named Ishbaal (or Ishbosheth) as their monarch, and declared war on the south.

The Philistines must have been highly satisfied with this state of affairs, for they knew that so long as the Hebrews were divided they were helpless prey. But David, too, knew this, and he therefore at once set himself the task of winning over the north. It was no easy task, for in his overtures he had to be most careful not to arouse either the jealousy of the southerners or the antagonism of the Philistines. But David was a man of quite extraordinary cleverness, and was not unequal to so difficult a situation. It took almost eight years before he attained his end—but attain it he did. The hapless young king of the north, Ishbaal, was assassinated by his own captains, and David became monarch of the whole land. A second time he was anointed in Hebron, but this time by the tribes of the north as well as the south.

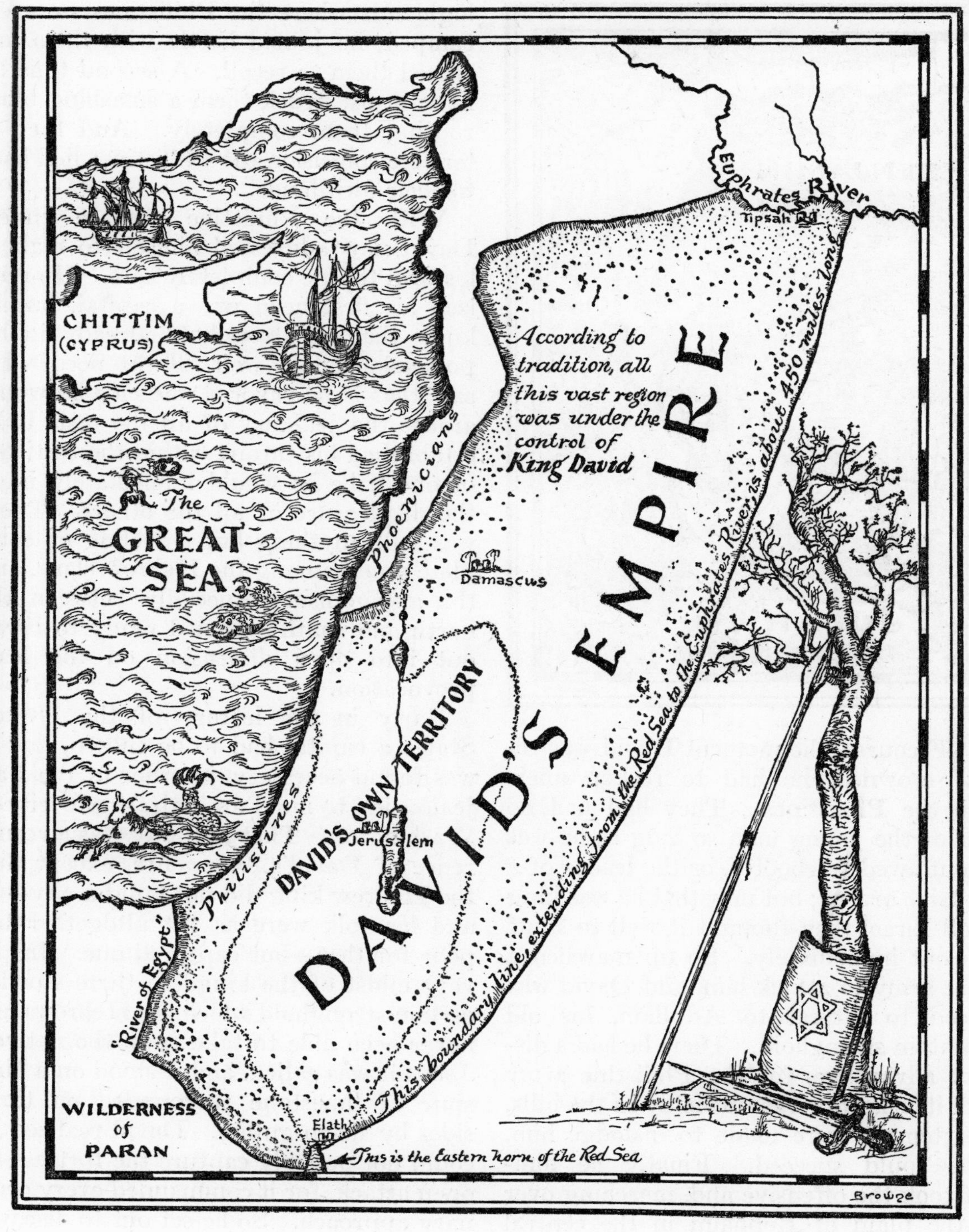
Euphrates River
Tipsah
CHITTIM
(CYPRUS)
According to tradition, all this vast region was under the control of King David
DAVID'S EMPIRE
This boundary line, extending from the Red Sea to the Euphrates River is about 450 miles long
The
GREAT
SEA
Phoenicians
Damascus
DAVID'S OWN TERRITORY
Jerusalem
Philistines
"River of Egypt"
WILDERNESS of PARAN
Elath
This is the Eastern horn of the Red Sea
Browne

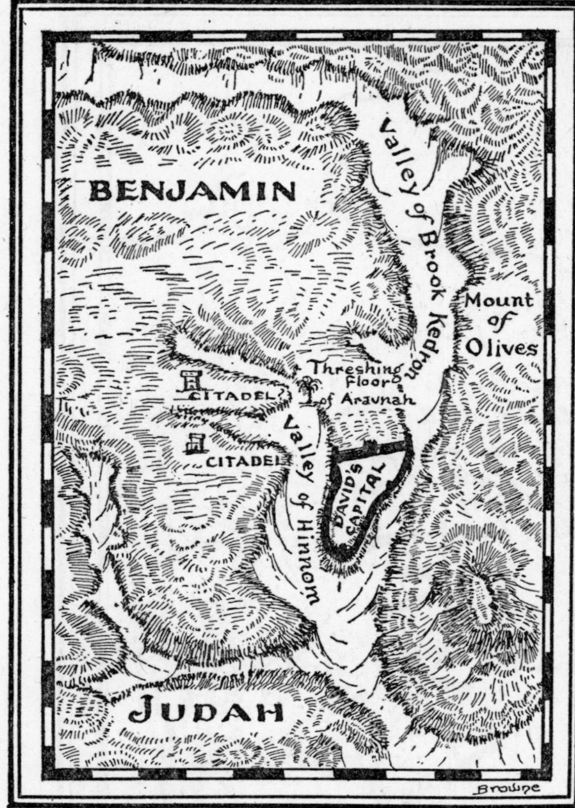

OF course, the moment David was recrowned, he had to reckon anew with the Philistines. They had had no fear of the young man so long as he was an outlawed freebooter, or the leader of a hill-tribe or two; but now that he was king of all Israel they thought it well to snuff him out immediately. So up marched a great army to attack him, and David was forced to retreat to Adullam, his old mountain stronghold. There he had a distinct advantage, for the Philistine army with its chariots was unwieldy in the hills. If attempts were made to dislodge him, none could succeed. Finally he himself took the offensive and, marching over to the plain of Rephaim in the central highlands where the Philistines were encamped, he joined battle with them and forced them to recoil. A second time his little army struck them a smashing blow, routing them completely. And then in terrible confusion the Philistines fled back to their own lands.

With the Philistine menace ended, David now addressed himself to making his own throne completely safe. He realized his first need was a capital, but he knew that no stronghold already in his possession could well fill the need. He saw that if he favored one city he would arouse the jealousy of all the rest; if he established his throne within the territory of one tribe he would immediately incur the displeasure of all the others. There was still anything but a feeling of complete union among the Hebrew clans, and the antagonism—especially between the north and south—seemed ready to break out into open dissension on the least provocation.

Early in the history of the United States a capital had to be chosen, and it was found necessary, in order to avoid all jealousies, to build an entirely new city—Washington. That in a way was a recurrence of David's experience, except that the Hebrew king did not build a city—he and his folk were as yet altogether too poor for that—but captured one. In the very midst of the kingdom there stood a certain stronghold which the Hebrews had never been able to take from the natives. Jebus it was called, and it stood on a high spur of limestone surrounded on three sides by sharp gullies. David realized he could not possibly capture the fortress by open attack, for it commanded every ordinary approach. So he set out to discover

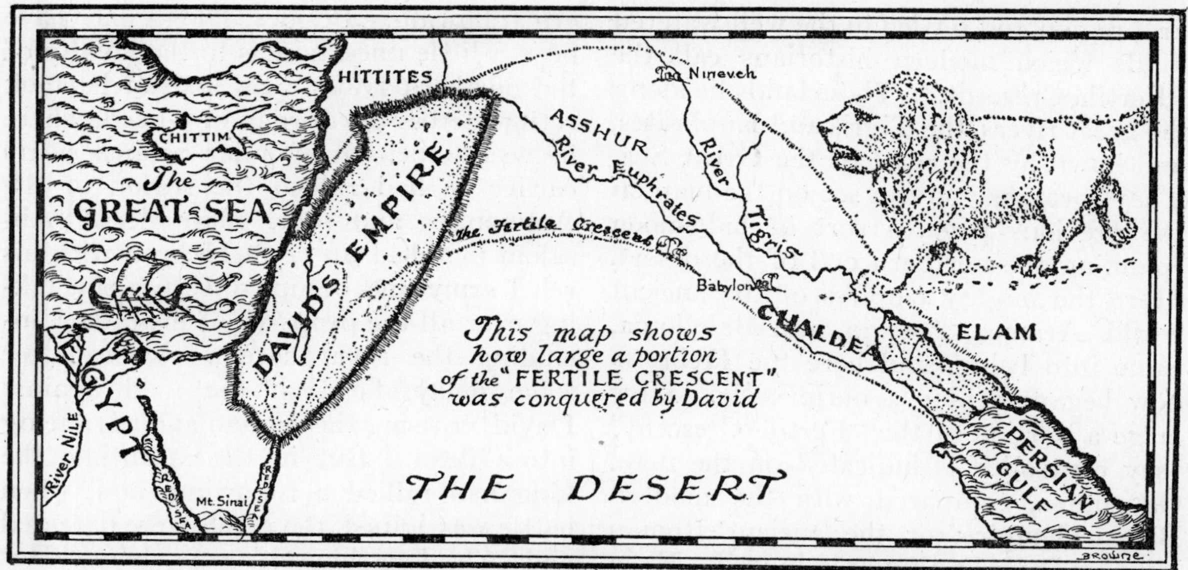

some extraordinary approach, and found it in a water-tunnel which led from a spring down in the gully right up into the very midst of the city. And through this tunnel he led an attack which so surprised the Jebusites that they were rendered helpless. The stronghold was taken and made the capital of Israel. Jerusalem it came to be called, and as Jerusalem it still stands there—the most significant city in the history of our world.

With this impregnable stronghold secured as his capital, David now felt free to turn on the ring of foes surrounding his little kingdom. First he carried war into Philistia, marching right down across the plain even as far as Gath, the chief city. The Holy Ark, which had been in Philistine hands so many years, was brought to the Hebrew capital and established there. And thus was settled the score with the enemy on the west.

Next David turned on the Moabites in the east. Trampling them into harmlessness, he then assailed the Ammonites. Next he subdued the Arameans in the northeast, who had tried to aid the Ammonites. Then, turning south, David broke the power of the Edomites, and their neighbors the Amalekites. And thus he completed the circle of conquest. David was now overlord of almost all the tribes and races in his corner of the world. He was no longer a petty king ruling over a strip of hill-country; now he was a veritable emperor. He held sway either directly or indirectly over all the land from the Great Sea (the Mediterranean) on the west to the desert on the east, and from the tip of the Red Sea in the south perhaps as far as the River Euphrates in the north. This, according to the Bible, was the territory which God had promised to the Hebrews in the beginning. Having conquered it, the children of Israel now took their place as one of the dominant races in the "Fertile Crescent."

The Semitic stock came into being in the Arabian Desert, but it attained civilization only when it emerged from that arid region and settled in the well-watered lands which modern historians call the "Fertile Crescent." These lands lie along the great rivers, the Tigris and Euphrates, and down by the coast of the Great Sea. They form, as you can see on the map on the previous page, a sort of half-moon spanning the northern end of the desert. Here the mighty empires of the ancient world, Aramea, Assyria, and Babylonia, came into being, and here the Hebrews now began to play a major rôle. How large a portion of the "Fertile Crescent" they controlled is indicated on the map. Of course, compared with the modern British Empire, or the ancient Roman Empire, it was a tiny area indeed. Even the most extravagant estimate would concede it a length of no more than 450 miles, and a breadth of about 175 miles. But compared with the empires of its own day, David's realm was of no little magnificence.

David had no easy time, however, in holding this realm together. His sudden rise to power turned his head, and he grew tyrannical and began to sin. And, as a consequence, great calamities befell him. Unrest began to spread among his people, and before long blood was spilled. One of David's own sons, Absalom, led a rebellion which almost destroyed the whole empire. Absalom played on the jealousy and disaffection of the southern tribes, which felt they were not shown sufficient favor by the king. And the conspirator was able to start so menacing a movement that David had to flee from Jerusalem to save his life. The king did not seek refuge in the north, however, for he knew that would have served only to heighten the hostility of Absalom's southern following. Besides, David may have been a little uncertain as to the loyalty of the northern tribes. So instead he took refuge across the Jordan in Gilead, where he was immensely popular because years earlier he had ridded the region of the Ammonites and other marauders. Absalom marched up from Hebron with his rebel army and occupied Jerusalem, taking over all the property of his father, including the royal harem. Then, after some delay, he took the field against David, crossing the Jordan and advancing into Gilead. But in the meantime the king had rallied a following, and, when battle was joined, the rebels were defeated and Absalom himself was slain. But David was in no position to exact vengeance; he had to shower the erstwhile rebels with favors before he could feel quite sure they would not renew hostilities. And this aroused the north, which had remained loyal to David during Absalom's revolt. No sooner, therefore, was one insurrection crushed, than another broke out. This second revolt was led by a certain Sheba, a man from the hill-country of Ephraim, and although it too was snuffed out, it did no little to sadden the last years of the king.

Nor where these two rebellions the only evils that befell David. A drought came, and three years of famine followed. And a little later a fell plague swept through the land, carrying off 70,000 men. Broken by these afflictions, David grew rapidly an aged and helpless man. Finally he abdicated entirely, appointing Solomon, the son of his favorite wife, as his successor. And then, after charging the new king to be faithful to God, David died and "slept with his fathers."

River Euphrates
CHITTIM
(CYPRUS)
Apparently Solomon claimed suzerainty over all this region but his hold on it was exceedingly feeble
The GREAT SEA
Phoenicians
ARAM which was lost when Rezon led a revolution
Damascus
Hazor
Megiddo
SOLOMON'S KINGDOM
Gezer
Jerusalem
DEAD SEA
Philistines
MOAB which was also lost
Thamar
EDOM which Solomon lost when Hadad led a rebellion
This region was all under the suzerainty of EGYPT
Browne

THE reign of Solomon is usually thought of as one of unparalleled magnificence. The Bible makes it clear, however, that there was a seamy side to this magnificence. At the very outset Solomon did away with his eldest brother, Adonijah, who had claimed the throne as his by right of birth. In addition Solomon executed two generals who had supported Adonijah, and banished a third. Thus he served notice on the kingdom that he intended to rule with an iron hand, and would brook no disaffection. Such an attitude was, of course, far from pleasing to the people. The Hebrews regarded their nation as a democracy, and they felt the king ought to be their servant, not their master. But they were helpless. Solomon, with the aid of the military organization which his father had established, made himself an absolute autocrat. His ambition seems to have been to reveal himself a man of power, a great oriental emperor whose outward splendor was in a class with that of the despots of Egypt and Babylonia.

But outward splendor is expensive, and therefore Solomon's greatest concern had to be the getting of wealth. Now David had acquired wealth by conquering the peoples around him. He had pillaged the lands of the Philistines and Arameans and the like, and had used the spoils to beautify Jerusalem. But Solomon was not a warrior. Indeed, far from seeking to make further conquests, he even lost part of the territory which his father had secured. Edom in the south revolted almost as soon as Solomon ascended the throne. An Edomite named Hadad, who had managed to escape when David nearly exterminated the nation, saw his opportunity now that a king of a different temper ruled in Jerusalem. He returned to Edom, called his wild brethren together, and organized a revolt which seems to have been in part successful. And thereupon Moab, taking courage from Edom's action, likewise rebelled. Next Syria freed itself. A certain sheikh named Rezon, who had also escaped the sword of David, now returned from the desert where he had long been hiding and raised the flag of revolt in Damascus. Solomon was powerless to stop him, and thus was a kingdom founded on the northeastern frontier of Palestine which was destined to plague the Israelites for hundreds of years to come.

Despite these revolts, Solomon still claimed to be suzerain over the whole of the empire his father had conquered. But, of course, he was unable to collect tribute save from the inhabitants of his own small kingdom. And this made the burden on Palestine almost beyond bearing, for Solomon needed a tremendous amount of tribute to carry out his ambitious schemes.

One of Solomon's first projects was the building of a series of fortresses to protect the frontiers. Several of these are indicated on the map on page 47: Thamar in the south, Gezer and others on the west, Megiddo at the entrance of the Vale of Esdraelon, the most desirable tract in the whole country, and Hazor in the north. But Solomon's far more splendid—and expensive—project was the beautifying of Jerusalem in the center of the land. Here he wanted to erect a magnificent palace and temple to show the world how vast was his power and how deep his devotion to Jehovah. But no Israelite was capable of planning and erecting such

structures, for none had seen any great palaces or temples. So Solomon had to call on his neighbors, the Phoenicians, for help. Phoenicia lay to the northwest of Palestine between the Lebanon Mountains and the Great Sea. As you can see by the map, it was a narrow strip of coastland—so narrow, indeed, that its inhabitants were almost forced to take to the sea to find any room in which to move about. Fortunately for them, their coast was not unbroken as in Palestine. On the contrary their coastline was heavily indented and possessed many fine natural harbors. Therefore the Phoenicians could do what was quite impossible for the people dwelling to the south of them: they could become seafarers. The Phoenicians had never once tried to invade the Hebrew kingdom, probably because they had never felt the need to spread inland. They had all the seven seas to roam. They were the great traders of the ancient world, and their galleys were to be seen in the ports of the furthest empires. Also they were the most noted industrial people of the time, and their dye-products, jewelry, silk, and glassware were to be found in all the great cities of the world.

It was natural, therefore, that Solomon should call on these neighbors for help. The Phoenicians knew all about architecture and interior decorating, for they had seen the palaces of all the great potentates of the world. More than that, they could also provide fine building material, for the forests of their Lebanon Mountains were thick with tall cedars. And the Phoenicians were delighted to dispose of both their knowledge and timber—for a price. So Solomon struck a bargain with Hiram, who was king of Tyre, one of Phoenicia's chief cities, and forthwith the building operations in Jerusalem began.

The site Solomon chose for his palace and Temple was the hill rising to the north of the stronghold now called

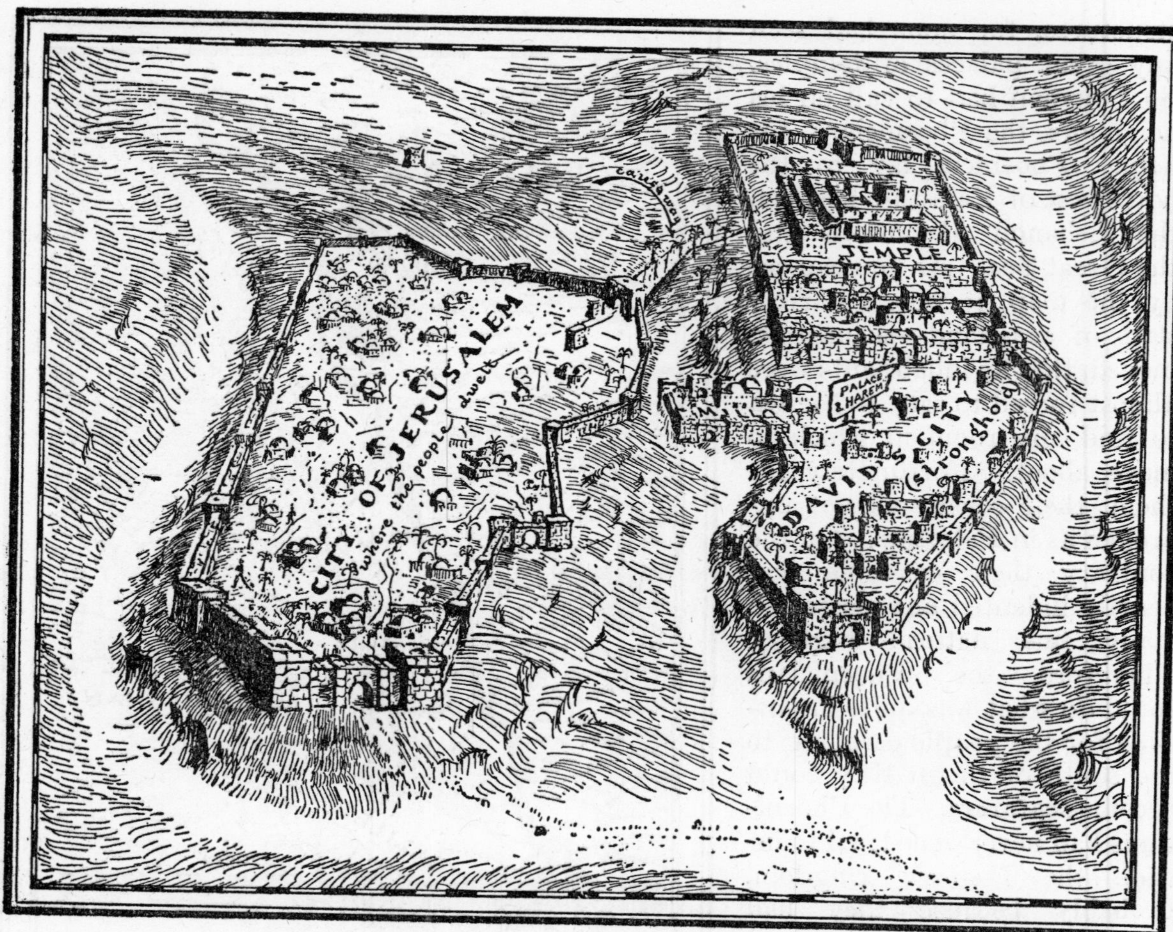

David's City. Mt. Moriah this hill was named in later years. Apparently the palace was the more magnificent structure, for it took thirteen years to build, whereas the Temple required only seven and a half. The sanctuary itself was but a very small building, 60 cubits long and 20 cubits wide—that is, about 90 feet by 30 feet. The royal residence was considerably larger: its assembly hall alone, built of huge cedar logs, was actually 150 feet by 75 feet in size. Of course, compared with those in Babylonia and Egypt, even this palace was a small structure. But small as it may have been, it was tremendously costly to erect. It required 30,000 Israelites to fell the timber in the Lebanon forests, and 80,000 state slaves to quarry and shape the stones. The logs were floated down the coast in rafts, picked up at Joppa, and then trundled up the hills to Jerusalem. The stones were transported on the backs of 70,000 slaves. The Phoenicians supervised the whole work, exacting as their pay an annual tribute of 200,000 bushels of wheat and 180,000 gallons of the finest olive oil.

Fortunately for Solomon, he was a brilliant organizer, and this alone made it possible for him to draw out of his little kingdom the great wealth he needed. Disregarding the old tribal divisions he substituted twelve federal districts, each with a governor in charge. These governors had to collect the produce for the Phoenician hirelings and also for Solomon and his court. The Bible tells us that each day the provisions for the royal court alone consisted of 330 bushels of fine flour, 660 bushels of meal, 30 oxen, 100 sheep, and an odd assortment of gazelles, roebucks, harts, and fat fowl. So much provender was needed because Solomon had a large family to feed. Not merely was there his standing army, his corps of servants, his counselors and secretaries to care for, but in addition he had his harem of a thousand wives and concubines. This harem, it must be realized, was more for show than comfort, for in those days a king's wealth was measured by the number of his wives. But whatever may have been the reason for the extensive harem, it was an expensive luxury.

And for all this immense entourage Solomon had to provide shelter as well as food. For his wives, some of whom were princesses from neighboring lands, he had to provide palaces, and for his army, which now could boast cavalry and chariots, he had to build garrisons and roads. All this required a vast number of workmen, for there were no steam shovels or derricks to reduce manual labor in those days. Accordingly Solomon had to resort to slavery. At first he drafted the non-Hebrew inhabitants of Palestine into his labor gangs. He took what Canaanites, Amorites, Jebusites, Gibeonites, and the like were still surviving in the land, and made them state slaves—precisely as his own ancestors had been made state slaves by Pharaoh of Egypt two centuries earlier. But since there were not enough of these non-Hebrews for all the work Solomon planned, he actually drafted Hebrews too. He forced his own people to supply 30,000 men to work as his serfs one month out of every three.

But it was impossible for Solomon to finance all his projects with revenues collected from his own realm, and he was forced after a while to take to trading. Situated as he was between two continents, he could very conveniently go in for commerce. He bought horses from the Egyptians in the south, and sold them to the Hittites in the north. And he levied a high tariff on all merchandise transported through his realm by foreign traders. Later he extended his activities and, with a fleet of merchant ships built for him by the Phoenicians, sent agents to distant lands to acquire gold and other precious commodities for him. This fleet was not built on the Mediterranean, for, as I have already remarked, there were no good harbors on the Palestinian coast. Instead it was built on the eastern horn of the Red Sea (the place is indicated on the map on the next page), for although Edom was restive, Solomon must still have controlled the caravan route to the port of Ezion-Geber. Thence his ships were able to go down the Red Sea and out to Ophir, a place either in eastern Arabia or western India, where gold was to be found in abundance.

And thus the Hebrews suddenly discovered the outside world. Until then they had remained an almost primitive folk pasturing their flocks and tending their

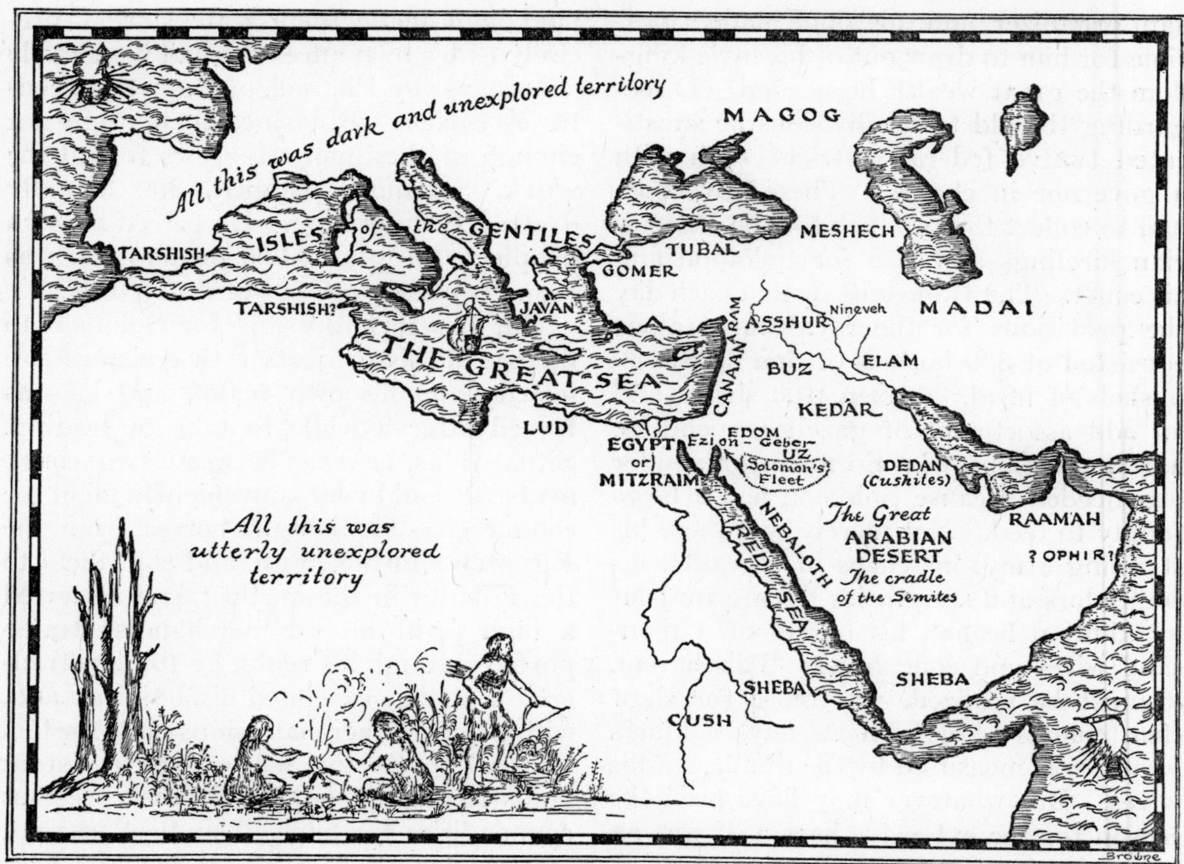

olive groves amid the remote hills alongside the Jordan. But now they became a cosmopolitan people, and the fame of their great king was spread far and wide. People came from all parts of the world to see the monarch. The queen of Sheba traveled with a train of attendants all the way from southwestern Arabia, about 1,500 miles away, to discover whether Solomon was really as wise as he was reputed to be.

But this sudden plunge into the vortex of civilization had dire consequences for Israel. The foreign princesses whom Solomon took into his harem brought with them their foreign gods and priests; and the Israelites ceased to worship Jehovah with perfect hearts. Moreover, the extravagance of Solomon was a great burden on the people, and some of them began to talk of ending the union of the tribes. Rebellion seethed in the masses, especially in the north, which still was not reconciled to serving a king who belonged to the south. Solomon's last years were not nearly so glorious as the first. He became lax in his religion and powerless among his people. And when at last he died, the whole structure his father had reared, and which he himself had tried to embellish, came tottering to the ground.

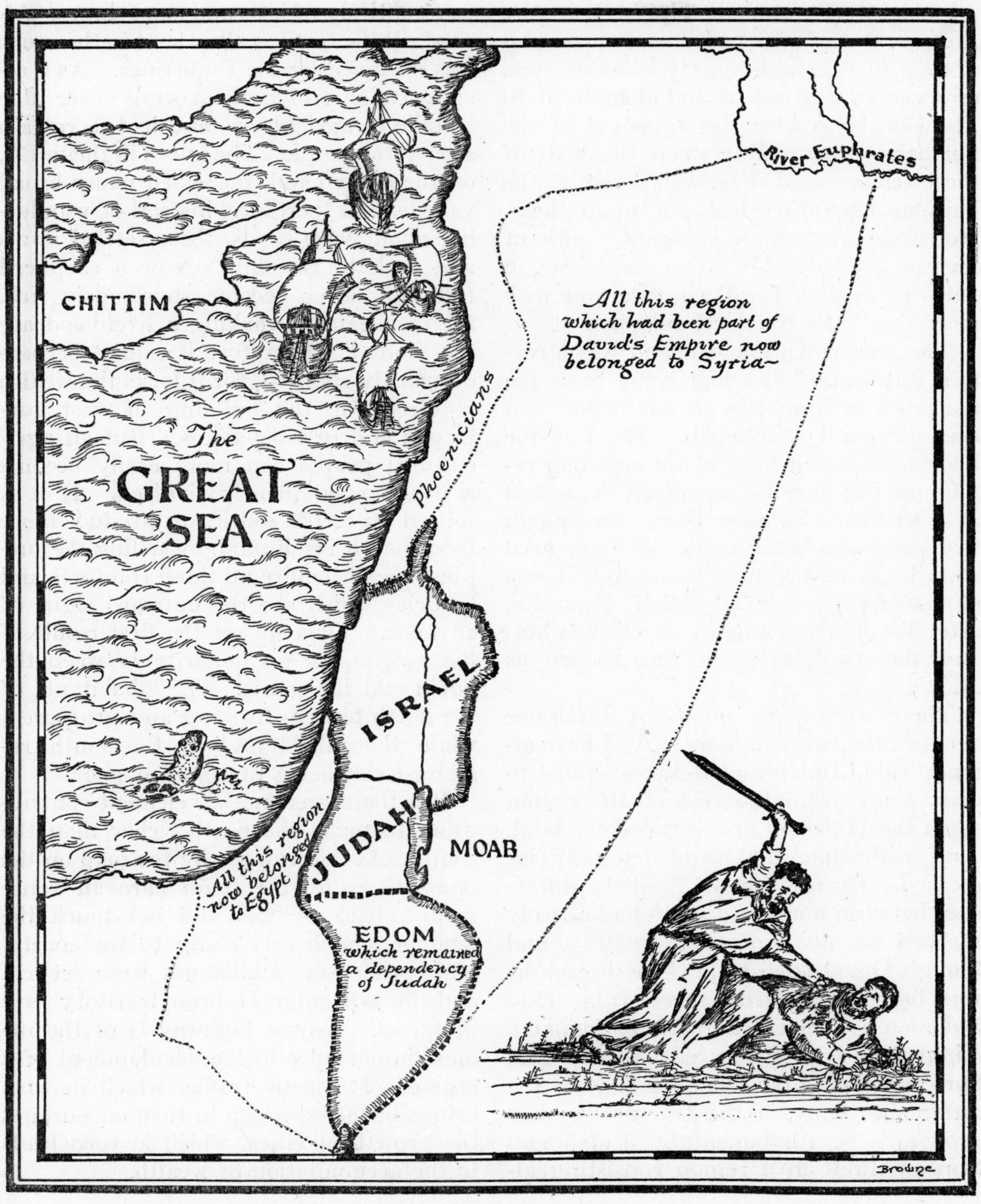
River Euphrates
CHITTIM
All this region
which had been part of
David's Empire now
belonged to Syria~
Phoenicians
The
GREAT
SEA
ISRAEL
JUDAH
MOAB
All this region
now belonged
to Egypt
EDOM
which remained
a dependency
of Judah
Brodine

ALMOST immediately after the death of Solomon came a revolution. The new king, Rehoboam, was crowned in Jerusalem and then went to Shechem to receive the approval of the northern tribes. But when the men of these tribes asked if he would reduce the burdens his father had put upon them, Rehoboam, being an arrogant youth of sixteen, replied: "My father chastised you with whips, but I will chastise you with scorpions." So the north rebelled.

The leader of the movement was a certain Jeroboam, who had come back for the purpose from Egypt, whither he had been driven by Solomon. He was the logical choice for king of the seceding region, and at once he was given the crown at Shechem. So now there were again two kingdoms in the land. The northern state took the name of Israel, but it was almost as frequently called Ephraim, after the name of one of its chief tribes; and the southern state was known as Judah.

There were many points of difference between the two kingdoms. As I have already said, Judah and Simeon tended to drift away from the rest of the nation when the Hebrews first invaded the land. And with time that tendency only increased. By the time of Saul the difference between north and south had already reached the point of open hostility, and though David tried to heal the breach he was only temporarily successful. Had Solomon not been so autocratic, the union might have been preserved much longer; but even this is far from certain, for the differences between the two groups had grown to be fundamental. Judah and Simeon dwelt in a region consisting almost entirely of hills and sand-dunes. Almost all the fertile valley land in the south was occupied by the Philistines. As a result, Judah and Simeon were never able to take to agriculture, and had to remain a pastoral people. The tribes in the north, on the other hand, possessed many broad valleys, and therefore, instead of wandering about with herds, these settled down and took to farming. Now a shepherd folk can never become enormously rich, for its means of making a livelihood are too limited. Therefore it cannot become outwardly civilized, for it lacks the wealth required for the building of vast fortresses and grand palaces. But an agricultural people can more easily become rich and consequently civilized. If it is settled on fertile soil it can produce more food than it needs, and, by selling the surplus, it can acquire all those comforts and luxuries which are the outward signs of advance. Thus we see the first result of the geographic dissimilarity between the north and the south. The inhabitants of the north took to farming and prospered, while the inhabitants of the south remained shepherds and stayed poor.

But there was another element contributing to make the north richer than the south. As you can see by the map on the opposite page, the main caravan route from Africa to Asia did not touch the land of Judah. It clung to the coastal plain where the Philistines were settled, and did not enter Hebrew territory save in Israel. Now a highway is of the utmost importance in the development of a region. It means traffic, which in turn brings business, which in turn encourages the growth of cities, which in turn leads to the accumulation of wealth.

But prosperity brings certain evils in its train. It provides an opportunity for the abler—and less scrupulous—men to outwit the rest and get more than their share of the wealth. A few people, the aristocrats, get to have far more than they can use, and the rest, the masses, are left with not even as much as they need. Both classes suffer, for the rich become in time lazy and corrupt, and the poor become spiritless and debased.

Another evil that came to blight the northern kingdom was religious corruption and moral decay. One reason for that was the continued presence of thousands of Canaanites in the ancient cities of the north. In the south, where there had never been many cities, the Canaanites had been dispersed throughout the countryside and thus had been stamped out. But in Israel, where they had had cities in which to congregate, they had survived. And although they were a subject people for centuries, still they clung to their ancient beliefs and practices. Indeed, instead of giving them up, these non-Hebrews succeeded in teaching them to their conquerors.

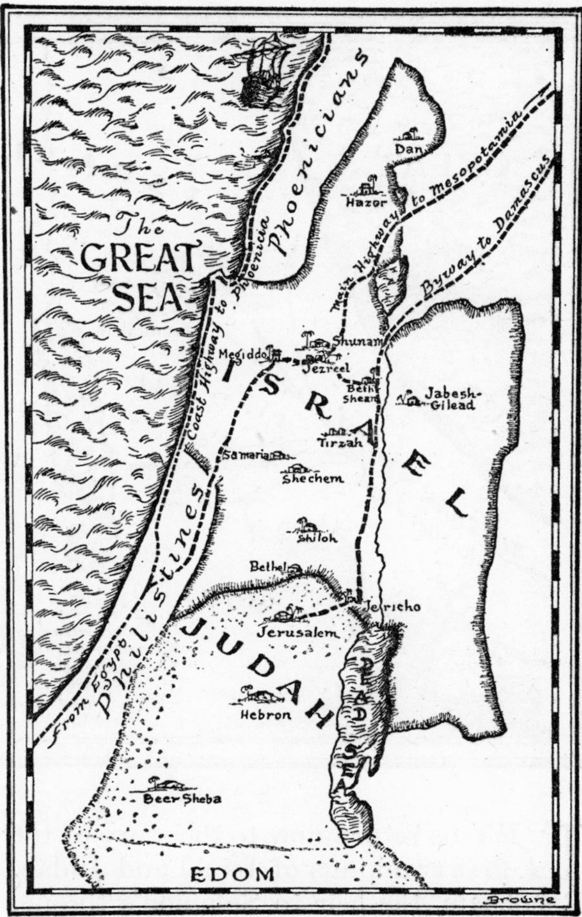

There was a further reason for apostasy in the northern kingdom. The continual stream of caravans from foreign lands brought the knowledge of many strange gods and cults to the Israelites. Judah in the south was safe from such foreign influences. Shut in among the hills, its men could remain unwavering in their loyalty to Jehovah. But Israel, with frontiers open to Phoenicia and Syria, and highways thronged with traders from every end of the earth—Israel could not escape corruption.

Such, in brief, were the differences between Israel and Judah. The northern kingdom was three times the size of the southern. It possessed all the fertile valleys and copious springs, most of the cities, and almost all the important roads. Compared with its rival it was advanced in agriculture, rich in commerce, and already on its way to religious and moral corruption. Judah was rocky, dry, isolated, and exposed only to the raids of the bedouins. It remained largely pastoral, and never saw much wealth. But perhaps for those very reasons Judah did not go so fast or so far toward destruction.

but also in a large inscription on the walls of a temple at Thebes in Egypt. Only a few of the cities which Shishak destroyed are indicated on the map above. The invader did not confine his depredations to Judah. Although he had sheltered Jeroboam during the days when the latter was a fugitive from Solomon, the Egyptian did not hesitate to raid the territory of which Jeroboam was now king. But Rehoboam in Judah suffered by far the greater loss. Many of his fortresses were burnt to the ground, and the capital itself was robbed of much of the treasure which Solomon had stored there. The Temple was stripped, and five hundred gold shields adorning the armory were stolen. And Rehoboam, son of the fabulously wealthy Solomon, was left practically bankrupt.

LET us return now to the story of the first two kings of Israel and Judah. Rehoboam, the heir to Solomon's throne, was spurned at Shechem by the rebellious northerners and forced to take refuge in Jerusalem. But he was far from reconciled to the loss of the north, and as soon as he was assured of the support of Judah he started to war on the rebels. The Bible records no incidents of this war, but I Kings 14:30 declares that it raged continually throughout the days of Rehoboam and Jeroboam. And this naturally gave the neighboring nations their long-awaited chance to plunder Palestine. Five years after Solomon's death, Shishak I of Egypt raided the war-torn land. The event is recorded not alone in the Bible,

Shishak withdrew, but the two little kingdoms did not soon recover from the blow he had struck them. Vassals now to Egypt, and desperately poor, they began to fall away into degeneracy. Even in Judah, which had always been more faithful to Jehovah, the people took to worshiping stone pillars and wooden idols on every high hill and in every grove of trees. In Israel it was worse still. Jeroboam built two royal temples in his own realm, one at Bethel on the southern border, and another at Dan in the extreme north. (Their locations are marked on the map on the preceding page.) Obviously his purpose was to keep his subjects from going over to Jerusalem in the enemy's territory to worship at the great Temple there. But at the new shrines the worship was marked by idolatry and vice. Jehovah was still nominally the god; but the rites were largely Canaanitish.

Rehoboam of Judah died about the year 923 B.C., after trying for some twelve years to crush the rebel kingdom in the north. Abijam, his son, succeeded to the throne and continued the war on Israel. But then peace ensued for a while, for Abijam's successor, Asa, was more interested in developing Judah than in accomplishing the downfall of Israel. Asa reigned some forty-one years, and during that time he labored most earnestly to cleanse Judah of the idolatry and vice which had crept into the land.

But Israel fared far worse during this half-century. Jeroboam, who had founded the kingdom, was succeeded by his son, Nadab. Within a few months of his coronation, however, Nadab was killed during a mutiny of the army, and the murderer, Baasha, usurped the throne. To ensure his dynasty, Baasha killed off all the other descendants of Jeroboam; but his own son, Elah, who succeeded to the throne, was in turn murdered by another usurper, Zimri. The army, however, did not favor Zimri, but chose instead a general named Omri to be king. Zimri, seeing his cause was lost, committed suicide after a reign of seven days, and then a new civil war began between Omri and another candidate for the throne, Tibni. Four years this wasteful contest continued, until Tibni was slain and Omri was left triumphant. The Bible tells us little about Omri save that during his reign the capital of Israel was moved to Samaria. The new site was on a hilltop in the very center of the kingdom. Omri, who was probably an able soldier, saw that the hill of Shomer—which means the "watch-tower"—was magnificently adapted for a stronghold. It rose some three hundred feet above a broad and fertile plain, and commanded the countryside for miles around. Omri built a mighty stronghold there—one which in later years played no small part in the preservation of Israel.

We know that Omri was an able soldier because a Moabite inscription tells how he marched down and captured that region. But in another direction he met with severe reverses. The Arameans from Damascus captured several of his strongholds, and, fearing further encroachments, Omri made a treaty with Ethbaal, King of Tyre, in Phoenicia. To bind that treaty, Ethbaal's daughter, Jezebel, was married to Omri's son, Ahab. The alliance strengthened Israel's position among the nations, but in another way it had a dire effect. Jezebel brought with her the religion of her native god, Baal Melkart, and when her husband succeeded to the throne, she used her influence to make all Israel worship this god. She built temples to Baal Melkart in Samaria and elsewhere, multiplied the number of his priests, and tried to kill off the prophets of Jehovah. By making the Israelites worshipers of the Phoenician god, Jezebel was trying to make them subjects of the Phoenician king. In those days there was no distinction between church and state, and a nation was as much a religious as a political organization.

But Jezebel's plot was thwarted by a

holy man named Elijah. He was one of that great galaxy of "troublers" in Israel whom we call the prophets. He saw the menace of Baalism—how it threatened to rob the Israelites both of their freedom and their moral character. So he went up and down the land agitating against Jezebel and her husband; and when Elijah was taken from this earth, another prophet, Elisha, continued the godly work. And in time this fierce agitation bore fruit, and the dynasty of Ahab came to a dreadful end.

But before that happened, many evils befell both Israel and Judah. The Arameans defeated the allied armies of both kingdoms, slaying Ahab in the course of one of the battles. A few years later Moab revolted and freed itself from the domination of Israel. And then Edom took courage and freed itself entirely from Judah. But such evils, being external, were of secondary importance. Far worse was the internal corruption that came to both the kingdoms. The Phoenician influence which Jezebel had brought to Israel crept over into Judah as well. This only aroused the prophets of Jehovah to greater activity, and before long the whole land was seething with unrest. Finally the revolution came. A young cavalry officer named Jehu, encouraged by Elisha, assassinated the king of Israel, flung Jezebel to the dogs, and made himself ruler. Then he corralled all the priests and worshipers of Baal in their temple at Samaria, slaughtered every last one of them, destroyed the building, and desecrated the site. Thus was the Phoenician cult, and the royal house which fostered it, rooted out of the land of Israel.

A similarly dreadful episode occurred in Judah six years later. There too the reigning monarch was assassinated, and the abomination of the Phoenicians was drowned in the blood of its priests.

OUR story has become involved, dreadfully involved. Perhaps it would be better for the reader not even to try to puzzle out the comings and goings of the many kings of Israel and Judah. Perhaps it would be enough merely to remember that for generations there was almost incessant strife in the divided land and, as a consequence, repeated foreign invasions. The Egyptians were the first to launch an attack, and then came the Arameans, or Syrians, as they were sometimes called. This second enemy proved far more destructive, especially after 845 B.C., when an upstart named Hazael became their king. Thenceforth neither Israel nor Judah had any peace. Hazael defeated the Hebrews in battle after battle, and finally reduced both their kingdoms to vassalage. He annexed Bashan and Gilead—indeed all of Israel's territory east of the Jordan. Then he trampled across western Palestine, plundered and ravaged as far south as Gath in Philistia, and ravaged at will over the kingdom of Judah. When Hazael finally returned to Damascus, he left Palestine prostrate. Israel was so reduced in size as to be no larger than Judah, and Judah was laid under heavy tribute.

But with the death of Hazael the whole situation changed. Damascus itself was suddenly plunged into a death struggle with its neighbors on the north and east, leaving the Hebrew kingdoms a chance to regain their freedom. But then almost immediately Judah and Israel again fell to warring against each other. Israel emerged the victor. An army of northerners invaded Judah, looted the palace and Temple, and carried off hostages to insure future good conduct. And thenceforth Judah remained a vassal of Israel until Israel was destroyed.

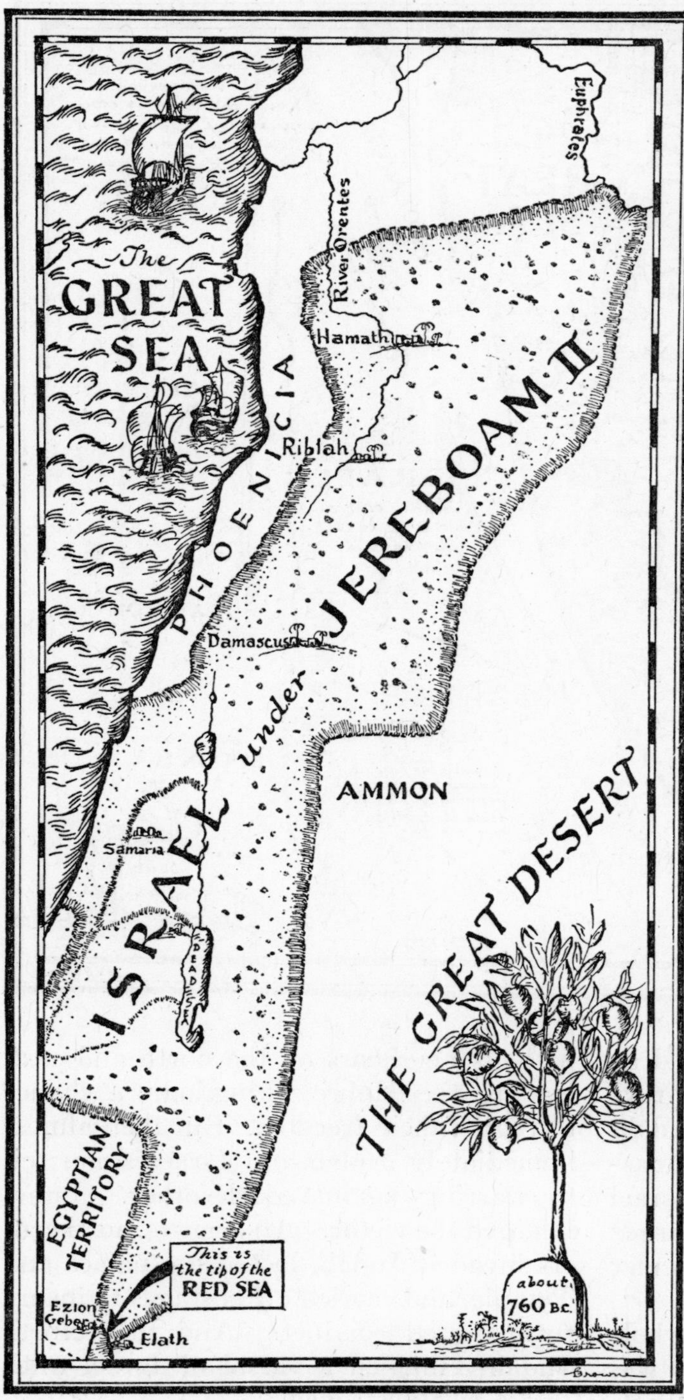

THERE followed a generation of prosperity and expansion for the Hebrews. The downfall of Damascus gave Israel a chance to reconquer all the north country as far as the River Euphrates, and gave Judah a chance to retake Edom down to the Red Sea. So now the Hebrews were masters again of almost all of the territory that David had conquered. They were still divided into two kingdoms, but one dominated the other. Judah, the southern kingdom, still had its own ruler, a young man named Uzziah; but he was counted a vassal of Jeroboam II of Israel. Uzziah was a person of considerable ability and he devoted himself to the task of strengthening his own kingdom. He fortified Elath, the port on the Red Sea, and colonized the coast region which until now had belonged to the Philistines. New resources were developed and for the first time in generations there was a measure of prosperity in Judah.

If Judah prospered it was but natural that Israel, the overlord, should prosper even more. The reconquest of Aramea yielded abundant spoils for King Jeroboam, and the ensuing peace gave his people a chance to cultivate their valleys and develop their markets. The whole country became flush with prosperity, and outwardly all was well with Israel.

BUT only outwardly was all well with Israel. Beneath the surface of prosperity and peace there was deep misery and bitter hatred. As was almost inevitable, the wealth of Israel had gone into the coffers of a few nobles, and the rest of the population was reduced to serfdom. These aristocrats no longer dwelt on the soil but in the capital or the other large cities, where they could live in luxury and show off their wealth. The rest of the inhabitants were sad and sodden, crushed by the corrupt ruling class. And the tragedy of it was that this unjust state of affairs was accepted as right and godly. The rich were quite certain they were also virtuous. They imagined that so long as they attended all the festivals and brought rich offerings of sheep and other animals to the temples at Bethel and Dan, so long they were doing all that the Lord required of them. The fine simplicity of their ancient desert religion was no more. The Canaanites and Phoenicians had had their influence, and the Hebrew festivals had become little more than drunken debauches. On these festive days the wealthy ones gathered at their shrines and amid great hilarity and license rejoiced in their good fortune. It seemed to them that Jehovah was immensely pleased with them, for not in centuries had there been so much prosperity in Israel. They quite literally believed they were living in "God's Country," and that ill-fortune could not possibly touch them.

But then there came the great prophets, men of godly spirit who dared to raise their voice in protest against the prevailing wickedness. We have already mentioned the prophets several times in this summary of Bible history. We have seen how Samuel helped to found the monarchy and how Elijah and Elisha helped to reform it. Were there space we might mention many other such men who sought at one time or another to utter Jehovah's word to the people. In the beginning the prophets were more magicians than anything else. They consulted oracles for the people, and told fortunes. But later they changed in character, and became preachers rather than soothsayers. They were the great evangelists of their day, and went up and down the country exhorting the people to keep far from the abomination of the idolators and remain faithful to Jehovah. They were a courageous lot, those prophets. They were not afraid even of kings. When David grew drunk with power and stole another man's wife, it was a prophet named Nathan who dared go to the king and tell him to his face he was an accursed criminal. It was a prophet, Ahijah, who stirred up the one attempt at revolution when Solomon was on the throne. And, as we have already seen, it was a prophet, Elijah, who alone kept the wicked Jezebel from ruining her husband's race.

Unhappily, however, we have record of exceedingly few sermons preached by prophets before the middle of the eighth century B.C. Not until the coming of that strange character named Amos do the real "literary prophets" make their appearance. It is significant that, though Amos preached in Israel, he came from a village in the hills of Judah. He was a simple herdsman from Tekoa, and only in obedience to the command of his God did he presume to preach at Bethel. His soul was revolted at the wickedness of the rich Israelites. So one Autumn, during the festival time, he went over to Bethel—it was only about 20 miles from his home in Tekoa—and began to speak God's word in the temple there. Bitterly he denounced the drunken throng, and loud did he cry that despite the present prosperity there would soon be terror in all Israel. For Jehovah, the God of Justice, would no longer abide the waywardness of the people. He demanded righteousness and they gave him only burnt offerings; He wanted them to practice justice, and instead they indulged in wild festivities. Therefore, Israel was doomed.

Thus did Amos, a simple peasant from Judah, dare to address the drunken lords and ladies in their temple at Bethel. But they would not hearken, and some forty years later the doom which Amos prophesied was fulfilled. Assyria came ravaging through the land, and Israel was utterly destroyed.

But before that calamity occurred another prophet appeared in Israel. Hosea was his name, and he too dared to protest against the evils in the land. According to tradition his home was in Gilead, and perhaps that was why he, though a subject of the northern kingdom, was capable of perceiving the wickedness of its ways. Gilead was the hilly region east of the Jordan, and shared to a degree the primitiveness of Judah. Hosea seems to have been a gentle and cultured man, and the burthen of his preaching was far less drastic and unforgiving than that of Amos. He too could see the certainty of Israel's doom if it persisted in its evil course; but with it he could see the possibility of repentance and forgiveness. For Jehovah to this prophet was not only a God of Justice but also a God of Mercy. Despite all the sins that the mighty in Israel had committed, Jehovah would forgive them. He would forgive them, declared Hosea, and save the land—if only the people would repent.

But the mighty in Israel did not repent. They continued to oppress the poor, to exploit the weak, and to conduct themselves perversely in the shrines of their God. And so the doom foreseen by these two men, Amos and Hosea, did come to the land, and Israel was destroyed.

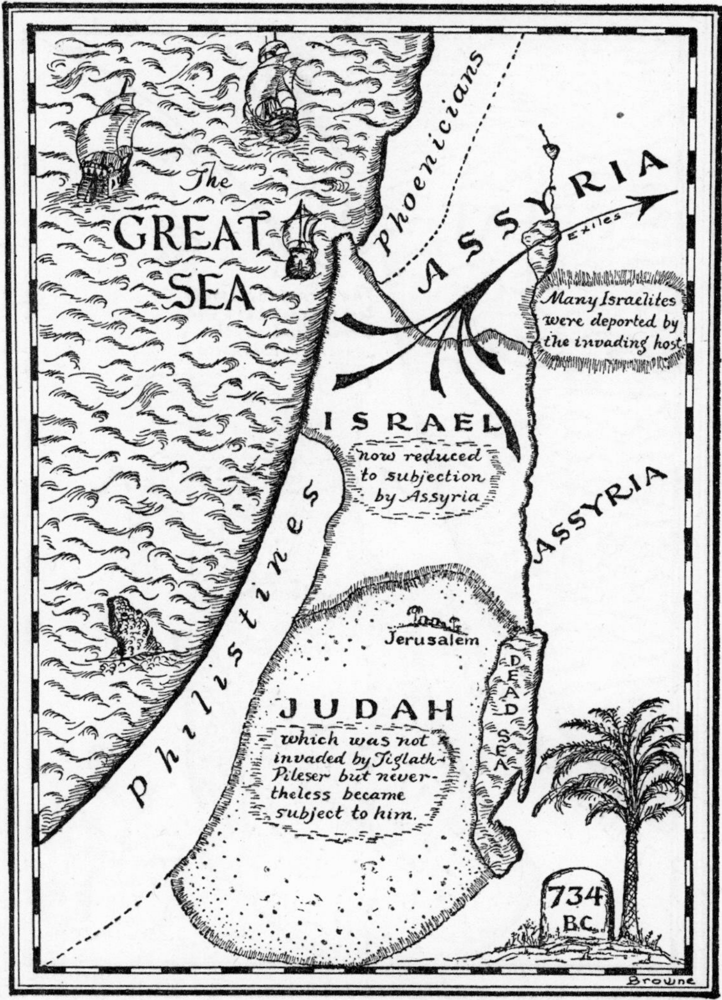

WHEN Jeroboam II died, the era of order and prosperity came to a swift end. The empire crumbled away, and the Hebrews were left with only their strip of hill-country along the Jordan. Jeroboam's son, Zechariah, reigned but six months before he was killed. His assassin, a man named Shallum, reigned only one month before he too was murdered. The new usurper, Menahem, managed to hold on to the throne several years, but his reign was marked by continuous strife. A devouring enemy, Assyria, was striding westward from Mesopotamia, and Israel lay helpless in its path. Assyria had been threatening to swallow up Palestine for some time past, but not until now was the act accomplished. A particularly able and energetic king, Tiglath-Pileser IV, came to the throne of Assyria in 745 B.C., and seven years later he marched over and invaded Israel. Menahem was in no position to offer resistance and hastened to pay the Assyrian an enormous tribute. Tiglath-Pileser then withdrew, but four years later he was back again. A new king had arisen in Israel, a military man named Pekah, who dared to attempt to throw off the Assyrian yoke. Allying himself with Rezin, the king of Damascus, he called on Judah to join in the revolt. But Ahaz, the king in Judah, refused, whereupon Pekah and Rezin invaded his realm. Ahaz, thoroughly terrified, called to Tiglath-Pileser for help, and the latter responded with alacrity. The Assyrian came storming down on Israel, annexed all the East Jordan region and all of what was later called Galilee, and carried off tens of thousands of Israelites into slavery. Damascus, the other rebel, he crushed completely, absorbing the whole kingdom. Of course, Judah was spared, but only at the price of vassalage.

IN Israel there was an immediate uprising against the king who had brought such trouble to his land. Pekah was swiftly put out of the way, and a new king, Hoshea, was seated on the throne. The favor of Assyria was purchased at the price of an annual tribute, and there was peace for the moment. But as soon as Tiglath-Pileser of Assyria died, Hoshea decided to rebel. Supported by Egypt, which was exceedingly anxious to create a buffer state between itself and Assyria, Hoshea refused to pay the annual tribute. Forthwith the new king of Assyria, Shalmaneser IV, swept down on Israel and took Hoshea prisoner. Not content with this, however, Shalmaneser continued on and laid siege to Samaria. He was determined to crush the kingdom thoroughly and thus put an end forever to all trouble from that quarter. But Samaria was not easily captured. Thanks to Omri's military astuteness in choosing its site, the city was able to hold out for three long years. Shalmaneser died before it fell, and it was left for his son, Sargon II, to complete the conquest. Finally, late in the year 722 B.C., Samaria capitulated, and the kingdom of Israel came to an end. The best element in the defeated population was deported to prevent the possibility of insurrection. The wealthiest and most powerful of the Israelites were taken captive by Sargon and settled in northern Mesopotamia and Media. (The regions are approximately indicated on the large map printed inside the covers of this book.) Only the humblest of the Israelites, the peasants and slaves, were left at home, for these showed little promise of ever attempting rebellion. To help them till the valleys and populate the market-towns of Israel, foreign colonists from northern Syria and Babylonia were brought in by Sargon. And thus the kingdom of Israel came to an end.

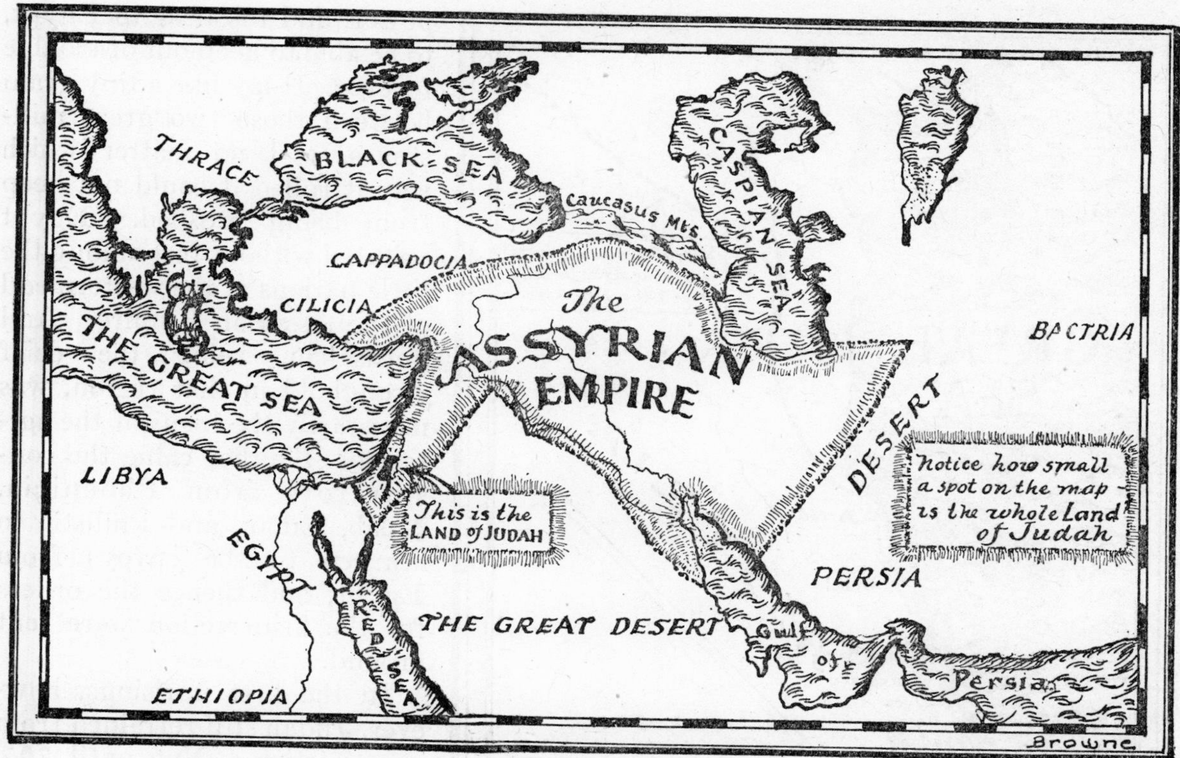

ACCORDING to tradition the kingdom of Israel consisted of ten of the original twelve tribes, and with the great deportation in 722 B.C. the legend of the Lost Ten Tribes began. It was imagined that the Israelites marched out of their land in one great body and then lost themselves in a far romantic land. Many an explorer coming across some strange people in Central America, or Japan, or Abyssinia, has rushed forth to declare that the Lost Ten Tribes have been found again. But no explorer ever really found them, and no explorer ever will. Those tribes did not wander off together to any distant land, but simply dwindled out of existence right where they were set down by the Assyrians. Many of the Israelites may have escaped from exile and joined the other two tribes of Hebrews; but quite clearly most of them simply merged with the races dwelling in Assyria and Media, and there faded out of history's picture.

A similar fate met all the other small nations of the ancient orient—all, that is, except Judah. Sargon did not go on from Samaria and seek to destroy Jerusalem too. Though he wiped out the northern kingdom, he spared Judah, for it had paid tribute faithfully. Thus the story of the Chosen People now becomes the story of its two southern tribes—really of its one tribe, Judah, for Simeon had by now largely merged with the Edomites in the desert. That is why from here on we no longer refer to the Chosen People as Israelites, or Hebrews, but as Judeans, or Jews.

THE destruction of Israel was a warning to Judah, and for a while the little kingdom accepted Assyrian domination without a murmur. But such docility could not be maintained for long. Judah was too far from the seat of Assyrian power, and too near to Egypt, to be able to keep out of trouble forever. It lay like a tiny grain between those two great millstones, and no matter which way it rolled it could not keep from being crushed. Egypt agitated without rest among the little nations at the western end of the Assyrian Empire. And Jerusalem, being the chief stronghold in that region, was necessarily the focus of the agitation. Thither came the conspirators from Phoenicia, Moab, Edom, and Philistia to hearken to the envoys from Egypt, and thence the orders for the insurrection were sent around.

In the first uprisings, however, Judah still refrained from overt action. Not until 705, when the great Sargon was assassinated and the Assyrian Empire seemed about to crumble, did Judah shows signs of rebelling. The new emperor, Sennacherib, was too busy crushing his enemies in the east to attend to Judah immediately. But four years later, after the east had been thoroughly subdued, Sennacherib gathered his army and thundered over to the west. He began with the Phoenician cities and then swiftly swept southward, pillaging and burning as he went. There was terror throughout the region, and Edom and Moab hurriedly sent their submission. Judah, however, made no move, trusting

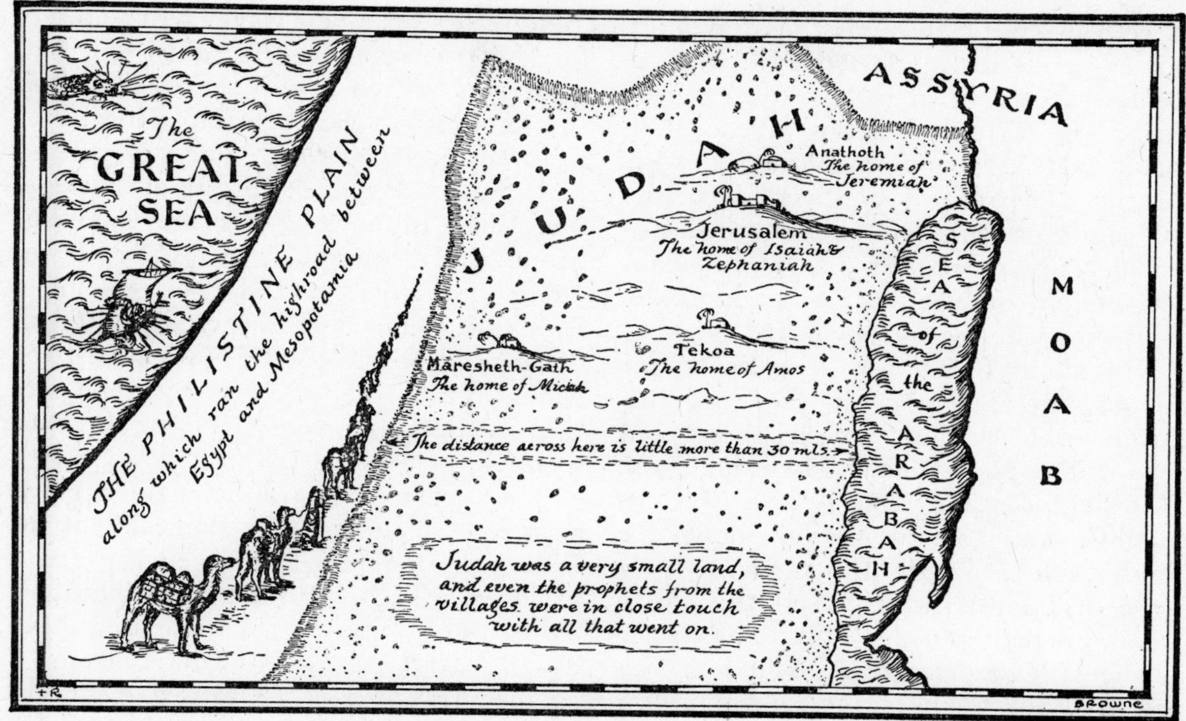

to Egypt to stay Sennacherib's march. But when at last Egypt did send an army against the Assyrians, it was ignominiously defeated. And then real panic broke loose in Judah. Sennacherib had routed the Egyptians at Eltekeh, on the southern border of Philistia, but instead of pushing on toward the Nile, he had doubled in his tracks and had begun to march toward Jerusalem. One Judean city after another went up in flames as Sennacherib's army pressed on into the hills. With feverish haste Jerusalem was put into a state of defense, but when the Assyrians actually appeared before the walls no resistance was offered. The king emptied his treasury, stripped his palace, even took off the gold from the doors and pillars in the Temple, and sent it all to Sennacherib as a peace offering. And in return Sennacherib spared Jerusalem and allowed the poor bankrupt Jewish king to retain his crown.

Sennacherib's invasion of Judah might never have occurred had one man had his way. That man was a prophet named Isaiah, and his importance cannot be exaggerated. Isaiah belonged to the aristocracy, and his chief influence was with the king and the princes in Jerusalem. Desperately he had pleaded with the king to turn a deaf ear to the blandishments of Egypt and make no move to throw off the Assyrian yoke. And though Isaiah failed in the end, still his work was not all in vain, for he did manage to stave off the rebellion for many years. And when at last Judah did raise the flag of revolt and was thoroughly chastised for it, Isaiah's influence became greater than ever. A wave of reform swept through the tiny land, and everyone in Judah from the king to the lowest serf tried to turn over a new leaf. The Temple itself was renovated, for it had become defiled by idol-worshipers. The reformation went even further and many social abuses were corrected. The new order was by no means perfect, but at least it was an improvement over what had preceded it.

Not alone Isaiah was responsible for this change, but also another prophet, Micah, who was not an aristocrat but one of the plain folk. He came from Maresheth-Gath, a village in the western foothills, and he went up and down the countryside arousing the peasants to a sense of their wrongs. And thus, with Isaiah preaching in the capital and Micah in the villages, the whole kingdom was prepared for the wave of reform.

But the results of the sudden reform were soon undone again. Fifteen years passed, and then all the old idolatry came back. Vile things were done to please the Phoenician god, Thammuz, and babies were sacrificed to the bloody god, Moloch. And all the reformers and the prophets of Jehovah were slaughtered or driven to cover.

For almost half a century a spirit of heathenism was rampant in Judah, and then another wave of reform swept the country. A new king, Josiah, sat on the throne, a young man who from childhood had probably been under the influence of secret friends of the reformers. The prophets cautiously emerged from their hiding-places and began to preach once more in the open. Zephaniah, a cousin of the king, and Jeremiah, a young man of a priestly family, were especially prominent as agitators for a new wave of reform. A terrifying chapter in oriental history had just been written, and it served to hasten the coming of the reform. Hordes of ravenous Scythians had suddenly poured forth out of the dark forests of Europe. They had plunged across the Caucasus Mountains, through Asia Minor, down along the borders of Palestine, leaving a wide trail of blood and ashes behind them. They very nearly got Jerusalem in their claws, and even though the city escaped, the inhabitants were left weak with terror.

That gave the prophets their great chance. Up and down the land they went, calling on the people to heed the dread warning. The awful Day of Jehovah's Judgment was at hand, they declared. And there was but one means of escape: repentance! "Return, O backsliding children!" they cried to the trembling people. "Return unto Jehovah or be destroyed!" So did the prophets cry with desperate sincerity.

And the people did return. Led by the terrified young king, they foreswore utterly their past wickedness. An ancient code of laws was discovered in the Temple at Jerusalem, a scroll said to have been written by Moses himself. In it were set down in harrowing detail the curses that would fall upon Judah if Jehovah's law was not scrupulously obeyed. And when Josiah, the young king, heard those curses, he rent his clothes in fear. Hastily he summoned all the free men of Judah to the Temple in Jerusalem, and there he arose and read to them the whole book. And there and then the people vowed to cleanse themselves of sin and rededicate themselves to Jehovah their Lord.

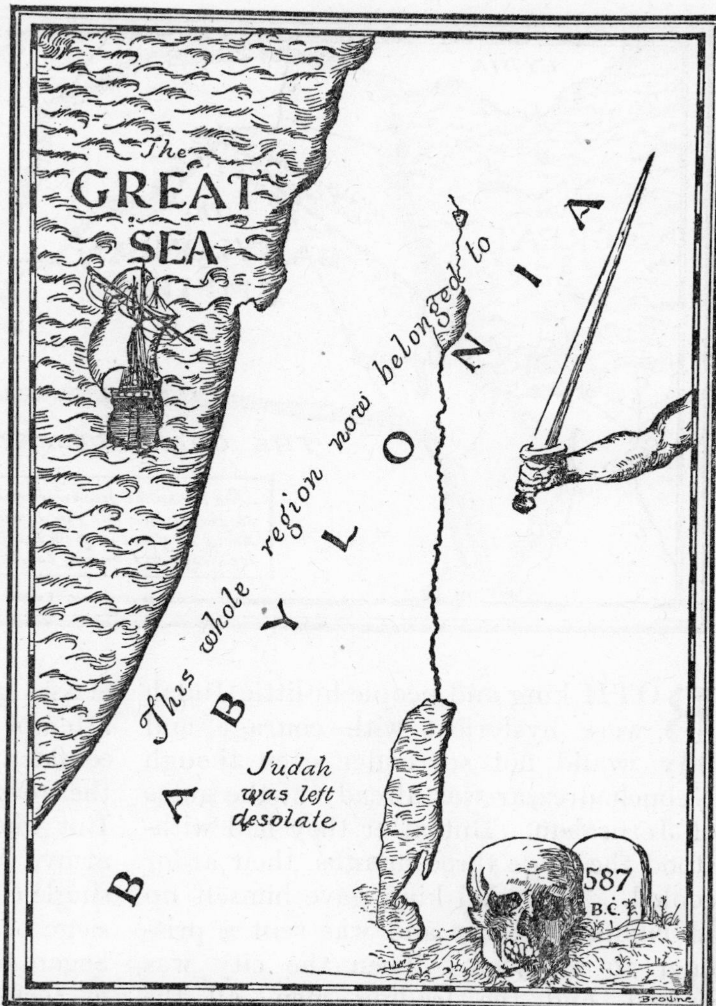

BUT soon there was another reaction, brought on largely by the new evils that came to Judah from the outside. After more than a century of triumph, Assyria began to crumble, and Egypt saw its long-awaited chance to snatch Palestine for itself. An invading army was sent northward in the year 608, but the King of Judah was determined to be free at last of all overlords, and he refused to surrender. Bravely he went out to join battle, but his handful of poorly trained troops proved no match for the disciplined and skilled Greek army which Egypt had hired for the invasion. In the very first skirmish Josiah was killed and his army routed. The Egyptians swept northward as far as the Euphrates, conquering all before them. But the triumph of Egypt did not last long. In the east a new empire arose to take Assyria's place, and the Egyptians were driven back to the Nile. So thereafter Judah had to recognize a new overlord, Nebuchadrezzar of Babylonia. But Jehoiakim, the foolhardy king then reigning in Judah, soon tried to withhold the annual tribute, and then trouble began anew. Nebuchadrezzar was too busy at the moment to attend to the little rebel, but he did order the governors of the neighboring provinces to let loose upon Judah bands of marauders, Edomites, Ammonites, and Samaritans. And these marauders harried the country-side until Nebuchadrezzar himself was ready to launch an attack.

At least one man in Judah saw the folly of the revolt: the prophet Jeremiah. From the beginning he had been opposed to insurrection, for he had realized how powerless was little Judah against Babylonia. But he had not been heeded. His first scroll of sermons was torn to shreds by the king himself, and Jeremiah was put in the stocks.

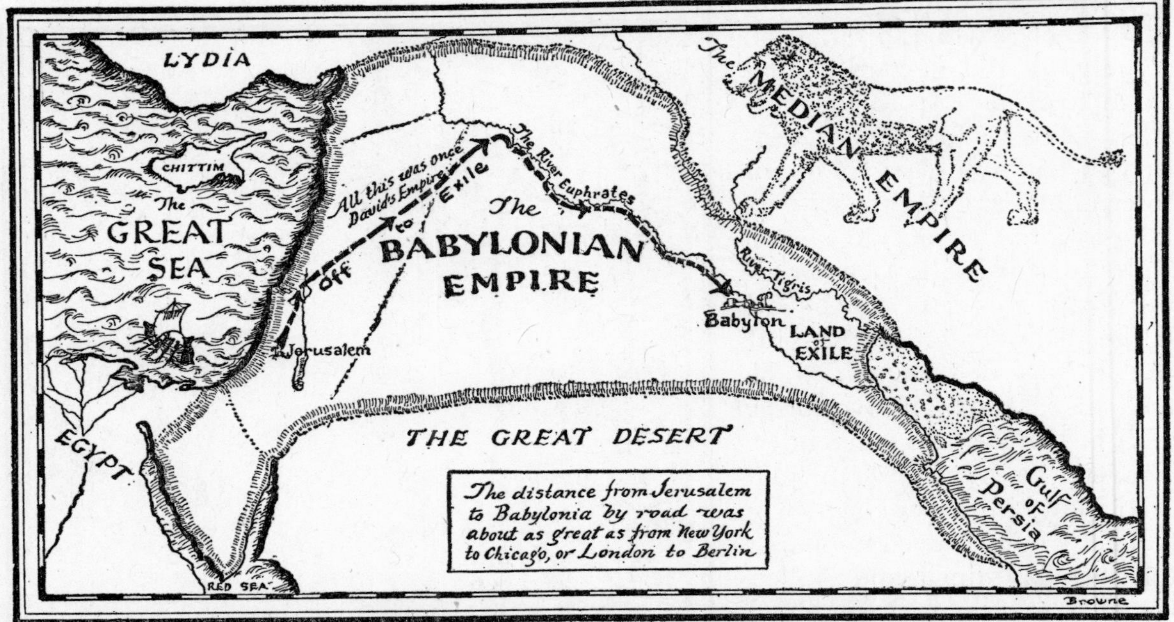

BOTH king and people in little Judah were hysterical with courage and they would not surrender even though Nebuchadrezzar was already at the gates of Jerusalem. But after they had withstood the siege three months, their ardor cooled. The rebel king gave himself up to Nebuchadrezzar and was sent a prisoner to Babylon. Then the city was sacked, and the leading men, all the landed proprietors and wealthy merchants, together with the entire standing army and all the skilled workmen, were deported in a body. The kingdom itself was spared, however. Nebuchadrezzar appointed one of the royal house to be the ruler, and then, confident he had stamped out the last spark of rebellion in Judah, the mighty emperor returned to Babylon. But Nebuchadrezzar had underestimated the stubborn patriotism of the Judeans. Although he had left none save the lower classes in the land, soon there was another attempt at rebellion. The Judeans were confident that Egypt, which had stirred up the revolt, would come to their rescue. But when the Egyptians did send up an army, Nebuchadrezzar destroyed it in a single campaign, and then returned to the siege of Jerusalem. His battering rams began to thunder against the north wall of Jerusalem, and finally, after a siege of a year and a half, a breach was made in July, 586 B.C. The king of Judah was captured, his sons were killed in his presence, his own eyes were put out, and then he was carried in chains to Babylon. To terrify the nation still further, seventy of the leading citizens were put to death. The walls of the city were entirely demolished, and all its inhabitants, perhaps 25,000 people, were taken into exile to Babylon. And thus was Judah brought low a second time.

THE thousands of Judeans left in the despoiled land were the very dregs of the population. A man of fine character named Gedaliah was appointed governor over them, and he tried with all his might to give the poor wretches some sort of government. But a rascally adventurer arose, assassinated the noble Gedaliah, and tried to organize a fresh revolt against Babylonia. Dreading the certain consequences, the more energetic of the population straightway fled from the land, forcibly taking the old prophet Jeremiah with them. They escaped to Egypt and settled down in the cities of Migdol and Tahpanhes, which, as you can see by the map, were commercial centers situated on the main caravan route going to Mesopotamia. Other of the fugitives settled in Memphis, while still others went far up the Nile to Elephantine. And thus the Jews, an erstwhile shepherd people, now perforce became traders.

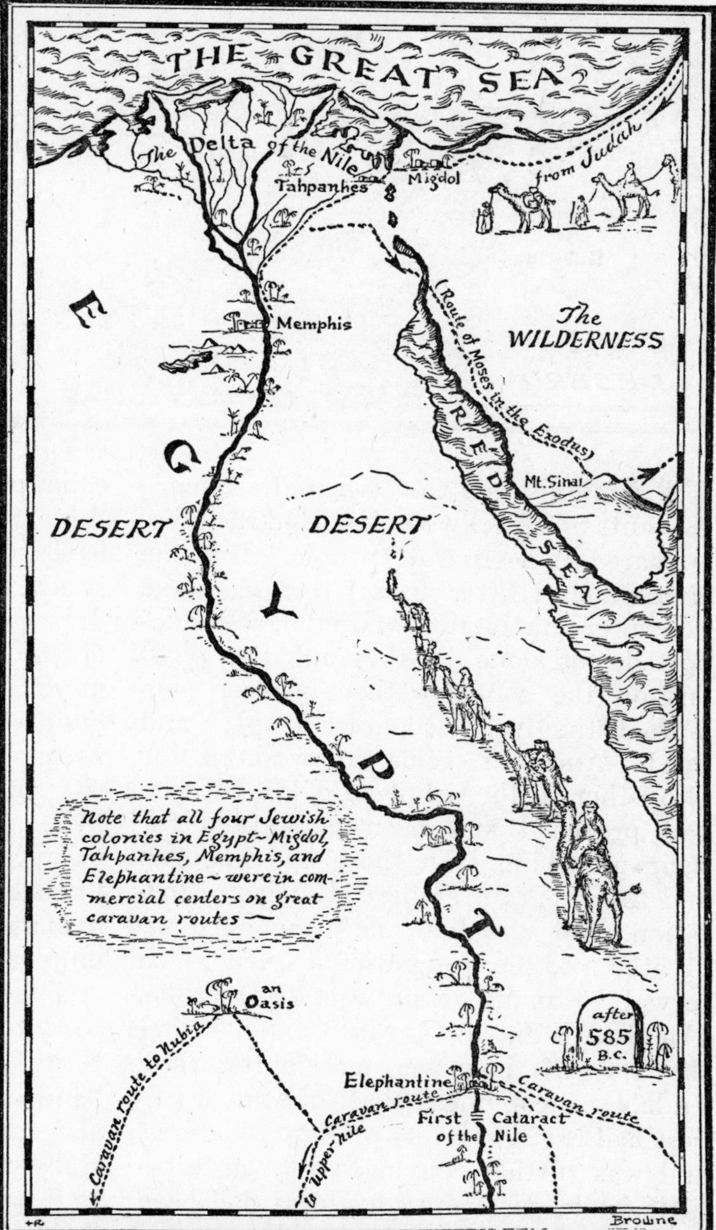

But with the vast change from pastoral life in the hills of Judah to commercial life in the market-places of Egypt, there came an equally vast change in the whole outlook of the people. They began to fall away from the religion of their forefathers, and took to the religion of the heathen people around them. Soon they began to cultivate the manners and vices of the Egyptians. The last recorded words of Jeremiah are a bitter attack on his fellow-Jews in Egypt for their apostasy; and, according to tradition, the heroic old prophet was beaten to death for uttering them.

IT is significant that when the inhabitants of Israel were deported they disappeared as a separate people. But one hundred and fifty years later, when the far fewer inhabitants of Judah were deported, not alone did they not disappear, but on the contrary they became even more distinctively a separate people—and lived. And that seems to have been due altogether to the prophets of Judah who had preached and been persecuted for their preaching. In those one hundred and fifty years preceding Judah's deportation, the prophets had managed to breathe into the tiny nation a spirit which served to make it quite indestructible. For Judah did not go into exile feeling that its sufferings were accidental. No, Judah was convinced that its own sinfulness had brought on its present afflictions, and was further convinced that in but a little while, when its sinfulness had been expiated, these afflictions would come to a final end. And it was this heartening belief that almost alone made it possible for tiny Judah to survive.

It is important to realize just how tiny Judah actually was, for then the miracle of its survival becomes even more impressive. After the catastrophe that occurred in 586, the inhabitants of Judah were left divided into three main fragments. First there was the dispirited remnant left behind in Palestine—poor, benighted peasants who were harried constantly by wild tribes from the desert. Then there were the fugitives who had congregated in scattered settlements in Egypt. Finally there was the community of exiles in Babylon. But all three groups together probably would not have sufficed to people an ordinary fair-sized American city like Paterson, New Jersey, or Des Moines, Iowa. Their total number could not have been much more than a hundred and twenty-five or a hundred and fifty thousand—about half as many Jews as there are today in the city of Chicago alone. And yet that little nation, dispersed across all the orient, tossed about in the welter of empires like a cork in a furious whirlpool, managed to live on and come out triumphant.

The story of that survival is largely the story of the handful that was dragged off to Babylon. And not even of all that handful, for many of those Jews deserted and took to the gods of the conquerors. Babylon was a mighty city whose outer wall was fifty miles in length, and so thick that four chariots could drive on it abreast. In it were mighty temples adorned with jewels and precious metals, and vast palaces brilliant with colored bricks and tiles. To the bedraggled Judeans, destitute wanderers from a backward little hill-country, the sight of all the magnificence of Babylonia must have been overwhelming.

But not all the exiles were swept off their feet by the grandeur of Babylon and its gods. The majority went the way of all majorities, but an heroic minority stood its ground and refused to be stampeded. Of course, the temptation to be satisfied with things in Babylon was almost irresistible. The exiles were not scattered throughout the empire, but settled together on the banks of one of the canals in Babylonia. Recently discovered inscriptions inform us that the specific canal was the Kabaru, which ran eastward from the city of Babylon to the ancient shrine of Nippur. Its waters flowed through as fertile a region as was to be found anywhere in the orient. The Jews dwelt in the villages along this canal, in the huddled little villages which had been built on low mud-mounds to escape the spring floods. Probably a goodly proportion of the exiles took to trading, for the canals which intersected this region in every direction were used as much for commerce as irrigation. The prophet Ezekiel, who was the spiritual adviser of the exiles, describes the place as "a land of traffic, a city of merchants, a fruitful soil, beside many waters."

The Jews were allowed every opportunity of making themselves comfortable in their new home. They were unhindered by their conquerors and allowed to manage their private affairs as they pleased. Chances a-plenty were given to those who desired wealth and station, for King Nebuchadrezzar of Babylonia —who not undeservedly was called the Great—put no obstacle in their way. He had destroyed the kingdom of Judah not out of any hatred for the Jews but simply because the existence of that kingdom had menaced his hold on Palestine. He could not afford to lose Palestine, for it was the one open approach from Egypt and therefore was the most vital region on the western frontier of the Babylonian Empire. Now, however, that Palestine was safe, Nebuchadrezzar wished the defeated and exiled men of Judah all the good in the world. And rapidly many of them began to get it.

But always there were the few who could not be at ease in Babylonia. They hated this strange land, for it was not their own. It was "unclean" to them. And longingly they thought only of the little hills whence they had been taken. In their minds those hills became ineffably lovely, and the men who once trod them seemed immeasurably great. Like beggars around a fire, the exiles warmed their hearts with tales of past glories, with glowing stories which they elaborated about Moses, and David, and Solomon.

Many of the exiles grew rich and forgot altogether the humble land whence they had come. But the rest plodded along in aching homesickness. They could not sacrifice to God in Babylon, for that would have meant a violation of their Holy Law which recognized Jerusalem as the only proper place for sacrifice. The best they could do was to devote one day of the week, the Sabbath, to undivided thought of their God. Perhaps on that day they prayed and fasted in little synagogues—that is, "assemblies"—their faces turned yearningly toward Jerusalem. And piteously they begged for the coming of the day of their redemption.

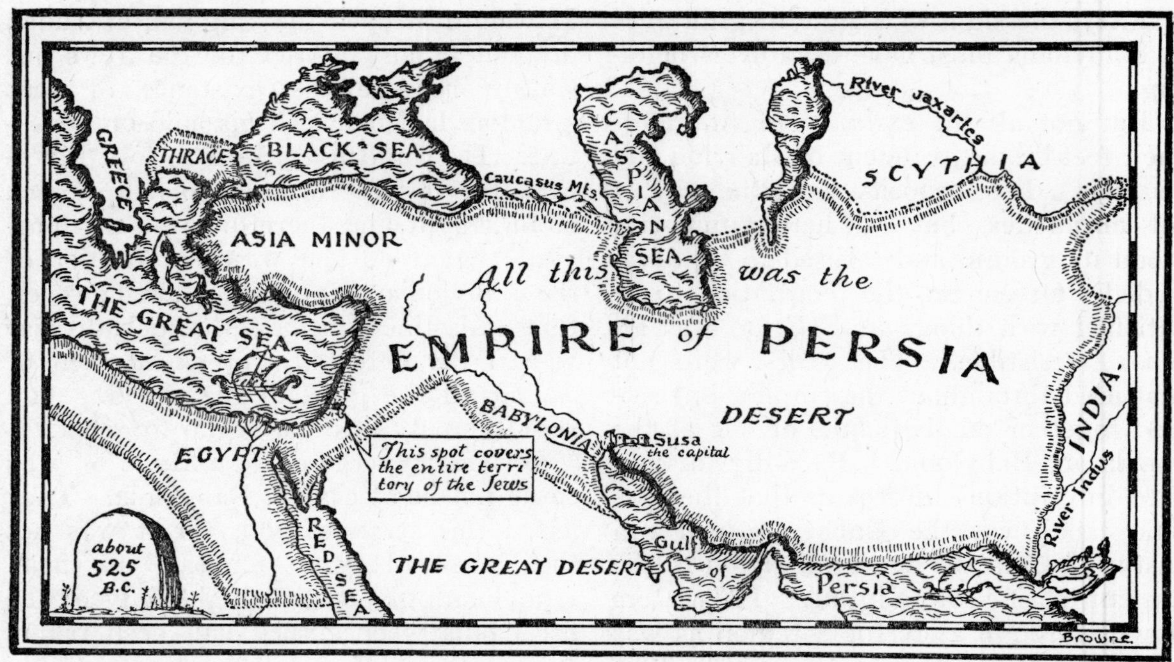

AND at last the day of redemption seemed about to dawn. A new empire was arising in the East, the empire of Cyrus, the Persian. Babylonia seemed certain to fall, for King Nebuchadrezzar was long dead and a weakling sat on the throne. Feverish whispering went on in the little settlement of the exiles, and then loud and heroic agitation. Finally in 538 B.C. Cyrus, king of the new empire of Persia, captured Babylon and the power of Assyria was destroyed forever.

Now Cyrus was a despot of the most enlightened sort, and one of his first acts after he conquered Babylon was to grant permission to the Jewish exiles to return, if they so desired, to their own ancestral homeland.

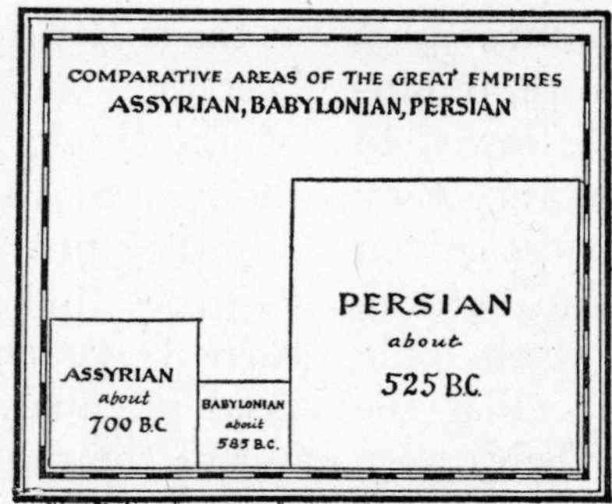

But not all of the exiles took advantage of Cyrus's decree. The rest found it too hard to tear themselves away from the shops and homes they had established in the "unclean" land, and they remained behind. Perhaps some of them even resented the decree, considering it a reflection on their Babylonian citizenship. They refused to think of themselves any more as Judeans; their boast was that they were "one hundred-percent" Babylonians. Even most of those who admitted freely that they felt themselves spiritual strangers in Babylonia—even they did not stir. Instead they gave money—and of course much free moral encouragement—to the few daring souls who did make ready to go back.

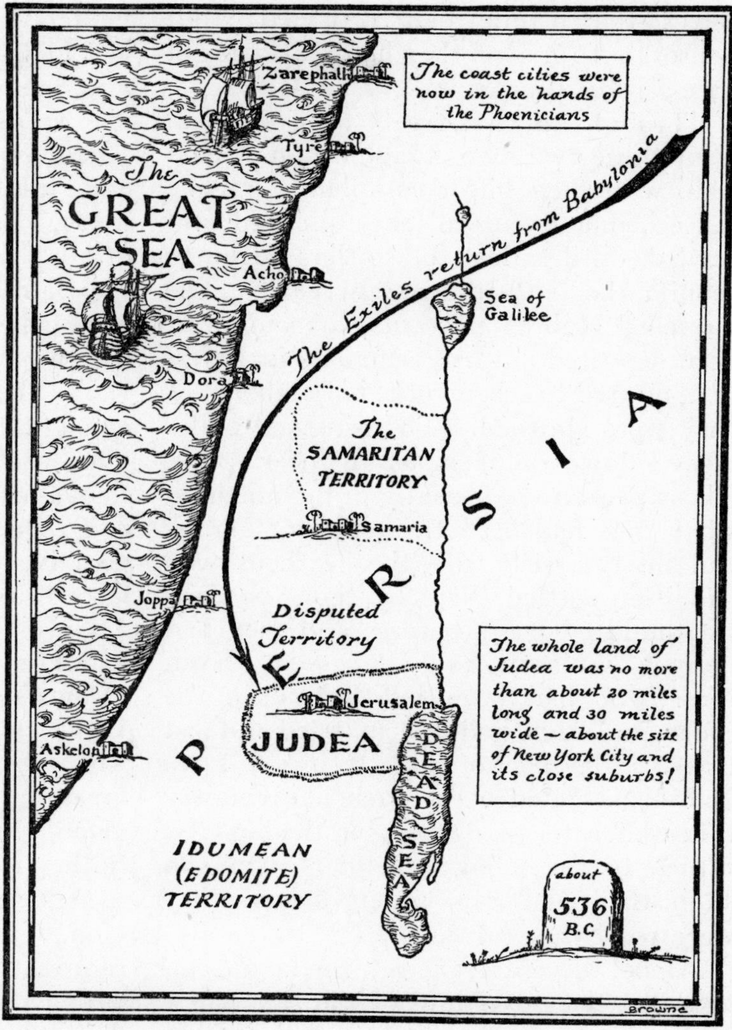

THOSE who returned were daring souls indeed. To get back to the old homeland they had to journey many months across the desert. And when they got back, only shambles greeted their gaze. Disappointments and hardships followed close on each other's heels from the very start. Jerusalem was a heap of ruins, and the fields roundabout were choked with wild growths and weeds. Houses had to be put up and cisterns dug; the fields had to be cleared and tilled. There was no time to dream great dreams or build glittering castles in the air. A rough stone altar was set up on Mt. Moriah—and that was all. They who had fondly hoped to build a house of prayer for all the peoples on earth were too busy trying to keep alive to make a house of prayer even for themselves. Seventeen years they struggled along in that fashion, and then almost all the zeal and idealism they had brought with them from Babylonia seeped out of their wearied souls. They were discouraged and miserable. Perhaps they cursed the day they had ever left the prosperous land of their exile.

And then once more the prophets reappeared. One was an aged man named Haggai, who had played in the streets of the old Jerusalem in his childhood. He preached in simple homely words, and with a fervor that recalls the preaching of Micah. The other was a young man named Zechariah, who had been born in Babylonia and who cast his prophecies in a new and rather artificial pattern. But though so different in character and style, these two men were altogether at one in their thought. A bitter famine was sweeping across the land, and to both Haggai and Zechariah it seemed that it had been sent as divine punishment. They believed it had come because the people had neglected God's Temple. For themselves the people had provided stout houses, but for God they had built naught save a rude altar.

Through all the streets of Jerusalem went those two men, Haggai and Zechariah, with their bitter complaints. They beseeched and cursed, they pleaded and reviled, until at last the settlers began to rebuild the long-ruined sanctuary. The wretched Hebrew peasants who had never been deported but had remained in Palestine, offered to share in the holy labor; but they were spurned. The returned exiles looked down on them as an inferior lot. Those peasants, especially in the north, in what once had been the realm of Israel, had intermarried with the heathens who had been settled there by the Assyrians two hundred years before; and they had become ignorant and debased. Even those who had been left behind in the south, in Judah, had intermarried and lost caste. The people just returned from Babylonia acted very much like country folk who, after many years in the big city, return to the village of their birth and snub the neighbors among whom they were reared.

Alone, therefore, the returned exiles labored at the rebuilding of the sanctuary, and with such tremendous earnestness that in less than five years their work was done. And then the people sat back in happy exhaustion and waited. Anxiously they waited for the grand reward the prophets had promised them. But the days passed—many days. Even years. And nothing happened. Whereupon the hearts of the exhausted Jews in Jerusalem turned to gall. They lost all faith in God and His prophets, and bitterly did they complain as they struggled along in their wretched little land. Fifty years of neglect had made the place a widerness, and now recurrent drought and famine made its redemption unspeakably difficult. Enemies from every side came raiding and plundering—Edomites from the south, Philistines from the west, and worst of all, those half-breed Israelite peasants, the Samaritans, from the north. (They were called Samaritans because their chief city was the old Israelite capital, Samaria. The region they inhabited is indicated on the map on the preceding page.) The whole land of Judah was no larger than a little county, but twenty miles from end to end! And within this restricted area dwelt a handful of people whose souls were filled with hatred and disgust.

Only a tiny minority still clung to God and His promise. They were called the "Pious," and they refused to give up hope. While the rest went astray, intermarrying with the heathens around them, and breaking all the other laws that had been given them, those pious ones kept the faith. Even the priests became corrupt, sacrificing unclean things on the altars of God. Cruelty and injustice and vice were rampant throughout the little land. And only a very few of the people, the "Pious," dared to protest.

The chief protestant was a prophet whom we know as Malachi, and though priestly ideas had taken fast hold on him there was still much of the old prophetic spirit ablaze in his preachment. But in vain did he raise his voice, for the day had almost passed when a prophet could command the respect of the mob. The Word of God had lost its power in Judah, and only the word of some earthly authority could carry any weight in the land now.

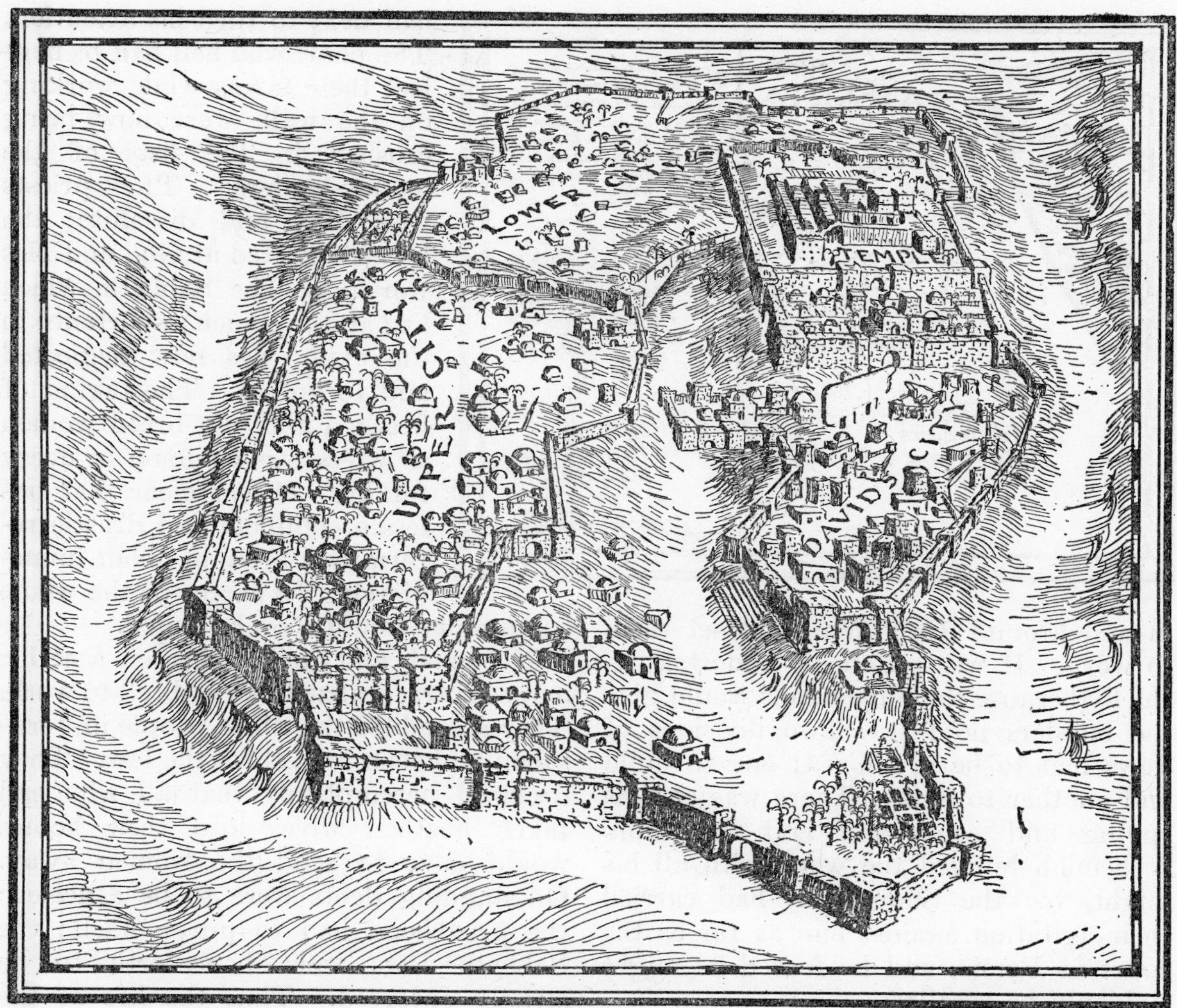

THE needed word of authority came just in time. It was brought from Babylon by a high official in the Persian court, a Jew named Nehemiah. Learning of the desperate plight of his brethren in Judah, this Nehemiah asked the king of Persia for permission to go back as governor of his people's homeland. The permission was quickly granted, for the king—like Cyrus long before him—well knew how important it was that the bridge called Palestine be held by a people who bore him good will. So, armed with all the authority of the great Persian emperor, Nehemiah started out on the three months' journey to Jerusalem.

His first undertaking, once he arrived in the ruined city, was that of rebuilding the wall. He realized that until the city was protected from its enemies the inhabitants could never be at rest. Accordingly he drafted all the able-bodied Jews

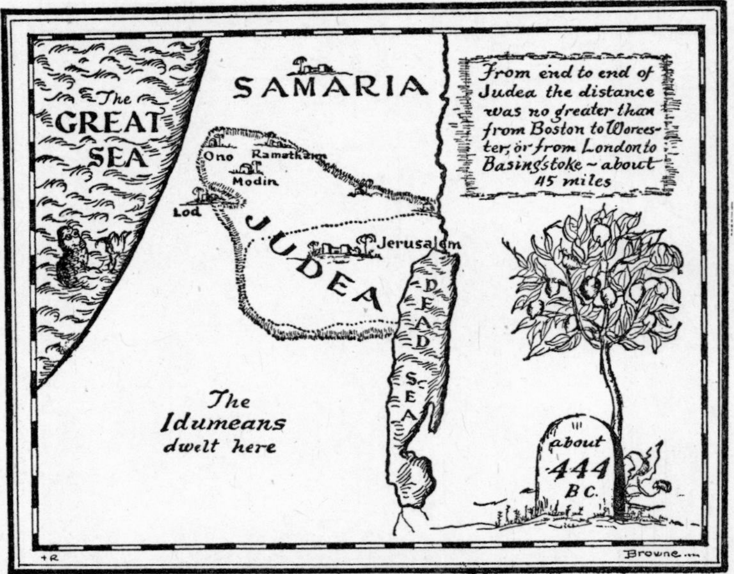

in and around Jerusalem, and set them to work. It was a difficult undertaking, chiefly because the Samaritans would give the builders no rest. Two divisions of Jews had to be organized: one to build and another to fight. There was endless spying and conspiring and deception. Nehemiah hurried the work with all his might, for the Samaritans had carried their agitation against him as far as the court of Persia, and he feared he might suddenly be recalled.

Finally, though laboring most of the time under fire, Nehemiah's men completed the wall. It extended much farther than the one it replaced, for it inclosed not merely Jerusalem, but also several little nearby villages. In effect it was the foundation of the restored Jewish state.

The rebuilding of the city wall was, however, but the beginning of Nehemiah's work. Within the community the morale was at its lowest ebb, and to this the leader had next to turn his attention. The poor, who had had to neglect their farms while working on the wall, were now being crushed in the fists of the money-lenders. The priests were lazy and dissolute; the laymen scoffed at God and His worship. The Sabbath, which had attained such importance in the exile, was now neglected and forgotten. The taking of heathen and half-breed women as wives was common in every family. It was clear that unless a complete and drastic reform was brought about immediately, the career of the whole community would soon be ended.

Nehemiah and another leader, a scribe named Ezra, realized this and fell to work. They assembled the whole people in Jerusalem and then read them the law. They declared peremptorily that all who had taken heathen wives into their homes would have to send the women away. Outstanding debts were to be canceled; the priesthood had to purge itself; the Sabbath laws were henceforth to be strictly enforced. Thus the life of the community was swept clean from end to end by the two reformers. From a lawless, reckless, godless populace, the Jews were suddenly transformed into a band of puritans. And the community was saved —for a while.

And now as never before the Jews who had remained in exile began to throng back to their homeland. From Babylonia they came in a steady stream; probably from Egypt and other lands too. Back they came to the little hills of Judea, once more to take up life there. But it was a life far different from that which their ancestors had known two centuries earlier. The newcomers were filled with a thousand new ideas gleaned from the foreign peoples among whom they had sojourned. They were no longer simple tribesmen with crude "small-town" ideas. They had traveled and seen the world. They were "civilized."

Yet for all that they were "civilized," their religion was hardly so vital, so simple, as it had been in the days of Micah or Jeremiah. It laid stress on showy externals, on essentially unimportant things—not eating certain foods, bringing regular gifts to the priest, observing certain festivals. And the exile was very largely to blame for this change. Even before the destruction of the old Temple, the seeds of a religion of priestliness had taken root in Palestine. But it had been unable to flourish then because the greater prophets had been most strenuously opposed to it, and the people themselves had been only feebly attracted by it. Now, however, that the Jews had seen the great temples and had witnessed the gorgeous ceremonies of priest-ridden peoples like the Babylonians, they eagerly took to imitating that sort of thing. And gone were the rebels, the true prophets, who might have decried the trend.

Year by year the power of the priests grew mightier among the Jews. Wealth rapidly accumulated in their hands, for each season the plain people had to take them the choicest portions of their flocks and harvests. Forgotten was the old democratic ideal of the prophets that all Jews were priests. Now only those who were supposed to come from the tribe of Levi were allowed to minister in the Temple; and furthermore only those of the family of Aaron of the tribe of Levi were considered holy enough actually to perform the sacrifices; and still further, only one directly descended from Solomon's favorite priest, Zadok, could possibly become the High Priest.

The High Priest was virtually the king of the land, and the lesser priests were the princes. They were no better, of course, than lay kings and princes. They were forever conspiring among themselves, cheating and murdering their way from one office to another. But for all their corruption, they did succeed in doing one thing: they kept the Jews alive as a separate people. They walled them in with their little rules and regulations, keeping them rigorously segregated from all the other tribes and peoples. Even the half-Jewish Samaritans were cut off completely and had to start a temple of their own in northern Palestine.

But despite the efforts of the priests, foreign influences did seep into the life of the people. Gradually their language changed from Hebrew to Aramaic, so that after a few generations they could not understand even their own Scriptures. In their synagogues each Sabbath—for those "meeting-houses" they had created in the exile had become common now throughout Judea—they had to read their Holy Writings through an Aramaic translation called the Targum. And many of their religious ideas changed too. Outwardly no sign of this change in thought was evident. None was there to hail it, and so none could rise to decry it.

But then came Alexander, and all was made open.

IN the fateful year 333 B.C. Alexander of Macedon became master of the Persian Empire, and a year later, on his march toward Egypt, he took possession of Palestine. (The little land was still the one bridge used by the empire builders.) But this Alexander, a mere boy in years, was quite unlike the ordinary world-conqueror. His aim seems to have been not so much the gaining of power as the spreading of culture. He dreamed of scattering throughout the world the seeds of Greek civilization. And so energetically did he try to realize his dream that, though he died at the age of thirty-three, his Greek colonies dotted all of the then-known world.

Alexander's effect on the Jews and their religion was greater than that of any other non-Jew in history. He was generous to them and gave them every liberty; but at the same time he located peaceful settlements of his own people throughout Palestine. The result was a growing familiarity with all things Greek. Jews began to affect the use of Greek words in their conversation, and began to give their children Greek names.

HELLENISM—the word comes from Hellas, meaning Greece—began to make itself felt in every walk of Jewish life, especially in the many Jewish settlements outside of Palestine. Unfortunately, it was not the Hellenism of classic Greece, the Hellenism that flowered in the genius of Socrates, Plato, Sophocles, and Phidias. Rather it was the Hellenism debased and sullied through long handling by Macedonians and other lesser tribes. But debased as it was, it nevertheless proved attractive. Even the priests in Jerusalem began to take to it. Indeed, they were attracted to it even more than the plain people. The story goes that they actually left the sacrifices unburnt on the altars in the Temple, and hurried off to the arenas to watch the Greek athletes there. Greek manners—and vices—became the great fashion of the day, for the more a Jew aped them the better seemed his chances of growing in power and station.

Of course, this change did not come about overnight, but took three or four generations. After Alexander died, his empire was divided into three kingdoms; and Palestine, being the bridge between two of them, naturally became the scene of constant warfare. First it belonged to the Ptolemies, who ruled over Egypt; but before long the Seleucids, who ruled over Syria and Mesopotamia, tried to annex it. The attempt failed, but it was nevertheless repeated several times, for Syria greatly coveted the "bridge." So for fully a century the little land was torn this way and that. Armies tramped up and down its highways continually, and there was war and confusion without rest. But finally the bloody contest was brought to end when, in the year 198 B.C., the Syrians drove the Egyptian army back to the Nile country and formally annexed Palestine.

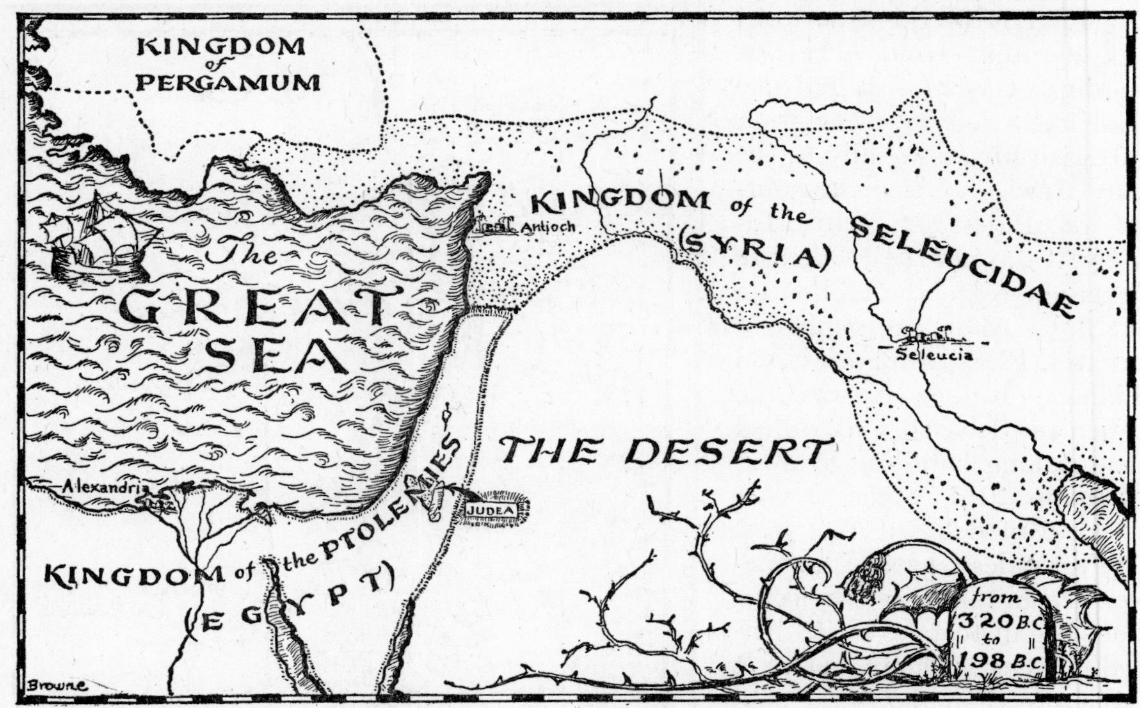
KINGDOM of PERGAMUM
KINGDOM of the SELEUCIDAE
(SYRIA)
Antioch
Seleucia
The GREAT SEA
THE DESERT
Alexandria
JUDEA
KINGDOM of the PTOLEMIES
(EGYPT)
from 320 B.C. to 198 B.C.
Browne

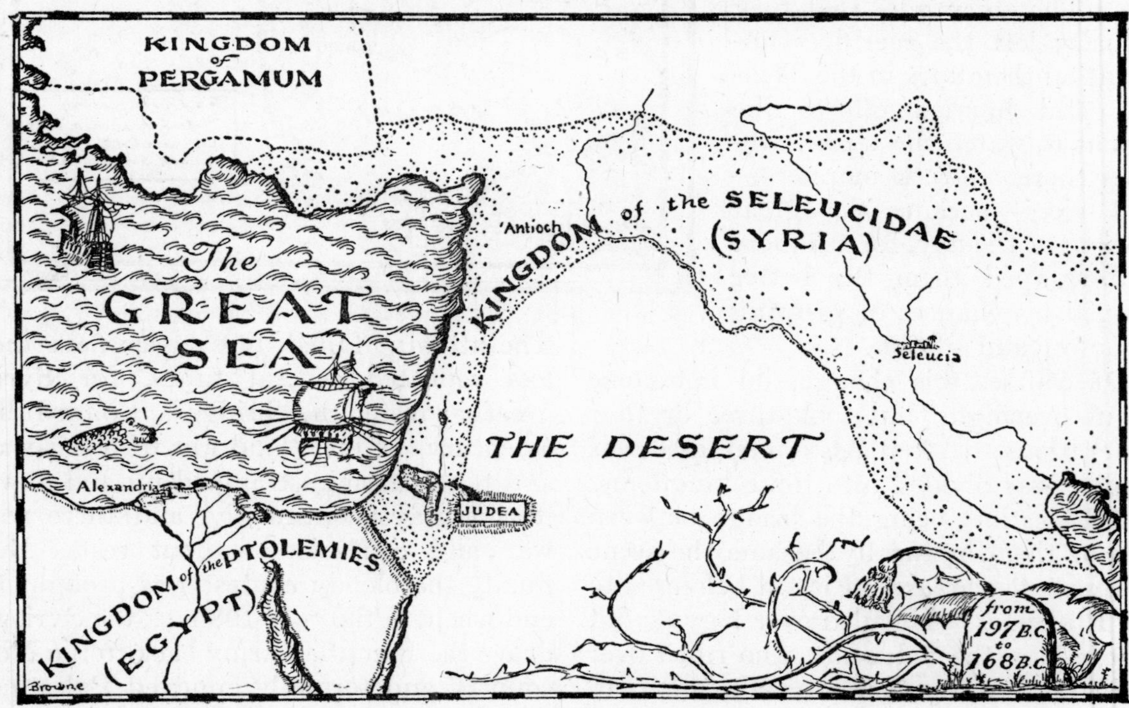
KINGDOM of PERGAMUM
KINGDOM of the SELEUCIDAE
(SYRIA)
Antioch
Seleucia
The GREAT SEA
THE DESERT
Alexandria
JUDEA
KINGDOM of the PTOLEMIES
(EGYPT)
from 197 B.C. to 168 B.C.
Browne

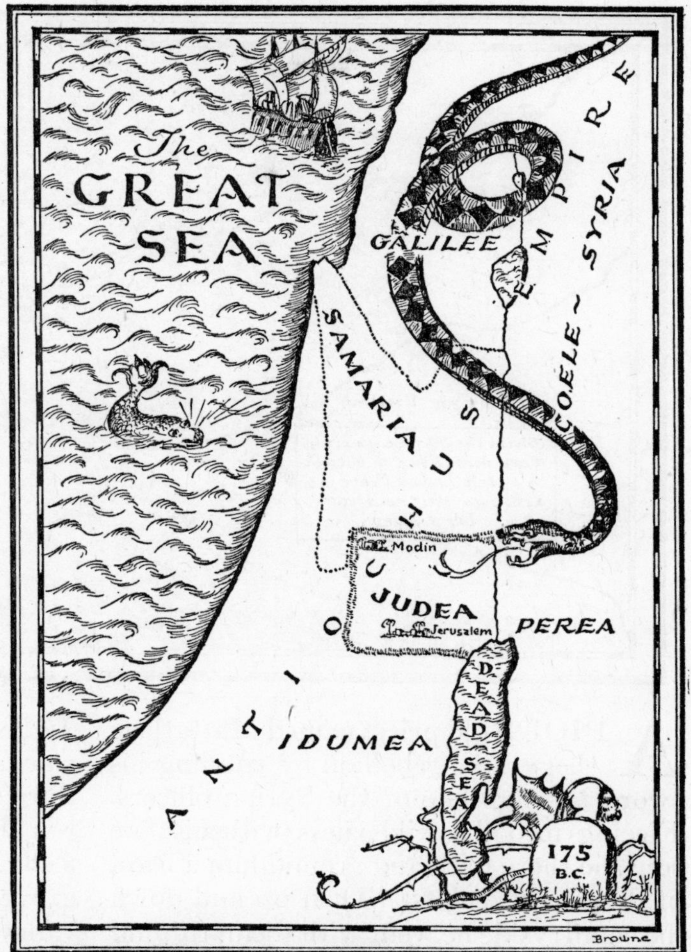

HELLENISM had been seeping steadily into Palestine during all that troublous century. Indeed, had nothing occurred to stem the tide, it might have so flooded the land that Jewish life and thought would in time have been drowned out completely. But one day there arose in Syria a king named Antiochus Epiphanes, who by his headstrong impatience spoiled everything. It is difficult to understand just what was wrong with this king. He seems to have been learned and markedly clever—but also at moments quite insane. He took great delight in poking fun at the whole matter of religion, and yet at the same time he tried to build a religion around himself. That is why he called himself Theos Epiphanes, which means "The Evident God."

Judea at the time was seething with unrest because the corrupt, Hellenized priests were at last being brought to book by a few of the pious Jews. It looked somewhat like a political uprising to Antiochus, and on his way home from a campaign in Egypt he stopped in the middle of the "bridge" to attend to the trouble. He looted the Temple and then simply ordered Judaism to cease. Just that! Evidently he thought it would be quite easy for him to stamp out this obscure and, as he thought, very odd little religion. His orders were that never more should the Sabbath, or the rite of circumcision, or the difference between "clean" and "unclean" food, be observed. Any person found with a Hebrew book in his possession was immediately to be put to death. Henceforth if there was to be any sacrificing it must be of swine's flesh, and to Antiochus or Zeus as god.

For a while starkest horror swept the land as the army of Antiochus began to put those orders into effect.

There were looting and murder, wailing and shame, as the minions of the Syrian tyrant tried to carry out his orders. And then, like the breaking out of a mad fire, the nation blazed into rebellion.

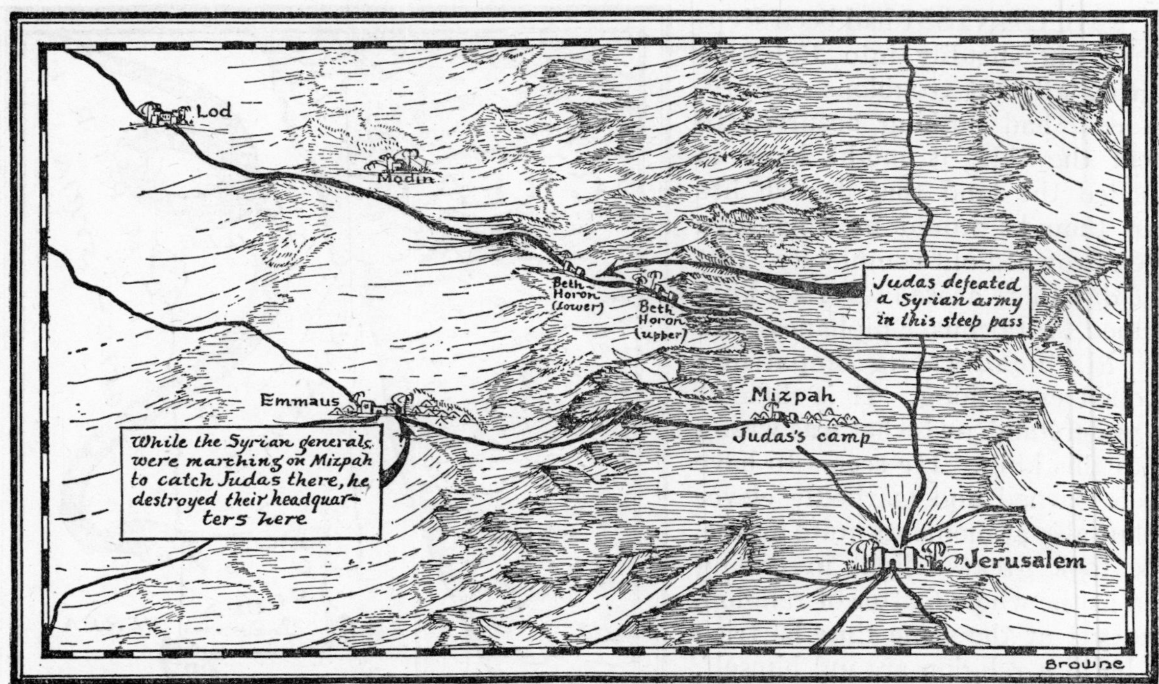

A PIOUS old priest named Mattathias began the rebellion by running his sword through one of the Syrian officers. Fleeing into the wilderness with his five sons, he there gathered around him a band of desperate zealots. Then up and down the countryside he went with them, tipping over the hated altars set up by the foreigners, and putting to death the renegade Jews who had sacrificed on them. It was magnificent, but it seemed insane. The tattered rebels were untrained, unequipped, unsupported—a tiny band of priests and peons fighting with little more than their bare fists. The great hosts of Syria, armed, disciplined, and led by the greatest generals of the day, outnumbered them ten to one. It seemed sheer suicide!

But it was not. Old Mattathias died soon after the beginning of the rebellion, but he was succeeded by one of his sons, Judas, who proved altogether a genius in warfare. His first victory over the Syrians was won in the hills through which ran the road from Samaria to Jerusalem. Judas surprised the Syrians there and drove them helter-skelter down into the valley. Then, arming himself and his men with the weapons of the slain, Judas prepared for the next encounter. It occurred in the steep pass leading through the Beth-Horons to Jerusalem. Another general had been sent with a new army from Syria, and Judas, with the courage of desperation, did not wait to be attacked. Learning that the enemy was marching toward Jerusalem, Judas stationed his men where the road was steepest and narrowest, and then proceeded to decimate the Syrians. The road at this point ascended in part by rock-cut steps, so that it was impossible for the Syrian army to

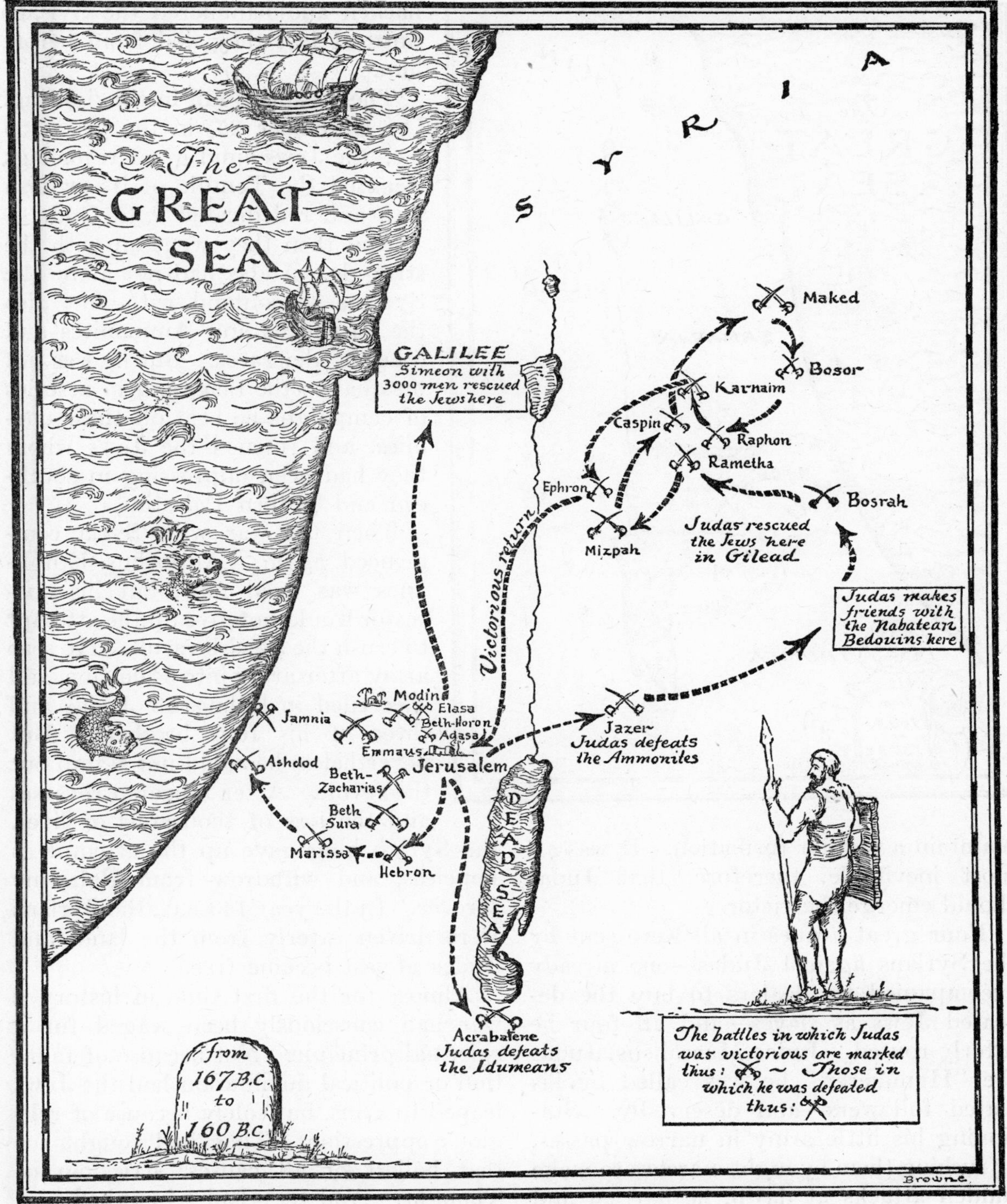
The GREAT SEA
S Y R I A
GALILEE
Simeon with 3000 men rescued the Jews here
Maked
Bosor
Karnaim
Caspin
Raphon
Rametha
Ephron
Bosrah
Mizpah
Judas rescued the Jews here in Gilead
Victorious return
Judas makes friends with the Nabatean Bedouins here
Modin
Elasa
Beth-Horon
Adasa
Jamnia
Emmaus
Jerusalem
Jazer
Judas defeats the Ammonites
Ashdod
Beth-Zacharias
Beth Sura
Marissa
Hebron
DEAD SEA
Acrabatene
Judas defeats the Idumeans
from 167 B.C. to 160 B.C.
The battles in which Judas was victorious are marked thus: ~ Those in which he was defeated thus:
Browne

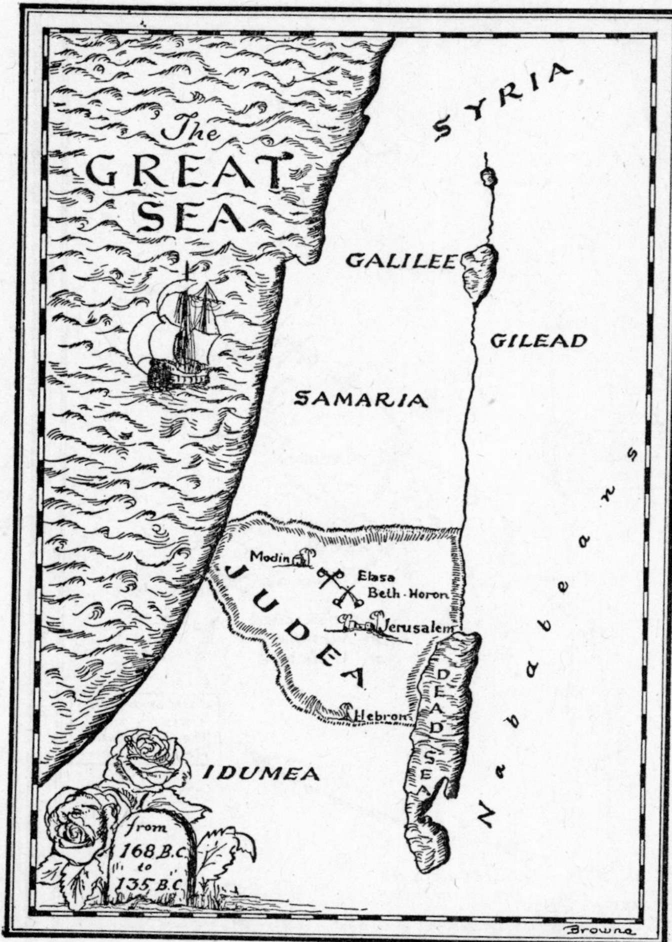

maintain a regular formation. It was almost inevitable, therefore, that Judas should emerge the victor.

Four great armies in all were sent by the Syrians against Judas—one already accompanied by dealers to buy the defeated Jews as slaves—and all four he utterly routed. Judas Maccabeus, Judas the "Hammerer," he was called by his elated followers—and deservedly. Stationing his little army in narrow passes, or rushing them by night marches to make sudden attacks at dawn, he harried and hacked and hammered the Syrians until at last they fled from before him.

There came a lull in the fighting. On December 25, in the year 165 B.C., the Jews amid great rejoicings cleansed the Temple of its swinish filth and rededicated it to God.

And then they went on with the struggle. Judas had not alone the Syrians to contend with, but also the Idumeans and Ammonites and other border races. But he was not unequal to the task, and in a series of campaigns he beat off these enemies, and rescued the Jews whom they had been oppressing in southern and eastern Palestine.

Then the war with Syria commenced again. Antiochus Epiphanes was dead now, but his successor would not give up the attempt to crush the Jewish revolt. He sent army after army into Palestine, and succeeded in killing off Judas and three of his four brothers. But nevertheless he could not stamp out the revolt. After repeated reverses and the loss of thousands of lives, the Syrian king gave up the attempt as hopeless, and withdrew from Palestine forever. In the year 143 B.C., the Syrians were driven utterly from the land, and Judea at last became free.

Almost for the first time in history a war had consciously been waged for a spiritual principle. Not because of taxation or political domination had the Jews leaped to arms, but solely because of religious oppression. They had fought for that holiest of all causes, Freedom of Thought. And they had triumphed.

BUT the triumph of the Jews had been too complete. The war which they had waged at first only for religious freedom ended in also winning for them political independence. And that added gain proved their undoing.

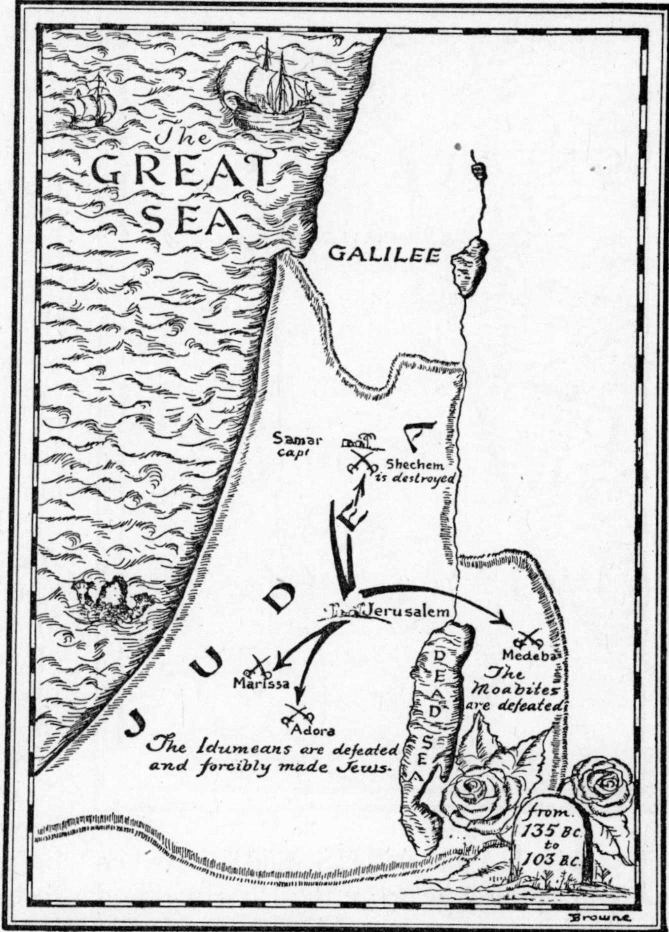

Simon, the last of the five sons of Mattathias, was succeeded on the throne by his son, the High Priest, John Hyrcanus; and with him the tragedy began. Drunk with his new-found power, this man undertook cruel and costly wars against his neighbors. In pursuance of his dream of carving out a great empire for himself, he invaded Samaria on the north and Idumea on the south. And not content merely with making those lands subject to his rule, he even compelled their inhabitants to accept his religion. Forcibly he converted the Samaritans and the Edomites to his own sort of Judaism. The grandson of old Mattathias, who gave his life for the right to worship his own God in his own way, was now spending all his days trying to wrest that very right from others.

But soon a group of protestants began to make themselves heard in the land of Judea. They were called the Pharisees, the "Interpreters," probably because they were pious men who spent much of their time studying and interpreting the Holy Scriptures. Pharisees may not mean "Separatists," as the scholars long thought. There is a possibility that the word comes from the Hebrew *parash,* which means "to make clear." The Pharisees cared not in the least for empire or dominion; their whole interest was in the Holy Law and its complete fulfillment.

Those who belonged to the party in power in the land were called the Sadducees, because they all sided with the supposed descendants of the ancient High Priest, Zadok. They were Hellenized aristocrats, and many of them were priests; but they showed but feeble interest in their religion. Essentially they were politicians. Sacramental ward-bosses, one might call them. The true spiritual leaders of the day were those Pharisees.

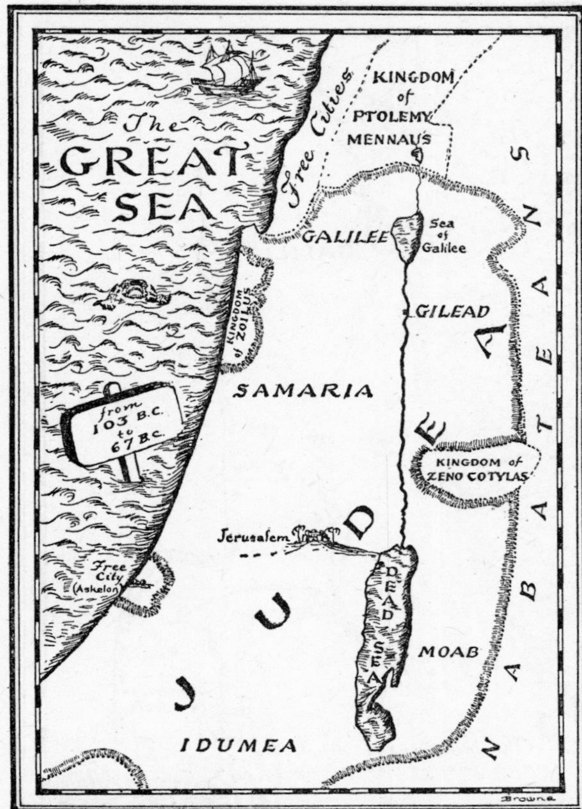

JOHN HYRCANUS died just when the conflict between the Pharisees and the Sadducees was reaching a crisis. He was succeeded by his son, Aristobulus, who continued the wars of conquest and added Galilee to the kingdom. After Aristobulus, his brother, Alexander Janneus, succeeded to the throne, and with him the dynasty sank to the very depths. Alexander's chief interests were war and pleasure. He brought unbounded distress to his subjects, and so taxed their patience that at last they rebelled and drove him into exile. But in a little while they repented and called him back, whereupon he, instead of showing gratitude, crucified 800 Pharisees, after slaying their wives and children before their very eyes.

Yet, despite his preoccupation with murder and revelry, the king found time to wage costly wars of conquest on the borders of his land. He extended the realm into Upper Galilee, down into the South Country, and over to the east into the territory of the Nabatean Arabs. These were relatively large gains, and they made the Judean realm once more a sizable bit of territory. Only three generations earlier, Judea had been little more than a city-state, as can be seen by the map on page 83. But now it was almost a real country again.

Alexander was succeeded by his widow Alexandra, and it was the folly of this woman that brought the dynasty of the Maccabees to an end. When she was an old woman of 73, one of her sons, Aristobulus II, started a civil war. Hyrcanus, the rightful heir to the throne, lost all save his life in the first encounter with Aristobulus; but instead of retiring and leaving the throne to the usurper, the defeated brother tried to continue the contest. In doing this, Hyrcanus was following the advice of a certain Idumean prince named Antipater. Antipater came of that half-breed stock in the South Country which John Hyrcanus had forcibly converted to Judaism two generations earlier. He was a man of great shrewdness and no scruples, and he thoroughly dominated Hyrcanus. He persuaded the weakling to call in the help of the Nabateans, a desert race that had moved up to the East Jordan country, and with 50,000 of these Arabs at his command, Hyrcanus joined battle with the usurper, Aristobulus, defeated him, and forced him to take refuge in Jerusalem.

AND now a new power enters into the tragic history of the Jews. Thus far we have learnt of at least six great empires that dominated the little land of Palestine and brought war to its inhabitants: Egypt, Aramea, Assyria, Babylonia, Persia, and Greece. Now comes the seventh and most terrible of all—Rome. By an extraordinary series of successes and accidents the tiny city of Rome had grown until at this time it ruled over almost all of the Mediterranean lands. It had absorbed Italy, then northern Africa, then Greece, and now was attempting the conquest of Asia Minor.

In 65 B.C. the Roman general Pompey defeated the kings who had inherited a large portion of the former Empire of Syria. It was natural then for him to turn to the bridge which connects Asia with Africa. Like every other world-conqueror he wanted that vital bit of territory, for in a measure it was the key to the whole of the orient. Nor was it difficult for Pompey to satisfy his desire. The Jews, divided now into three parties, played directly into the Roman's hands. Aristobulus was intrenched in Jerusalem, beleaguered there by Hyrcanus and his Arab army. Meanwhile the Pharisees in the land, sick of the unending evils which the kings had brought them, were begging for a chance to get rid of royalty entirely. All three of these parties, Aristobulus, Hyrcanus, and the Pharisees, sent deputations to Damascus, where Pompey was encamped, asking him to intervene.

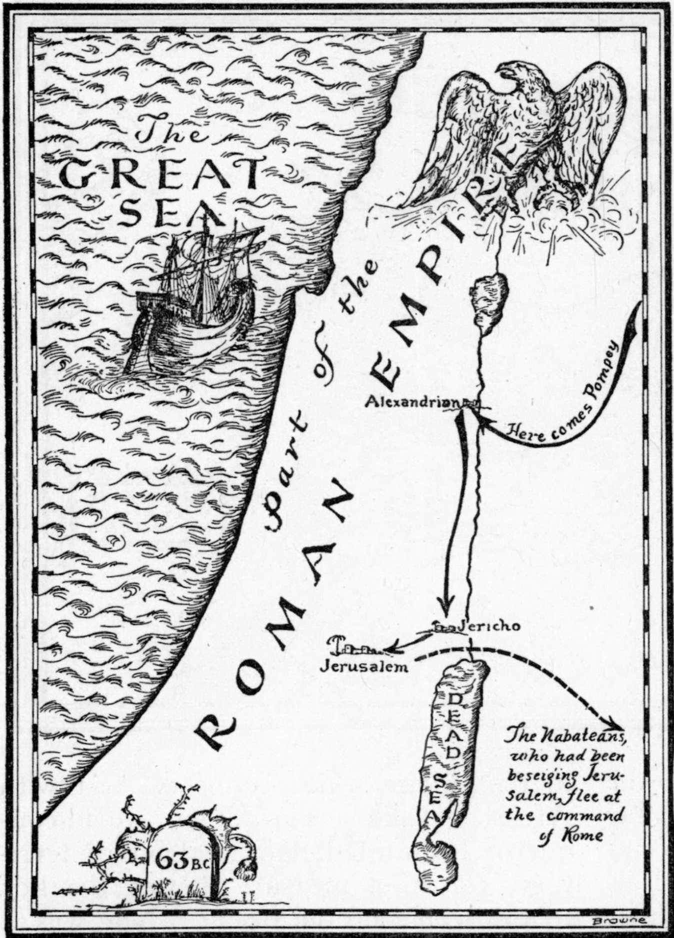

THE three requests for intervention furnished Pompey with a perfect excuse for invading Palestine. Of course, the Arab army which had been besieging Jerusalem fled the very moment it heard of the approach of the Roman host. Aristobulus, suspecting that Pompey would not favor him, shut himself up in the fortress of Alexandrion (or Alexandrium); but his courage failed him at the last moment, and he abjectly surrendered when Pompey arrived. Aristobulus's followers, however, were less easily cowed, and when Pompey reached Jerusalem they refused to lay down their arms, but instead intrenched themselves on the Temple hill. And so strong were the fortifications that it required three months before the rebels were forced to surrender. Even then it was only because Pompey took advantage of the religious scruples of the Jews, and attacked them on a Sabbath day, when they would not strike a blow in their defense, that he was able to make a breach in the walls and capture the stronghold.

With the capital in his hands, Pompey proceeded immediately to put the fear of Rome into the hearts of the Jews. His first act was to put 12,000 of the rebels to the sword. His next act was to investigate the Temple. He had heard much about this strange edifice, and was very curious to enter it. But the Jews had strict laws forbidding all save Israelites to enter the inner courts, and all save the High Priest to enter the Holy of Holies. Pompey, however, paid no attention to these laws, and unceremoniously tramped right into the holy place. He even dared to lift the veil and go into the Holy of Holies. But then, strangely enough, he withdrew without laying a finger on any of the treasure in the place. Perhaps he was overawed, for it must have been the first temple he had ever entered where there was no image of a god. But even though he did have the grace not to strip the Temple, the Jews never forgave him for having entered it.

POMPEY tried to settle the civil strife in Palestine by imprisoning Aristobulus and giving Hyrcanus the title of Ethnarch, which meant "governor of a nation." But it was only a sorry fragment of a nation that Hyrcanus was permitted to govern. His territory was cut down until it included little more than the central hill-country around the city of Jerusalem. The rest of the country was given into the hands of the governor of Syria, a Roman official. The large cities along the seacoast, and in the territory east of the Jordan, were made independent, for to a large degree they were not Jewish in population. Most of them had been built up as Greek colonies during the time of Alexander the Great, and they were still largely pagan.

But even though the Jews were left with so little territory, they still knew no peace. The sons of the defeated Aristobulus had been taken captive to Rome, but, escaping thence, they had returned to stir up trouble in Jerusalem. Hyrcanus and his patron, Antipater, were temporarily overthrown, and only with difficulty did they manage to regain their power. A second time they were attacked, and a third. Then Crassus, the Roman general in charge of the East, needing money to carry on his wars, marched down and plundered the Temple treasury. A little later the Jews revolted, but then another general, Cassius, came down and took swift vengeance by selling 30,000 of the rebels into slavery. Thus evil followed evil, and the wretched little land was crushed and torn in the talons of Rome. Finally events took a new turn. Pompey lost his hold over the Roman Empire and was succeeded by the great Julius Caesar.

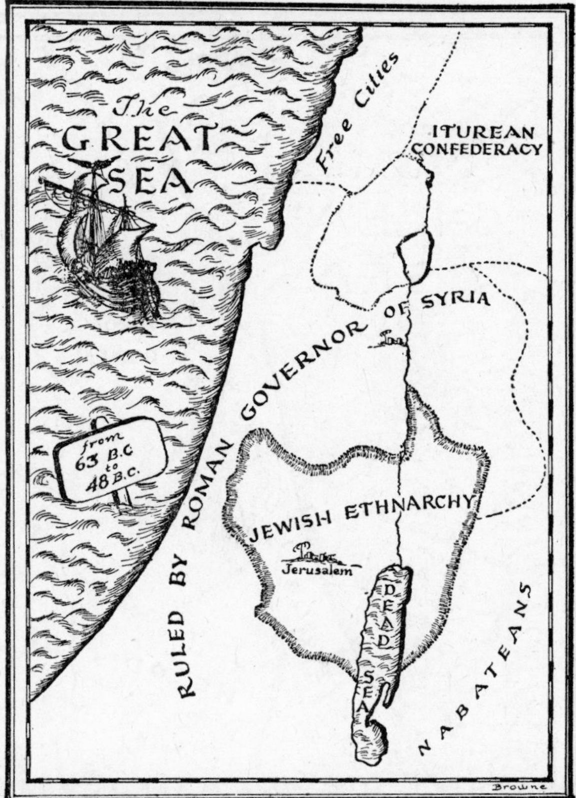

It was then that Antipater, who until now had remained largely in the background, came forward and asserted himself openly.

This Antipater was a man of astounding shrewdness, and he saw the wisdom of throwing in his lot with Caesar while the latter was still engaged in his life and death struggle with Pompey. As a result, when Caesar emerged the victor and became master of the Roman Empire, Antipater came in for a rich reward. He was appointed no less than procurator over Judea—a position which was really of far greater importance than that of Hyrcanus, who was merely the nominal ruler with the title of Ethnarch.

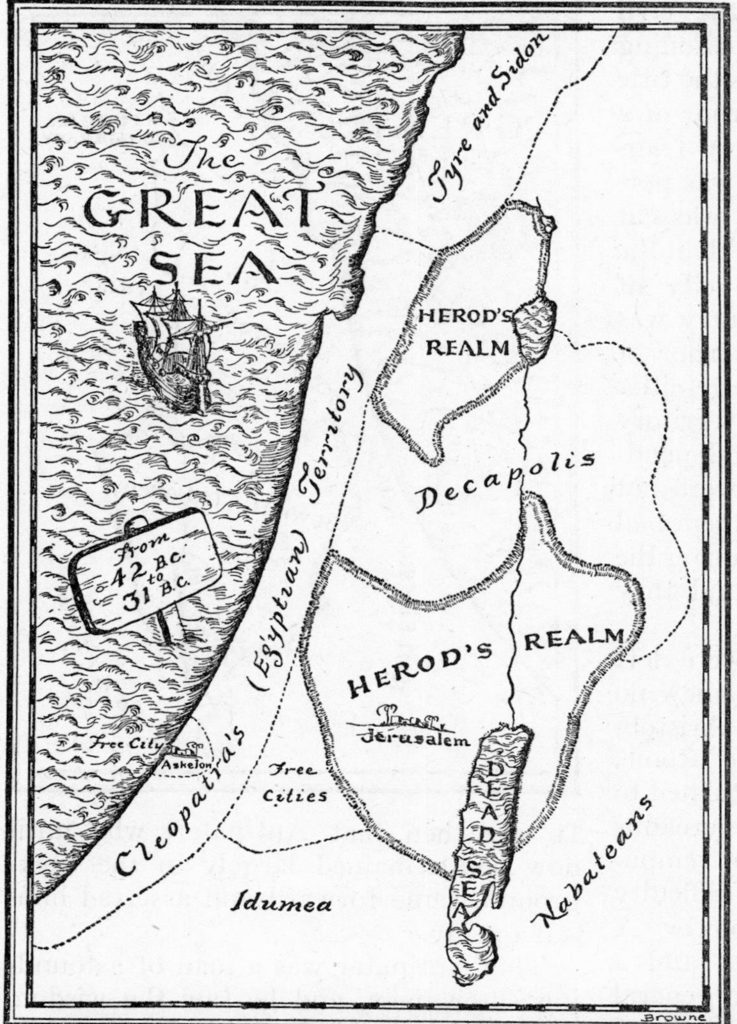

ANTIPATER did not enjoy his power for long. Four years after his elevation to the procuratorship he was treacherously poisoned by a rival politician. But his death brought no relief to the Jews; on the contrary, their plight now became worse than ever, for Antipater's power fell into the hands of his son, Herod, one of the craftiest men that had ever ruled over Judea. Like his father, Herod realized that the supremacy of Rome could never be broken, and that therefore it was wisest always to side with whoever happened to be ruling the empire. Caesar having been assassinated, Herod now fawned on Mark Antony. Herod sent him bribes and flattered him with fine speeches, and as a reward was confirmed as governor of Judea and Galilee, though still under the nominal rule of the doddering old Hyrcanus. The central and eastern parts of the land remained independent of all Jewish rule. The ten Greek cities which dominated these regions were organized into a separate state called the Decapolis. The whole of the coastland was given by Mark Antony to Cleopatra, the fascinating queen of Egypt, with whom he was in love.

But even with the land thus divided there was no peace. While Mark Antony went down to Egypt, the Parthians, a fierce race dwelling south of the Caspian Sea, swooped down and pillaged Palestine. They took old Hyrcanus, slashed off his ears, and drove out all of his supporters. The young Herod, after many adventures, managed to escape to Rome, and there he was given the empty title of "King of the Jews." Then, with a strong army at his heels, he returned to Palestine, and after a six-month siege he captured Jerusalem. And thus it came about that Herod the Idumean, descendant of a half-breed desert folk, became king in Zion.

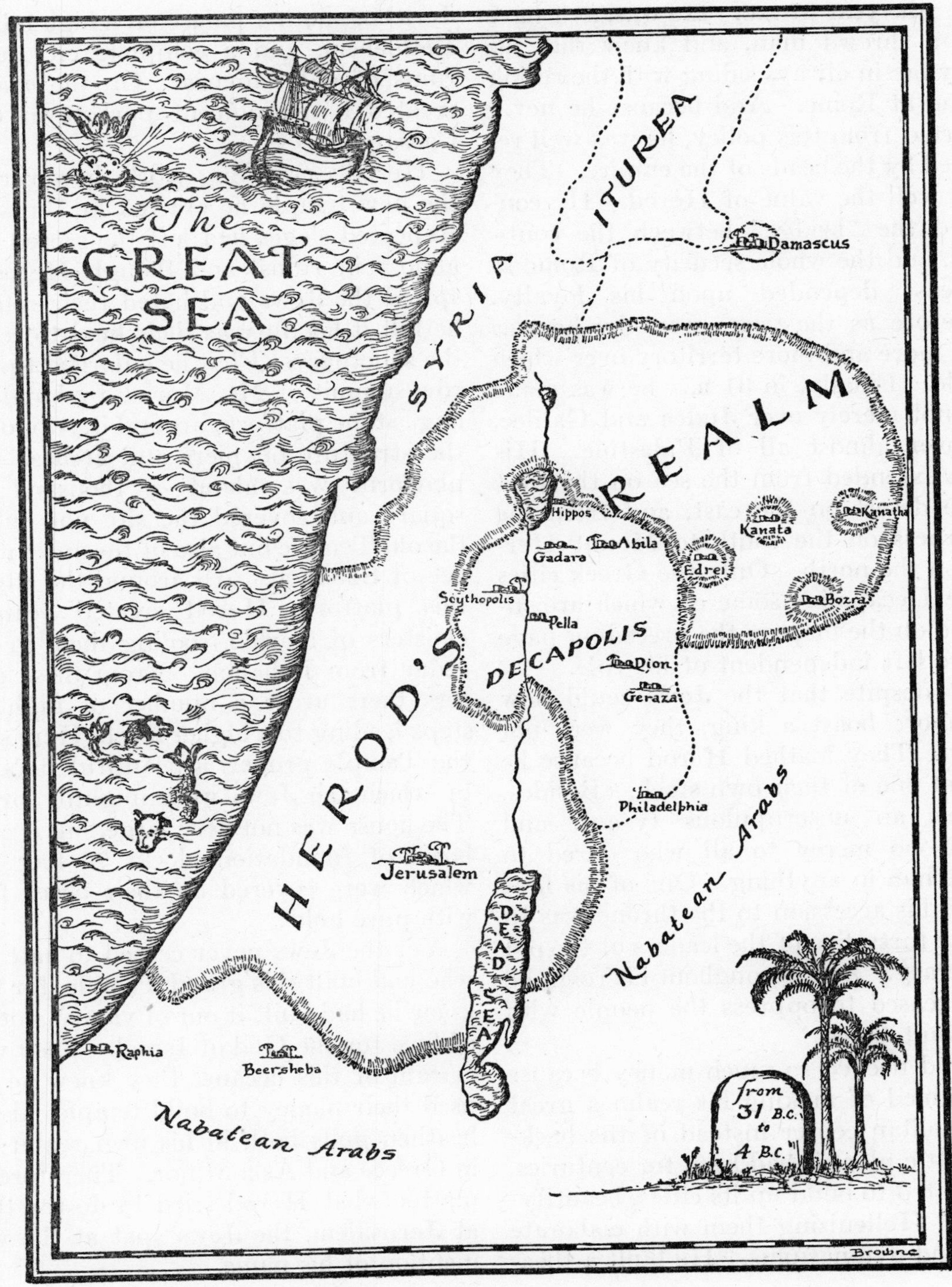
The GREAT SEA
SYRIA
ITUREA
Damascus
HEROD'S REALM
Hippos
Kanatha
Kanata
Abila
Gadara
Edrei
Scythopolis
Bozra
Pella
DECAPOLIS
Dion
Geraza
Philadelphia
Nabatean Arabs
Jerusalem
DEAD SEA
Raphia
Beersheba
from 31 B.C. to 4 B.C.
Nabatean Arabs
Browne

HEROD became king of the Jews in the year 37 B.C. He was, as I have said, a shrewd man, and knew that his safety lay in always siding with the ruling faction at Rome. And because he never departed from this policy, he was well rewarded by the heads of the empire. They knew well the value of Herod. He controlled the "bridge" between the continents, and the whole security of Rome in the east depended upon his loyalty. Therefore as the years went by he was given more and more territory over which to rule. Finally, in 31 B.C. he was made king not merely over Judea and Galilee, but over almost all of Palestine. His realm extended from the sea on the west to the desert on the east, and from the wilderness on the south to Mount Hermon on the north. Only the Greek cities of the Decapolis—some of which are indicated on the map on the preceding page —were left independent of his rule.

But despite that the Jews could now once more boast a king, they were not happy. They loathed Herod because he was not one of their own stock. Besides, he was an unscrupulous tyrant, and showed no mercy to all who dared to oppose him in anything. One of his first acts on his accession to the throne was to execute forty-five of the leaders of the old aristocracy. And throughout his reign he never ceased to oppress the people with exorbitant taxes.

Herod needed so much money because he dreamed of making his realm a great cosmopolitan center instead of the backward little place it had been for centuries. He wanted to build up its cities, beautifying and Hellenizing them with elaborate baths and gymnasiums. He built a theater and stadium in Jerusalem, a palace in Jericho, another palace on a high hill near Bethlehem, and a complete city on the ruins of old Samaria. On the coast he created a magnificent port town called Caesarea.

Herod's crowning work, however, was the new temple he erected in Jerusalem. Repeated sieges had left the sacred place almost in ruins, and though Herod despised the Jews and hated their religion, he felt it his duty as their king to rebuild the sanctuary. First he enlarged the narrow summit of Mt. Moriah by building a huge stone platform around it, supporting the structure on piers and arches. This platform was about a thousand feet square and covered the site not only of the old Temple but also of the ancient palace of Solomon. All around the edge of this platform Herod erected beautiful cloisters of marble, roofing them in with cedar from Lebanon. From these cloisters there arose a number of flights of steps leading to a higher level. Here stood the Temple proper, a beautiful structure of which the Jews were mightily proud. The house was not very large, but it could boast of foundation blocks 70 feet long which were covered on their outer faces with pure gold!

Yet the Jews never ceased to hate him who had built this grand Temple, for they knew he had built it out of vanity, not out of love for the God of Israel. They were certain of this because they knew he had used their money to build temples also to heathen gods both in his own realm and in Greece and Asia Minor. Therefore, no matter what Herod tried to do for them at Jerusalem, the Jews spat at the very mention of his name.

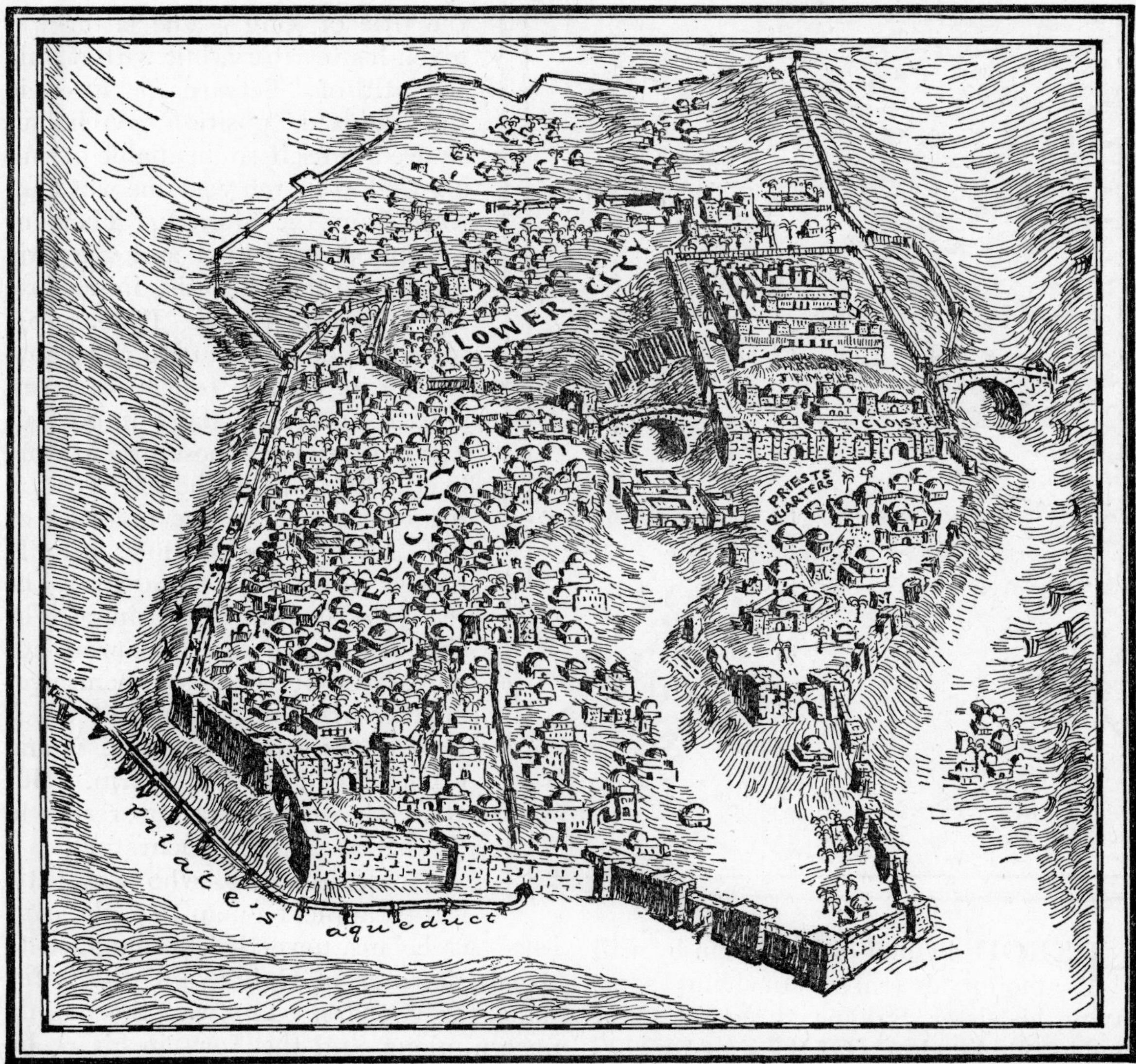

So Herod, for all that he became a mighty king, knew little joy in life. All his days he was surrounded by conspirators, and never till his death was he free of the web of intrigue. The Jews hated him, and many of the Roman politicians regarded him with envy. And as Herod grew older and his infirmities increased, he grew increasingly suspicious and cruel. Toward the very end he became quite mad, and ordered executions right and left. Finally, in the year 4 B.C., the royal maniac died, leaving an order that all the leading Jews be butchered so that the people might mourn at his funeral. But no attention was paid to the command, and Herod was buried amid the rejoicings of the populace.

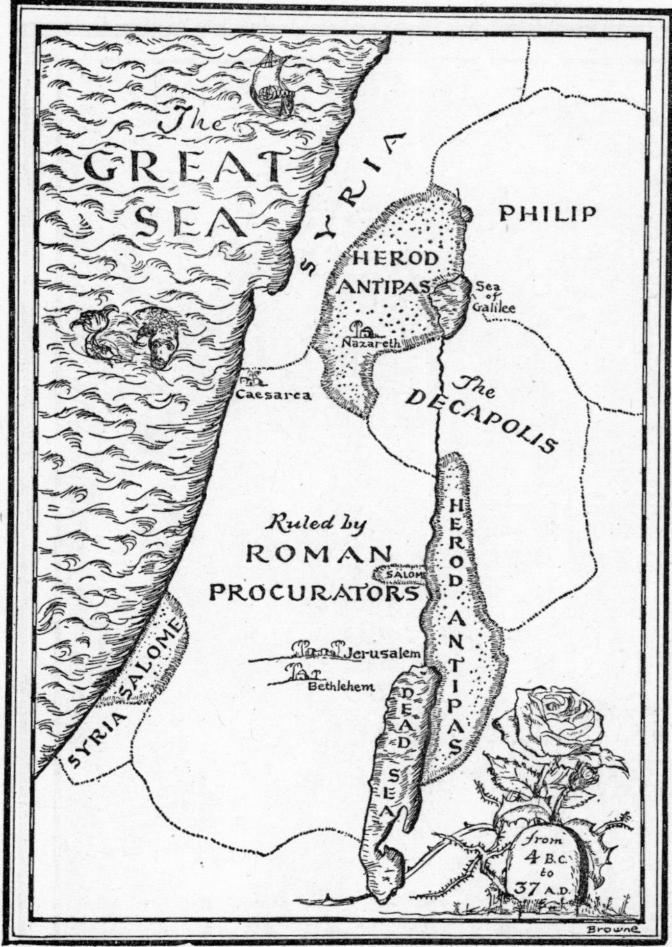

HEROD divided his kingdom by will among his three surviving sons, leaving his sister, Salome, three cities and a palace at Ascalon. Of the sons, Archelaus was left the crown and the territory of Judea, Samaria, and Idumea; Herod Antipas was given Galilee and the East-Jordan region called Perea; and Philip was given the northeast territory. But the Roman emperor refused to confirm certain provisions in the will, especially the one which gave to Archelaus the title of king. The latter was given his territory, but with it only the title of "Tetrarch." Even in this limited position Archelaus showed himself so incapable of ruling that after ten years he was banished from the country. Then for a generation Judea and Samaria were placed under the immediate rule of the emperor. Procurators were sent down from Rome to govern the region, to collect its taxes, and to decide its more important legal questions. These procurators lived at Caesarea, the new city on the coast; but on the occasion of the Jewish feasts they usually moved down to Jerusalem to be ready to quell any uprising. The civil and ceremonial laws were administered by the Jews themselves in their own courts, chief of which was the great court of priests and rabbis called the Sanhedrin. But all really serious matters rested in the hands of the procurators.

Herod Antipas, who was little less tyrannical a man than the banished Archelaus, nevertheless managed to remain tetrarch of Galilee and Perea for some forty years. He was thoroughly unscrupulous, and the Jews in his realm hated him bitterly. His chief fame rests upon the crime he committed in executing a Jewish prophet named John the Baptist. Philip, who ruled in the northeast, seems to have been a wise and just man; but unfortunately his province contained practically no Jews.

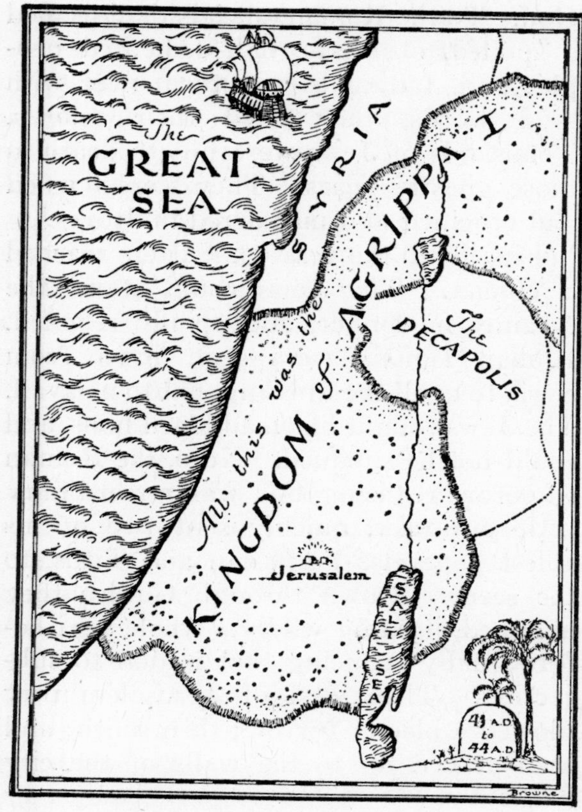

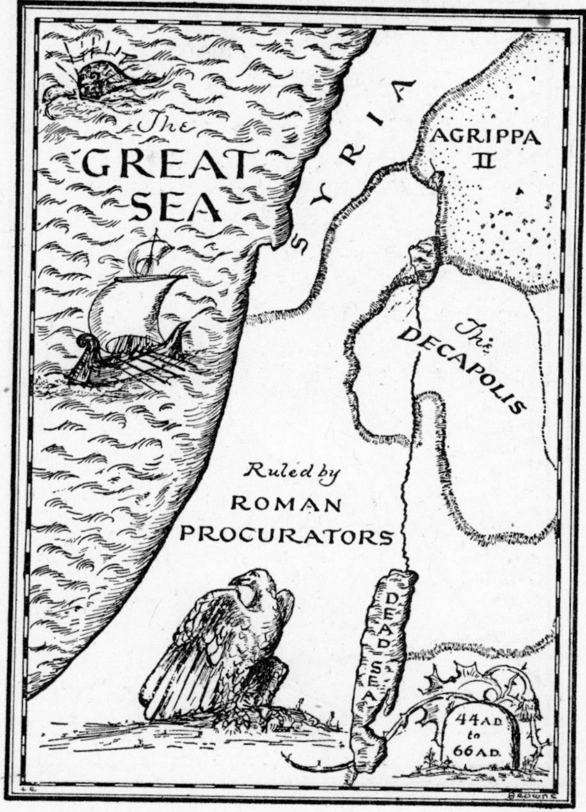

WHEN Philip died, his tetrarchy was given to a nephew of his who had been living at Rome and was a favorite of the emperor Caligula. This nephew, Agrippa I by name, managed to cast suspicion on the loyalty of his uncle, Herod Antipas, and thus he became master also of the latter's territory. Finally he succeeded in adding to his realm the regions which for a generation had been in the control of the procurators. And thus it came about that once more the government of all Palestine—save of course the Decapolis—rested in the hands of a Jewish king.

Agrippa, for all that he was an adventurer, made a rather good king. He saved the Jews from insult at the hands of the Romans, reduced their taxes, and made every effort not to outrage their religious feelings. Indeed, his rule seemed to presage a new day for his people, a day of peace and comfort after a long, long night of torment.

But certain of Agrippa's friends at the Roman court grew jealous of his growing power and conspired against him. He died suddenly—in all probability at the hands of a secret assassin. And with him the line of the Jewish kings ended forever. His son, Agrippa II, was allowed to rule only over the northeastern tetrarchy; the rest was given over once more into the hands of the Roman procurators.

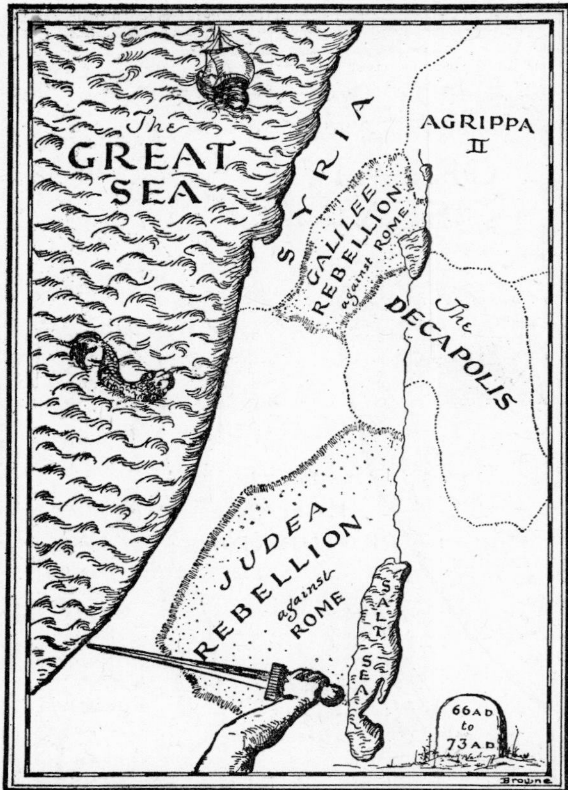

THE fierce struggle between Roman and Jew began once more in Judea and Galilee. Seven Roman governors followed each other in rapid succession, each more cruel than the last. They drove the people to despair and madness by their wanton violations of religious feeling.

Perhaps those governors were not altogether to blame. They were at their wits' end. They had been able to handle all sorts of people in every part of the world—but these Jews were altogether beyond them. They were the only people on earth who would rather die than offer sacrifices to the image of an emperor. They were willing to give up everything, their wealth, their homes, their land, their very lives—but they would not give up their God. To the Roman officials they seemed a spoiled, obstinate, half-demented people; and, failing to win them over with kind words, they tried their swords. Thousands of Jews were put to death in those ghastly years. They were burned and crucified and massacred in droves.

Finally, in the year 66, matters reached a climax. The Jews could stand the tyranny no longer, and openly rebelled. Roman legions were sent down from Syria to quell the uprising, but to no avail. The Jews fought like maddened lions, and could not be subdued. Nero, the Roman emperor, realizing this was no ordinary little outbreak, quickly sent two of his ablest generals, Vespasian and Titus, to the scene. Down through Galilee they marched, fighting wildly a whole year before finally reducing that region to subjection. Then west of Jerusalem they plowed a bloody furrow; then south; and then at last up to the walls of the city itself.

It is chiefly from the writings of a Jewish general named Josephus, a man who deserted his forces and then tried to do penance by recounting the heroism of those who stayed true, that we know what happened during the siege. Jerusalem became the scene of one of the most devastating contests in all history. The besieged within the city were divided into three camps, each wrangling with the other over who should be leader and how the war should be carried on. One held the lower city, another the upper, and a third the Temple area in between. Two of the factions began to quarrel over the possession of the town granaries, and, after repeated raids and massacres, someone set fire to the whole vast store so that

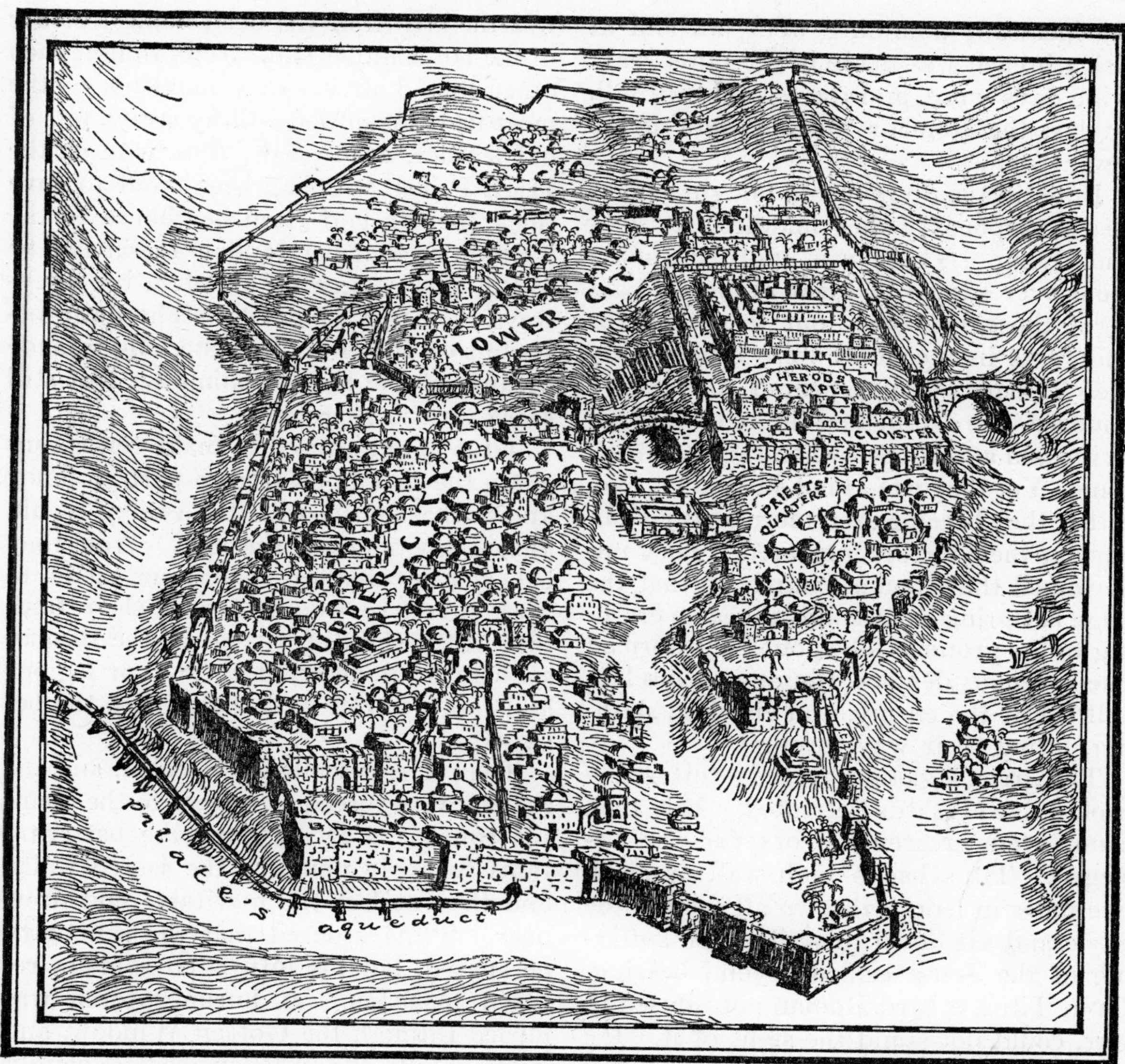

it was completely destroyed. There they were, a million or more Jews butchering each other in an ancient, dirty, high-walled city hardly a mile square in size—the food supplies gone, and the dread Roman already at the gates!

And yet they would not surrender!

Vespasian had been called back to Rome to be crowned emperor, and Titus, his son, began the siege. His artillery hurled great boulders a quarter of a mile into the heart of the city. Great mounds were built close against the north wall and huge battering rams were placed on them. Every tree within ten miles of the city had been cut down to make those rams. And then day and night the thunder of the rams was to be heard. Fifteen days the incessant pounding went on, and at last a breach was made in the outer wall. Nine days more, and the second wall fell. At last the Romans were masters of the lower city.

But still the Jews would not surrender. In the upper city they huddled, starving and dying. There was murder among them over scraps of meat or bread. At night those who stole out to pick herbs and roots in the fields were crucified by the Romans who captured them—five hundred were crucified in one day—or were slain and robbed when they returned home. Yet they would not surrender. No, rather they became even more madly stubborn as their terrors increased. They undermined the Roman mounds so that the huge battering rams suddenly came crashing to the ground. Then out they stormed like ravenous demons, flinging themselves full tilt at the enemy, and clawing, slashing, biting their way through.

The great legions wavered—tottered—broke! And Titus retreated. But then came even greater horrors for the besieged. Titus had a high wall of earth five miles in length thrown all around the city—and sat down to wait. The suffering of the Jews seemed beyond bearing. Even Titus, a hard Roman not unused to war, could not stand the sight of it. He begged the mad zealots to surrender and have done with it all. But no. No surrender. Never!

A month passed. Two. The Romans returned to the attack. One wall fell, but a second had been raised by the Jews in the meantime. The second fell. But still the heroes fought on. They were taking their stand in the inner fortress now. The narrow streets ran with blood. Sickening was the stench of the dead bodies rotting in the hot summer sun. Jews fought each other in the streets over handfuls of the most loathsome food—filthy straw, bits of old leather, even offal. The wife of the High Priest, who had been wont to have thick carpets laid from her house to the Temple so that her sandals might not be soiled, now staggered about in the alleyways in search of crusts. The daily offerings on the altars were no longer made because of the lack of animals. But still there was no surrender.

Titus again offered to make terms, but again the zealots refused to parley. They knew what terms with the enemy would mean—giving over the city. And they believed the city was God's, not theirs, to give. And so wondrous was their faith that at the sight of it some of the Roman soldiers even deserted their own legions and ran to throw in their lot with the besieged.

The fortress walls were scaled, and the zealots were forced to retreat to the Temple courts. For six days the battering rams savagely pounded the sacred walls, and then at last the inevitable end drew near. Titus ordered that the sanctuary be spared, but his infuriated soldiers refused to listen. A burning torch was hurled through the Golden Window, and immediately the wooden beams caught fire. Into the Temple courts the soldiers dashed, massacring the thousands who had taken refuge there.

And then there was quiet for a moment.

But again the resistance blazed forth. The zealots retreated to the upper city, to their last inch of ground, and once more defied the enemy. Almost a whole month they held out there before they crumpled for good. They were starved out and exhausted; their strength was utterly spent. The Romans came raging in, slaying until their arms were tired. Every alley and room and corner was choked with bleeding corpses. Then fire was set to everything—houses, buildings, walls—and the conquerors stood back to watch the flames.

And thus was old Jerusalem destroyed.

It is said that more than a million Jews died in that siege. Of those who survived, 97,000 were made slaves. They were deported to labor in the mines of Egypt, or were forced to fight wild beasts in the Roman arenas. Titus himself carried away the noblest of the zealots to march in his triumphal procession through the broad streets of Rome. A great arch was built there to commemorate his ghastly triumph, an arch on which were carved figures of his young captives carrying the sacred vessels of the Temple. That beauteous arch is still standing in old Rome; and the ruins of the blood-soaked wall still stand in old Jerusalem. Only there are no Romans now to look on that arch and rejoice in the triumph it commemorates. The Jews alone are left, and they come to pray at their old wall even to this day. The Romans have gone—gone the way of the Egyptians and Assyrians and Babylonians and Persians and Greeks. Only the Jews still live.

In the year 70 it seemed as if the Jews had indeed reached their end. But it was not their end; it was but a new beginning. Jewish Independence ends with the destruction of Jerusalem, but not Jewish life

and thought. They were driven out of their ancient homeland and scattered to the far ends of the earth. But wherever they went they took with them their Holy Law, and with it the high hope which the prophets had instilled in their hearts. No matter how sad was their lot in the lands of their exile, no matter how low their station, always they retained their belief that a time must come when they would yet triumph. And I cannot help but feel that because of that belief the Jews still survive to this day.

A CHRONOLOGY OF BIBLE HISTORY

A CHRONOLOGY OF BIBLE HISTORY

IT is altogether impossible to work out an exact chronology of all of Bible history. Save for a few isolated dates verified by the Egyptian, Moabite, and other non-Hebrew inscriptions, we are compelled to resort largely to guess-work in any effort to give the years of almost all the events in early Hebrew history. Hundreds of Bible scholars have attempted to draw up chronologies, and no two of them have quite agreed. Some have relied entirely on the Bible record, accepting all its round numbers, its "forties" and "seventies," as literally correct; others have gone to the opposite extreme, accepting almost none of the Biblical figures and relying wherever possible—and sometimes when quite impossible—on non-Hebrew records. The chronology given below follows a middle course. It is based largely upon that of Dr. George Adam Smith in his excellent "Atlas of the Historical Geography of the Holy Land," and is probably as reliable as any that our present limited knowledge of ancient history can provide.

I hope no reader will attempt to learn all these dates by heart, for that would be a waste of time and effort. Only the ten dates printed in italics are of such outstanding importance as to deserve to be memorized by the ordinary student. What is far more valuable than remembering a lot of dates is remembering the sequence of events. That ingenious man, Dr. Hendrik Willem Van Loon, once told me a clever way of getting the utmost out of a chronology. Draw up a list of the most important events, he suggested, and write each on a separate slip of paper. Throw all the slips into a hat, shuffle them thoroughly, toss them out on a desk, and then try to put them together again in their proper chronological order. If you can do that without error, you know the whole sequence of the story.

I recommend that the reader try Dr. Van Loon's game with the major events in the list below. It will fix his mind on the one important element in Bible history: that golden chain of cause and effect which makes that history one of the most fascinating and instructive in the annals of man.

A CHRONOLOGY OF BIBLE HISTORY

? ALL DATES IN THIS PERIOD ARE UNCERTAIN ?

AGE OF THE PATRIARCHS

- ABRAHAM leaves Ur of the Chaldees and after many wanderings settles in Canaan
- ISAAC dwells in Canaan
- JACOB in his last years moves with his household to Egypt
- JOSEPH attains great power in Egypt

THE EXODUS

- MOSES leads the Hebrew Slaves from Egypt
    - The Covenant is made at Mount Sinai
    - The Hebrews worship the Golden Calf
    - Korah rebels and is destroyed
    - Miriam and Aaron die
    - *Sihon, King of the Amorites,* is defeated at Jahaz
    - *Og, King of Bashan,* is defeated at Edrei
    - Reuben, Gad, and half of the tribe of Manasseh are given the land east of the Jordan
    - Moses dies after seeing the Promised Land
- JOSHUA leads the invasion
    - Jericho is captured
    - The Gibeonites submit to Hebrew domination
    - The land is divided
    - The Tabernacle is established at Shiloh
    - Joshua dies

THE RULE OF THE JUDGES

- OTHNIEL delivers the southern tribes from *Edomite* oppression
- EHUD defeats *Eglon, King of the Moabites*
- SHAMGAR struggles with the *Philistines*
- DEBORAH and BARAK defeat the *Canaanites* under *Sisera*
- GIDEON routs the *Midianites* and *Amalekites*
- ABIMELECH rules over the men of Shechem
- TOLA rules for 23 years in Ephraim
- JAIR rules for 22 years in Gilead
- JEPHTHAH repulses the *Ammonites*, east of the Jordan
- SAMSON struggles with the *Philistines*
- IBZAN, whom tradition identifies with Boaz of the Book of Ruth
- ELON rules for 10 years and is buried at Aijalon
- ABDON restores order in Central Israel after a feud with Jephthah
- ELI: The Ark is captured by the *Philistines*
- SAMUEL anoints a King over Israel

? ALL DATES IN THIS PERIOD ARE UNCERTAIN ?

THE MONARCHY

1020? SAUL is anointed first King in Israel *1020?*

The *Philistines* are defeated at Michmash

So are the *Amorites*

And the *Amalekites*

David joins Saul's court, slays *Goliath*, and later flees because of Saul's jealousy

David becomes a freebooter in the South Country

Saul and Jonathan die in battle with *Philistines* at Mt. Gilboa

ISHBOSHETH is accepted as King by the tribes east of the Jordan

1000? DAVID is crowned King of Judah 1000?

Civil war ensues, but finally David triumphs

Nathan and Gad are prophets at this time

995? *Jerusalem* taken from *Jebusites* and made the capital 995?

Philistines defeated at Baal-Perizim; other enemies conquered

The Empire is established

Absalom rebels; Sheba leads an insurrection

David dies

962? SOLOMON succeeds to the throne 962?

THE TEMPLE IS BUILT

Zadok is made the sole High Priest

Solomon builds palaces and roads with the forced labor of the Canaanites and his own people

Rebellion led by Jeroboam in vain

Solomon dies

935? THE DIVIDED KINGDOM *935?*

	JUDAH (SOUTH)	ISRAEL (NORTH)	
	REHOBOAM, son of Solomon	JEROBOAM I crowned by rebels	
930?	*Shishkak of Egypt* invades Palestine		930?
923?	ABIJAM wars against Israel		923?
920?	ASA reigns in peace and prosperity		920?
918?		NADAB son of Jeroboam	918?
915?		BAASHA murders Nadab	915?
	Civil War		
891?		ELAH, who is murdered by	891?
888?		ZIMRI, who usurps throne but commits suicide 7 days later	888?
		Civil War	
		OMRI becomes King in Samaria. Encourages worship of the Phoenician Baal and Astarte. His son, Ahab, marries Jezebel, a Phoenician princess	

	JUDAH (SOUTH)		ISRAEL (NORTH)	
876?		ELIJAH	AHAB ascends the throne	876?
874?	JEHOSHAPHAT		Elijah denounces Jezebel	874?
			Struggle with Baal worship	
			Ahab defeats the *Arameans*	
			Makes alliance with Judah	
853?			AHAZIAH: Moab revolts	853?
852?			JORAM: petty wars	852?
849?	JEHORAM	ELISHA		849?
846	Edom revolts			846
844?	AHAZIAH		Elisha foments rebellion	844?
842?	ATHALIAH, the queen-mother murders her grandchildren and usurps the throne		JEHU exterminates the house of Omri and usurps throne	842?
839	*Hazael of Damascus* invades Palestine			839
836?	JOASH			836?
	The Temple is repaired			
814?			JEHOAHAZ	814?
798?			JOASH	798?
797?	AMAZIAH			797?
	Civil War			
	Jerusalem is sacked by Joash, and Amaziah is taken prisoner			
783?			JEREBOAM II reconquers	783?
778?	UZZIAH reconquers lost territory	AMOS	Moab, Gilead, etc.;	778?
			Great prosperity	
	He usurps the office of High Priest in the Temple			
743		HOSEA	ZECHARIAH reigns 6 months	743
			SHALLUM reigns 1 month	
740?	JOTHAM		MENAHEM murders Shallum	740?
738			*Assyrians* invade Israel	738
737?			PEKAHIAH	737?
736?	AHAZ	ISAIAH	PEKAH murders Pekahiah	736?
735	Ahaz is attacked by Pekah and *Rezin of Damascus*			735
734			*Assyria* invades Israel	734
732	Judah is *Assyrian* vassal		*First Deportation*	732
730?			HOSHEA murders Pekah and	730?
727?	HEZEKIAH		usurps throne. Refuses to pay tribute to Assyria, Israel is invaded	727?
725			Siege of Samaria begins	725
722			*"TEN TRIBES" DEPORTED*	*722*
715			Samaria is repeopled by "heathens" brought in from Assyria	715

KINGDOM OF JUDAH

ISAIAH — MICAH

705 HEZEKIAH, who is still King, allies himself with Egypt and rebels against Assyria 705

701 *Sennacherib of Assyria* invades Palestine 701

685? MANASSEH is taken captive by Assyrians and restored only as a vassal prince 685?

ZEPHANIAH — JEREMIAH — HABAKKUK? — HULDA — NAHUM? — URIAH

641? AMON, King of Judah 641?

639? JOSIAH, King of Judah 639?

627 The wild *Scythians* sweep down the Palestine coast 627

Josiah rebuilds the Temple

621 Hilkiah, the High Priest, finds the "Book of the Law." 621

Josiah's reforms commence (2 Kings, 22, 23)

608 Josiah is slain at Meggido in battle with Egyptians 608

608 JEHOAHAZ reigns 3 months as a vassal of Egypt 608

608 JEHOIAKIM is vassal of Egypt until 608

604 *Babylon* becomes the supreme power in the Orient 604

599 Judah withholds tribute from *Babylon*, and the land is invaded and plundered by *Nebuchadrezzar* 599

597 JEHOIACHIN is taken captive when Jerusalem falls 597

1st Great Deportation

EZEKIEL

597 ZEDEKIAH made King by Nebuchadrezzar 597

Jeremiah warns against rebellion, but in vain

589 Judah rebels against Babylonia 589

587 Jerusalem besieged by Nebuchadrezzar 587

586 *TEMPLE RAZED AND JERUSALEM DESTROYED* *586*

Zedekiah is taken prisoner and blinded; princes beheaded

2d Great Deportation

BABYLONIAN EXILE

OBADIAH?

586 GEDALIAH appointed governor over remnant left in Judah, but is soon murdered. The rebels flee to Egypt carrying Jeremiah with them 586

582 *3d Great Deportation* 582

Close of the Book of Ezekiel

Conditions grow increasingly difficult for the exiles

The "Unknown Prophet" preaches to the exiles

538 *Cyrus of Persia* takes Babylon and permits the Jewish exiles to return to their home land *538*

537 ZERUBBABEL and JOSHUA lead the 1st Return 537

THE SECOND COMMONWEALTH

The Altar is restored in Jerusalem
536 Samaritans attack the returning exiles 536
521 HAGGAI and ZECHARIAH, two prophets, cry out for rebuilding of the Temple 521
520 Temple restoration begun 520
516 *THE SECOND TEMPLE IS COMPLETED* 516
The tiny settlement in the restored Judea struggles along unsuccessfully until
458 EZRA comes leading the 2d large group of returning exiles 458
The *Samaritans* under Sanballat resent their rejection by the Judeans, and begin hostilities
445 NEHEMIAH a man of great influence at the Persian Court leads the 3d large group of returning exiles 445
The walls of Jerusalem are rebuilt
Thorough reforms are instituted
444 Ezra reads the "LAW" to the Judeans 444
432 The Samaritan intrigues compel Nehemiah to go back to Persia to reëstablish his influence there 432
420? *Samaritans* build their own temple at Mt. Gerizim 420?
HIGH PRIESTS rule Judea from now on
350 Revolt in Judea against Persia, resulting in much bloodshed 350
345 and ending in the exile of the leaders to Hyrcania in Asia 345
332 *Alexander the Great* marches down on Judea *332*
331 After defeating the Egyptians, *Alexander* returns through Judea 331
320 *Ptolemy I* (*Soter*) *of Egypt* occupies Judea, which now becomes a subdivision of Coele-Syria, tributary to Egypt 320
But the land is never at peace, for it is a constant cause of war between the Egyptian and Syrian Empires
264 War over Palestine breaks out anew between Egypt and Syria 264
Egypt still triumphant
250 About this time the *Septuagint*, a Greek translation of the Pentateuch, was made at Alexandria 250
GREEK INFLUENCE becomes very marked in Judea
218 Palestine overrun by *Antiochus III of Syria* 218
217 The land is taken by Egypt but later made tributary again 217
203 to Syria, only to be recaptured by Egypt, and then a third 203
200 time, to be recaptured by Antiochus of Syria 200
197 Palestine is finally ceded to Syria 197
175 *Antiochus IV* (*Epiphanes*) ascends throne of Syria, and soon loses patience with the Jews because of the constant intrigues of their corrupt rulers, the priests 175
169 Temple plundered by Antiochus Epiphanes 169

168 Altar to Zeus is erected in the Holy of Holies, and a Syrian garrison is stationed in Jerusalem to crush the Jewish religion 168

167 MATTATHIAS, the Hasmonean, resists the Syrian officer at Modin *167*

THE MACCABEAN REVOLT

166 JUDAS MACCABEUS victorious over the Syrian hosts 166
Possible date of the Book of Daniel
165 *The Temple is purified* 165
Judas wins great victories
164 Antiochus Epiphanes dies 164
163 Judas suffers defeat at Beth-Zechariah: his brother, Eliezar is killed in battle 163

Judas makes overtures to Rome. He is killed in a battle with the Syrians

161 JONATHAN, brother of Judas, continues the war against Syria 161
159 *Syrians evacuate Judea* 159
157 Syrian War renewed because of treachery of the Hellenized among the Jews 157
153 Jonathan is made High Priest 153
142 Jonathan is executed by the usurper of the Syrian crown 142

142 SIMON, last of Mattathias's five sons, made High Priest 142
Jewish independence is recognized by Syria
139 *Rome recognizes the Jewish State* 139
Simon slain by his son-in-law and is succeeded by his son

135 JOHN HYRCANUS I. Syria continues the war on Judea, and John Hyrcanus appeals to Rome for help. Syria withdraws, and John Hyrcanus then wages war against the Samaritans and Idumeans, forcibly converting the latter to Judaism 135

About 109 *Judea at height of prosperity,* but discord is rife, especially between *Pharisees* and *Sadducees* About 109

103 ARISTOBULUS I succeeds John Hyrcanus, continuing the wars of conquest 103

102 ALEXANDER JANNEUS becomes ruler. He favors the Sadducees and oppresses the Pharisees. He greatly enlarges the frontiers of the land 102

78 ALEXANDRA, widow of Alexander, becomes queen of Judea. She favors the Pharisees. The religious parliament called the *Sanhedrin* is reorganized 78

66	HYRCANUS II and his brother, ARISTOBULUS II, become co-regents of the land. They quarrel, and Hyrcanus calls in Aretas, King of the Nabateans (Arabs). The latter invades Judea and takes Jerusalem; whereupon Aristobulus II appeals to the Roman legate.	66
63	*Pompey of Rome* captures Jerusalem and makes Hyrcanus his vassal. Aristobulus II is sent a prisoner to Rome, whence	*63*
56	he escapes and leads an abortive revolt in Judea. There is continual strife and intrigue, but finally he is poisoned and his son is executed	56
47	*Antipater of Idumea* is made procurator of Judea by Caesar. He appoints his eldest son, *Phasael*, governor of Jerusalem and his second son, *Herod*, governor of Galilee	47
42	*Mark Antony* takes possession of Palestine, and appoints Herod and Phasael his tetrarchs	42
40	*Parthians* invade Judea, capture Jerusalem, mutilate Hyrcanus II, and proclaim	40
	ANTIGONUS king of Judea; but three years later	
37	HEROD, aided by a Roman army, captures Jerusalem, executes	37
20	Antigonus, and becomes king of Judea	20
	About this time Herod rebuilds the Temple	
4	Herod dies	4
4	ARCHELAUS rules over Judea and Samaria;	4
	HEROD ANTIPAS is tetrarch of Galilee and Perea; *Philip II* is tetrarch of Gaulanitis, etc.	
3	Revolt against Archelaus and other Roman appointees, led by Judas the Galilean, founder of the Zealots	3
2	Archelaus recognized as Ethnarch by Rome	2
	Continual insurrection and unrest in Palestine	
A. D.		A. D.
6	ROMAN PROCURATORS rule Judea: Archelaus is deposed	6
26 *29*	Ministry of *Jeshua of Nazareth*	*26* *29*
30	Martyrdom of *Stephen*	30
34 56	Apostolic journeys of *Saul of Tarsus*	34 56
41	AGRIPPA I is made king of Palestine	41
44	HEROD II, titular king of Judea	44
49	AGRIPPA II, titular king of Judea	49
59	*Paul* is sent a prisoner to Rome	59
66	*Revolt against Rome Renewed*	66
70	Titus besieges Jerusalem	*70*
	DESTRUCTION OF JERUSALEM	

DISPERSION OF THE JEWS

	ISRAEL		THE ENEMIES		
	1020? Judges	INDEPENDENT PEOPLE	*Continual war against Canaanites, Philistines*		
1000					1000
	United Kingdom 935?		*Midianites, etc.*		
			EGYPT	930?	
900					900
	Divided Kingdom Israel-north Judah-south			839?	
800					800
			ARAMEA (*Syria*)	738	
700	722				700
	Judah		*ASSYRIA*	627	
			Scythian invasion	608	
600			*Egyptian invasion*	604	600
	586 Babylonian Exile 536		*BABYLONIA*	538	
500					500
			PERSIA		
400					400
	High Priests				
300			*Alexander*	332 320	300
			GREECE	*Ptolemies of Egypt*	
200					200
	167	INDEPENDENT		*Seleucids of Syria* 197 167	
100	Maccabean Kings				100
	63		*Nabatean (Arab) invasion*	66	
				63	
A.D.	Idumean Rulers		*Parthian invasion*	40	A.D.
	6 Roman Procurators 41 Agrippa II 44 Roman Procurators		*ROME*		
100	70 DISPERSION of the JEWS				100

A SUMMARY OF THE BOOKS OF THE JEWISH SCRIPTURES

SUMMARY OF THE BOOKS OF THE JEWISH SCRIPTURES

BY the name Bible we mean all those writings which together make up the most sacred literature of Judaism and Christianity. The word is of Greek origin and is derived from *ta biblia,* which means simply "the books." It consists in all of some 66 books, 39 of which belong to the Old, or Jewish, Testament, and 27 to the New, or Christian, Testament. It was the Rabbis of old who decided what books should or should not become part of the Jewish Testament. The writings which they rejected became part of what we call the Apocrypha. The accepted books were divided into three groups: the Law (*torah*), the Prophets (*nebiim*), and the Writings (*ketubim*). The order of the books within these groups was not chronological, and it has varied in different versions. In this synopsis the arrangement of the Jews is followed, for though that arrangement may not be the most widely accepted in the world today, it is at least the most ancient.

THE LAW

This division consists of the so-called Five Books of Moses, or the Pentateuch. Each book receives its name from its opening word or words.

(1) *Genesis* tells the story of how the world was created, of the first adventures of the human race, and of the origin of the Hebrews. Its obvious purpose is to give the Chosen People its place in the whole scheme of existence. The first eleven chapters deal with the early history of mankind, and the thirty-nine remaining chapters recount the adventures of the Patriarchs, the fathers of the Jewish race. The narrative groups itself around five principal characters: Adam, Noah, Abraham, Isaac, and Jacob.

(2) *Exodus* is so named because its opening portion tells the story of how the Israelites fled from Egypt. The book consists of forty chapters, but only the first eighteen of these deal with historical matters. The rest give the laws, including the Ten Commandments, which the Israelites solemnly swore to observe when they made their covenant with Jehovah at Mt. Sinai.

(3) *Leviticus* continues the law code begun in Exodus. It is chiefly concerned with the priestly regulations regarding the offering of sacrifices and the observance of the Holy days.

(4) *Numbers* is so called because of the numbering or census of the people which is given twice in the book. It continues the historical narrative begun in Exodus, telling what happened to the Israelites while they wandered through the Wilderness.

(5) *Deuteronomy* contains an account of the last great discourses of Moses. It repeats in somewhat different language and with rather different emphasis the

laws laid down in the earlier books of the Bible.

The Prophets

This part includes various books which are distinctly historical in their character, as well as others which contain the magnificent sermons of the great prophets of old. The classical arrangement is as follows:

(6) *Joshua,* the first in this section, really belongs with the Pentateuch. It tells the story of the exploits of Joshua who succeeded Moses as leader of the people and directed the invasion of Canaan.

(7) *Judges* recounts the dreadful difficulties which the Hebrews had when they tried to maintain themselves in the Promised Land. It describes with convincing directness and simplicity the anarchy which prevailed among the tribes soon after they broke their way into Canaan. There was no king to unite them, but only tribal chieftains, or "judges," many of whom were men of a very low order.

(8) *Samuel* consists of two parts in our versions of the Bible. It takes its name from the prophet and judge who plays the chief rôle in the first part of the book. I Samuel carries the narrative through to the death of Israel's first king, Saul. II Samuel continues the narrative through to the last years of King David.

(9) *Kings* is also divided into two parts in our versions. It tells of the death of David, the reign of his son Solomon, the division of the land into two rival kingdoms, and the sorry events that ensued until both kingdoms were carried away captive.

(10) *Isaiah* is the next book according to the Jewish arrangement, and reports the prophet's utterances on a great variety of occasions. Very little is known about Isaiah beyond the fact that he was a man of aristocratic birth, lived in Jerusalem, and had great influence over the kings of his day.

(11) *Jeremiah* contains the prophecies of one of the noblest of all the preachers of Bible times. He was active during forty of the most stormy and tragic years in the life of the people of Judah.

(12) *Ezekiel* was a priest, and preached to the Jews who had been carried away captive to Babylonia. In a sense he was the spiritual adviser of these exiles, and to him is due much of the credit for the preservation of the ancient faith during the years in Babylon.

(13) *Hosea* is the first of the twelve minor prophets listed in the Jewish Scriptures. He lived in the eighth century B.C. and preached to Israel, the northern kingdom, just before its destruction. The burthen of his prophecy was that Jehovah was a God of love and would have mercy on Israel if only it would repent its sins.

(14) *Joel* is a short book of sermons which cannot be exactly dated. Some scholars say the prophet lived during the time of the divided kingdom, but nowadays it is usually agreed that he appeared much later, probably just after the time of Nehemiah.

(15) *Amos* is the earliest of the prophets whose sermons are recorded in the Bible. He came from Judah and preached to the northern kingdom, warning it that Jehovah, who was a God of justice, would destroy Israel for its sins.

(16) *Obadiah* contains a series of sermons denouncing Edom for having joined hands with the enemies of Judah.

(17) *Jonah* tells the story of a prophet who was commanded by Jehovah to go out and save the heathens who dwelt in Nineveh. It is one of the most beautiful books in the Bible, for it reveals with rare poignancy the truth that God loves not alone the Israelites, but all the peoples of the earth.

(18) *Micah* was a peasant who prophesied in Judah about the time of Isaiah. In his sermons he seems to sum up the doctrines of Amos, Hosea, and Isaiah. The most famous passage in his book is that which reads: "He hath shewed thee, O man, what is good; and what doth the Lord require of thee; but to do justly, and to love mercy, and to walk humbly with thy God?"

(19) *Nahum* preached against Nineveh, that is, Assyria. He lived shortly after the time when that great empire had terrorized over Judah.

(20) *Habakkuk,* of whom practically nothing is known, prophesied in Judah at about the same time as Nahum, but directs his complaints against the Babylonians rather than the Assyrians.

(21) *Zephaniah* was another of that group of great preachers who instilled in the Judeans the faith which made it possible for them to survive when their kingdom was destroyed in 586 B.C.

(22) *Haggai* prophesied to the little community of Jews who dragged their way back to Palestine after the Babylonian exile. The burthen of his preaching is that there can be no happiness or prosperity in the community until the Temple of Jehovah is rebuilt on Mt. Moriah.

(23) *Zechariah* was a partner with Haggai in the attempt to awaken the returned exiles to a realization of their duty to rebuild the Temple. He was, however, a much younger man than Haggai, and preached in a more stilted and artificial style.

(24) *Malachi* means "My Messenger," and may have been a title of honor given to some unknown prophet rather than a proper name. We cannot be certain of the date of this book, except that it belongs to the period after the return from the Babylonian exile. Its most famous verse is that which declares: "Have we not all one father? Hath not one God created us?"

Writings

This group contains books of varied character and subject matter. Some are collections of pure poetry; some are philosophic works; still others are histories.

(25) *Psalms* is attributed to David, but only 73 of the 150 hymns in it are directly ascribed to the ancient minstrel king. Many of the rest are ascribed to various other great Hebrew worthies, among them Moses, the sons of Korah, and Solomon. This book has been far and away the most popular in history, both with Jews and Christians. It consists entirely of songs of praise and petition, which, because of their simple beauty and profound sincerity, are able to express the hopes and the longings of men in any and every age.

(26) *Proverbs* is a collection of wise maxims and parables both of a religious and a very worldly nature. The whole book is popularly attributed to Solomon, but many of its verses are specifically ascribed to other and less well-known men.

(27) *Job* is really a dramatic narrative

which tells of the troubles which befell a pious man, and then discusses the problem of why evil should ever afflict the righteous.

(28) *Song of Songs*, or, as it is often called, the *Song of Solomon,* is a most beautiful work of poetry. The ancient Rabbis believed it to be a parable telling of God's love for Israel, and the Church Fathers interpreted it as a parable describing the love of Jesus for the Church. Most modern scholars, however, believe it to be simply a love lyric describing the passion of a man for a woman.

(29) *Ruth* in most of our translations is put after the Book of Judges because the story it tells is laid in that very early time. It is a beautiful pastoral story telling of how a Moabite woman became a true daughter of Israel and was found worthy of being the ancestress of none other than the great King David.

(30) *Lamentations* is attributed to the prophet Jeremiah, and is a book of dirges over the fall of Jerusalem.

(31) *Ecclesiastes,* a book attributed to the wise King Solomon, is made up of many profound reflections on life. Its most famous verse, of course, is the refrain, "Vanity of vanities, vanity of vanities, all is vanity."

(32) *Esther* tells the story of a Jewish maiden who became queen of Persia and saved her people from destruction at the hands of a cruel minister named Haman. It is curious that the book contains no single mention of the word God.

(33) *Daniel* tells the story of a young Jew who was carried away captive to Babylon and then, because of his great wisdom, was advanced to the position of governor of the land. The book contains many strange verses describing what the prophet believed would happen in the "end of days." Evidently it was written at a time when the Jews were in great despair and when they looked forward hungrily to the coming of a new order on earth.

(34) *Ezra* commences with the proclamation of Cyrus, king of Persia, who in 536 B.C. allowed the exiled Jews to leave Babylon and return to their homeland. It tells of the families that returned to ruined Judea, and of the adventures that occurred to them there.

(35) *Nehemiah* tells how that great leader, having learnt of the sad state prevailing among the returned exiles in Jerusalem, left his high position at the Persian court and went back to help them. The book recounts how Nehemiah rebuilt the walls of Jerusalem and brought about many reforms in the life of the people.

(36) *Chronicles,* like Samuel and Kings, is divided into two books in our versions. It is really a supplement to the other historical books of the Old Testament, for it begins by tracing the descent from Adam down to the sons of Jacob, and then continues with a rapid outline of the history of the Israelites from the time of David through the Babylonian exile.

THE CHRISTIAN SCRIPTURES

IT came to pass toward the end of the reign of Herod that there lived in the city of Hebron, or perhaps in the nearby village of Juttah, a priest named Zacharias. As was the custom in Israel among the men of his sacred profession, Zacharias had a wife, Elizabeth, who was also of the priestly family. They were aged folk, and very humble and poor; but they were pious and contented for all that. Indeed, their only sorrow was occasioned by the fact that they had no child.

But one day, when Zacharias was ministering at the golden altar in the Temple at Jerusalem, an angel came to him and announced that his secret prayers to God had been heard and his wife was about to bear a child. Zacharias was naturally amazed, for he was already a man full of years. In his incredulity he asked for some assurance of the promised blessing, whereupon the angel declared that the priest, because of his unbelief, would remain dumb till the day that the child was born.

As soon as his act of service at the Temple was ended, Zacharias, now dumb as well as aged, returned to his home. And behold, it came to pass just as the angel had promised, and Zacharias's wife, Elizabeth, conceived and became with child.

Six months after he appeared to Zacharias in the Temple, the same angel came to Nazareth, a remote village in the hills of Galilee, and there appeared unto a lowly virgin named Miriam, or Mary. This young woman was betrothed to a poor carpenter at Nazareth named Joseph, and she was much astounded to learn that, though she was not yet married, she was about to become a mother. The Holy Ghost had sought her out and found her worthy of bearing a child who would grow to be the Redeemer of the world, and would be known as Jehoshua (or Jeshua), which means "God the Savior."

Now this Mary was a kinswoman of Elizabeth, and, having heard of the miracle that had occurred to the aged woman, she made haste to go up to Judea to confer with her. Mary remained some three months with Elizabeth, and then returned to Nazareth. But when Joseph, the carpenter to whom Mary was betrothed, saw that she was with child, he determined on casting her off. He was a kindly man, and did not want to report the girl to the authorities; but he refused to consider marrying her now, for he believed she had sinned. Before he could take any action, however, he too was visited by an angel and was assured that the child Mary was about to bear had been conceived through the operation not of a man but of the Holy Ghost. So Joseph no longer hesitated, but straightway took Mary to wife.

Meanwhile the event announced to the aged Zacharias in the Temple was fulfilled and Elizabeth bore a man-child. She named him Jochanan, that is, "God is gracious," but, in accordance with the Greek fashion of the day, the child was known as John. And that child grew to be a prophet. Having been dedicated to God's service as a Nazirite, he never touched wine or strong drink, and denied himself all other pleasures of ordinary life. John assumed the garb of the ancient holy men, wore a robe of camel's hair fastened around the body by a leather girdle, and ate locusts, wild honey, and other such desert foods.

According to the Bible, it came to pass at about the time when John was born that the Roman emperor passed a decree ordering all his subjects in Palestine to go up to the capital to be registered in the census. This decree compelled Joseph and his wife Mary to leave their home in Nazareth and travel to Judea just when she was about to bear her child. One night they got as far as the village of Bethlehem, but found the tavern there so crowded with travelers that they were compelled to seek shelter in the stable among the cattle and the beasts of burden. And behold, there in the stable the pangs came over Mary, and she bore her child. Wrapping him in swaddling clothes, she laid him in a manger by her side. And thus was Jesus ushered into the world of men.

Now Joseph and Mary were strict Jews, and naturally enough they felt it incumbent upon them to rear their child according to the Holy Law. When the infant was eight days old he was circumcised and given the Hebrew name of Jeshua, which in Greek was Jesus. And on the fortieth day Mary repaired to the Temple and, in accordance with the Jewish custom, presented her offering of purification. She brought her little one with her on that journey, and she marveled much to see an aged man named Symeon, and a prophetess named Anna, recognize the holy child and openly declare him to be none other than the promised Messiah of Israel.

Soon after the holy family left Jerusalem and returned to their lodging place at Bethlehem, certain Magi or Wise Men from Persia came to the capital and began to inquire where they could find him that was born King of the Jews. They declared they had seen his star in the east and had come expressly to worship

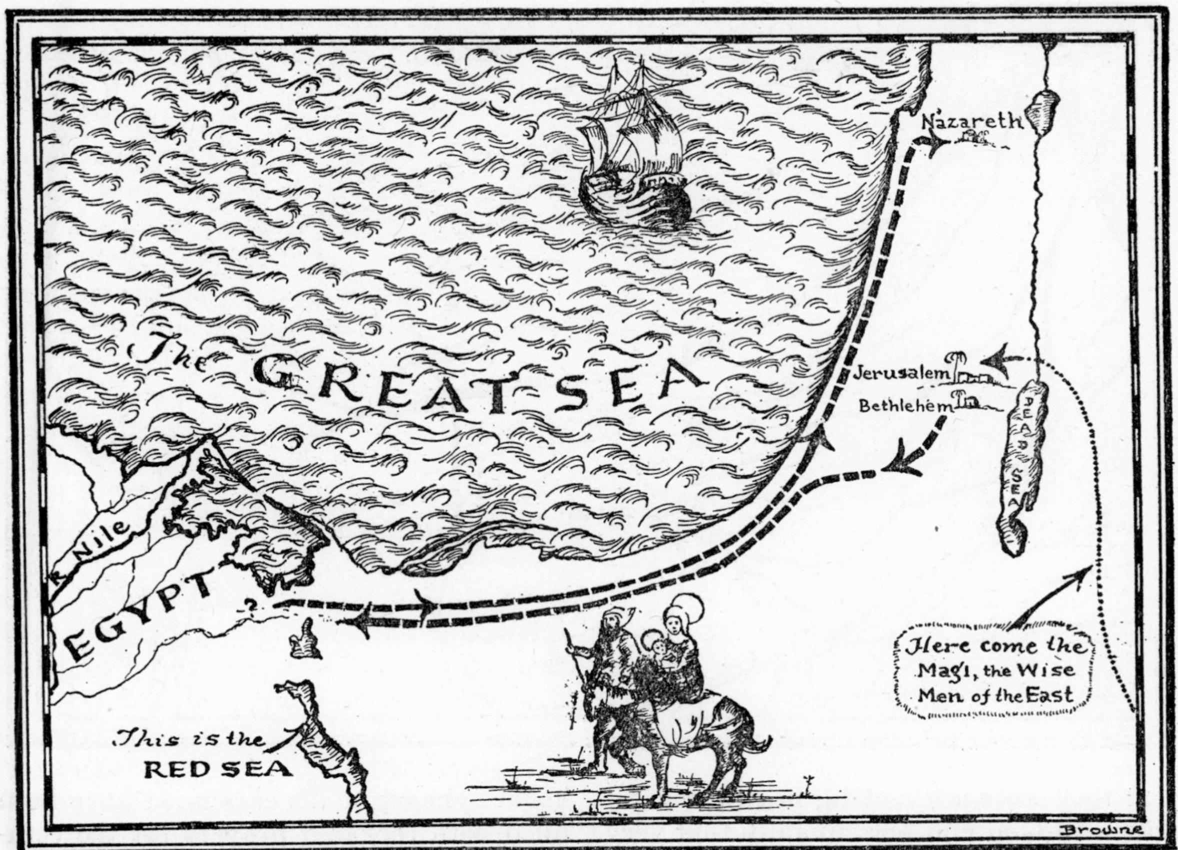

him. But when King Herod heard of this, he was filled with alarm, for he had no desire to lose his throne. By means of a low stratagem he discovered where the infant lay, and at once he began to plot to destroy him. But Joseph was forewarned in a dream, and just in time he took his wife and the child and fled with them across the wilderness to Egypt. And only when Herod died did the holy family return to Palestine. Joseph brought his wife and child to Nazareth and once more took up his work there as a carpenter.

The map on the next page gives some indication of the geographical position of Nazareth. The village itself was very small; indeed it was so obscure that it never once receives mention in the Old Testament. But though small, it lay in the very heart of Lower Galilee, and therefore was far from secluded. Not far away from it were the great highways radiating in all directions, and because of these highways, Nazareth lay open to all the many influences coming from the cities and lands of the East and West.

Galilee had once been a place inhabited largely by half-breed Jews, but from the time of the Maccabees it became a center of the most intense Jewish patriotism. The people there were not as well educated as those in Jerusalem, but for all

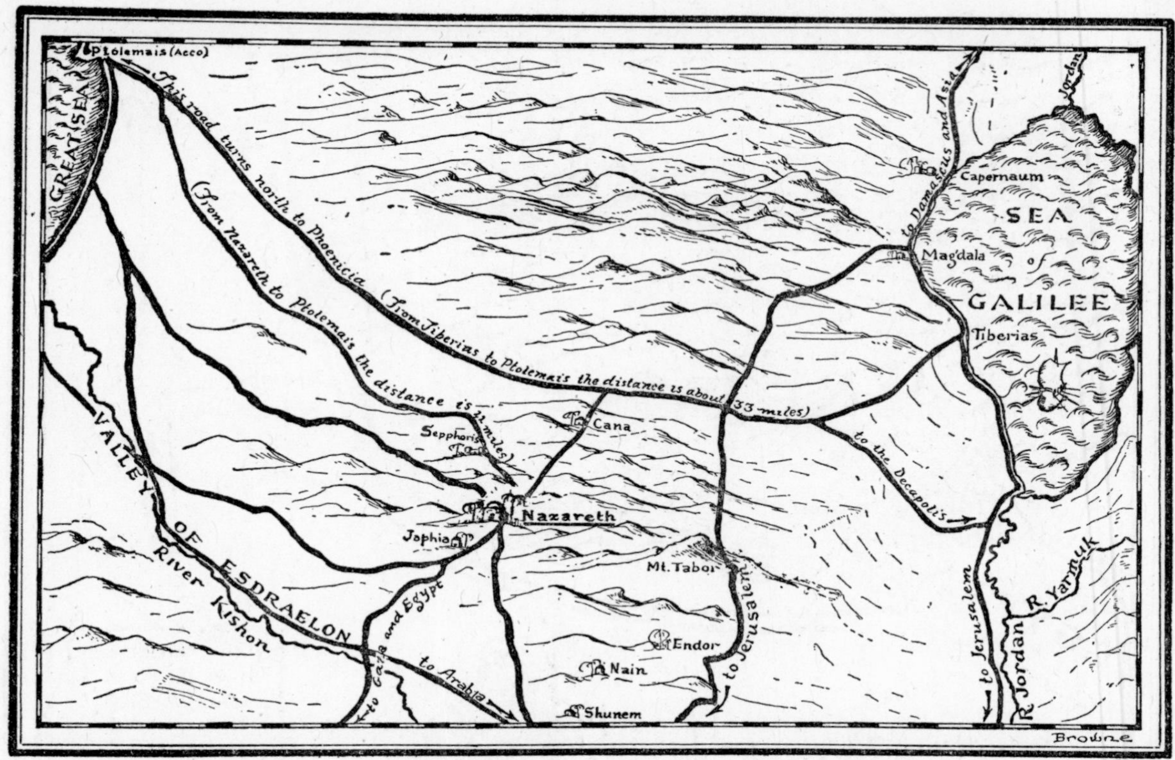

that they were not lacking in extreme devotion to God and fervent faith that very soon He would send the Messiah to rescue them from the talons of Rome. Indeed, the spirit of rebellion against Rome was fiercer in Galilee than almost anywhere else in Palestine. About an hour's walk from Nazareth lay the important city of Sepphoris, and we know from history that this was for a time a stronghold of the revolutionists. All around Nazareth there were other cities and villages where the spark of rebellion lay always ready to be fanned. And from this we can imagine what must have been one of the great influences in the early life of Jesus. In the alleyways of Nazareth he must have heard constant talk of the wickedness of the Roman oppressor, and in the synagogue his ears must have been filled with repeated prayers for the coming of a Redeemer. For the Jews were convinced that the intolerable evil could not last much longer. Of old the prophets had taught them that a day of release must come, a day wherein their God would send them a wondrous leader, a Messiah—that is, an "Anointed One"—who would miraculously overthrow the hated enemy and then reign in peace forevermore. And the more horrible the persecutions, the nearer seemed the advent of this Anointed One. Each day was thought to be the very last, and every hour the people pricked up their ears for the sound of the Messiah's trumpet. And it was in such an atmosphere that the child Jesus grew to boyhood.

ONLY one episode of Jesus' boyhood is reported in the Gospels. When he was twelve years of age he was taken up to Jerusalem by his parents to celebrate the festival of Passover, and there he astonished all by entering into a learned discussion with the aged rabbis. Otherwise, however, his youth seems not to have been in any wise extraordinary. He remained in Nazareth and plied the trade of his foster father, Joseph, working as a carpenter in and around the village.

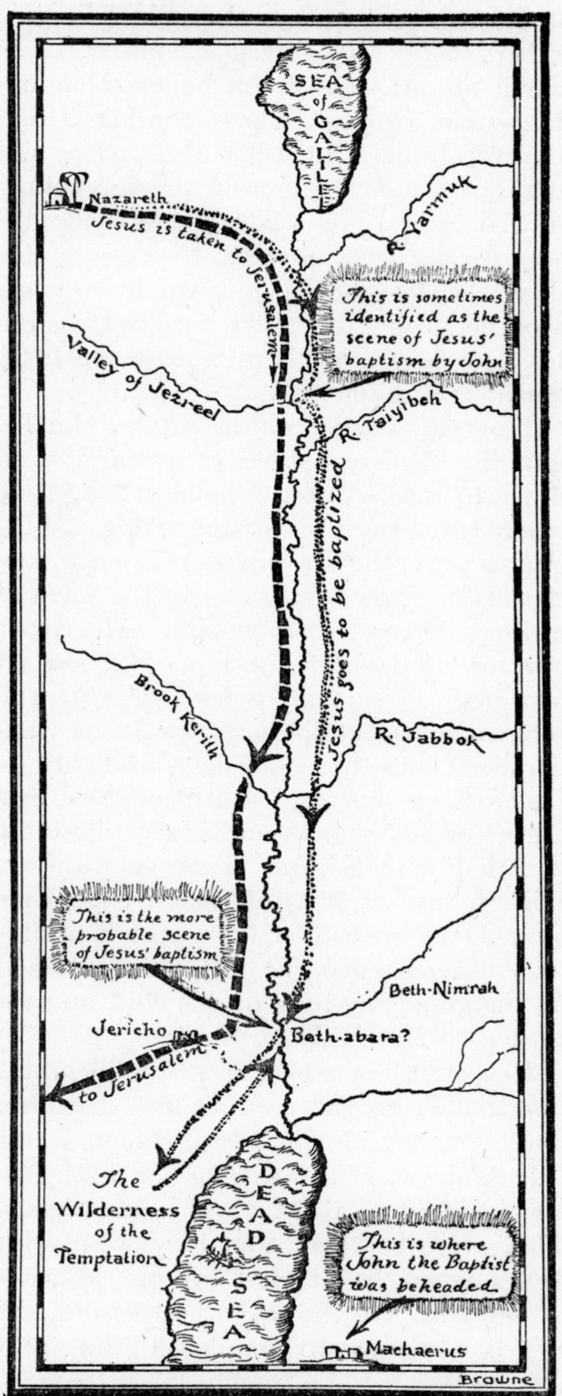

Now while Jesus remained in seclusion in Nazareth, John, the son of Zacharias and Elizabeth, came forth and began to preach in Judea. As I have already said, he assumed the garb of the ancient prophets and began to call on the people to repent of their sins. He took his stand at Beth-Abara, which was probably not far from Jericho, and began to baptize the people in the River Jordan. John believed that the Day of the Messiah was about to come, and therefore he was tremendously concerned that the Jews be prepared for the event. Just as a heathen who desired to become a Jew had to be baptized before he could be counted "clean" enough, so every Jew, said John, also must be baptized. For the Jews, he declared, were almost as sinful now as the heathens, and in their present state were not ready to enter the Kingdom of Heaven when it suddenly swooped down on the earth.

And many thousands in Israel believed that which John declared, and in swarms they made pilgrimage to Beth-Abara to be baptized by him. Indeed, we are told that the river-bank became like the street of a crowded city. Some believed that

John was none other than the Messiah; others believed he was Elijah come to earth again; still others believed he was the great prophet whose coming Moses had foretold. But John declared he was none of these, but merely the forerunner of Another. He was but preparing the way for a greater prophet the very latchet of whose shoes he was not worthy to loose. For he, John, baptized with water, but lo, the other would baptize with the Holy Spirit and with fire!

Now about six months after John began his ministry, Jesus arose and went down to Beth-Abara to be baptized. And when Jesus came out of the water and began to pray, the heavens were opened, and the Holy Spirit, embodied in the form of a dove, descended upon him. Moreover, a voice cried out from above, "Thou art my beloved son in whom I am well pleased." After the baptism Jesus wandered off into the wilderness, probably on the western shores of the Dead Sea, and there for forty days and forty nights he wrestled with Satan. There amidst the thickets and caverns of that dreadful region Jesus withstood the great Temptation and emerged the victor. Sustained by the angels he took up his staff and returned to Beth-Abara.

It was on his return from the Temptation that Jesus gathered his first disciples. Two young Galilean Jews, Simon Peter and Andrew, who formerly had been followers of the Baptist, now joined Jesus. They were brothers, and they went with Jesus when he started on his journey homeward. On the way the disciples met a fellow-townsman named Philip, and they persuaded him to join the little company. Philip agreed and then tried to win a fourth disciple, a man named Nathanael who was from Cana, a village very near Nazareth. But Nathanael could not believe that anything good could come out of a hamlet like Nazareth, and was most reluctant to join the group. When, however, he saw how miraculously wise was Jesus, his doubts disappeared, and he declared, "Rabbi, thou art the son of God, thou art the king of Israel."

On the third day after the departure from Beth-Abara, Jesus with his five disciples reached the village of Cana, and there he performed his first recorded miracle. A marriage was being celebrated, and Jesus and his followers were invited to share in the festivities. But there not being enough wine to go around, Jesus turned six large vessels of water into wine, and thus kept the joy of the occasion from being marred.

That helped confirm the faith of the four young men who had joined Jesus as his disciples. When the feast was over they followed him to the city of Capernaum, as did also Jesus' mother and brethren. According to the Gospel of John, Jesus remained there only a few days, for the Passover was approaching, and, being a pious Jew, he wished to go up to Jerusalem for the holy season. His disciples accompanied him and when they came to the Temple they received further evidence of the character of him whom they called their Rabbi. In one of the outer courts of the Temple there was a market where the pilgrims coming from distant parts could purchase animals for the sacrifices, and where those who came from distant parts could exchange their foreign coins for the sacred shekel which alone was accepted as currency by the priests in the Temple.

Naturally there was much cheating at these tables, and throughout the market there was a noisy bickering and haggling which profaned the holy place and made it seem no better than a bazaar. Jesus was revolted by the scenes in this outer court, and with a scourge of small cords he proceeded to drive the sheep and the oxen out of the place. Then, overthrowing the tables of the money-changers, he commanded them all to clear out.

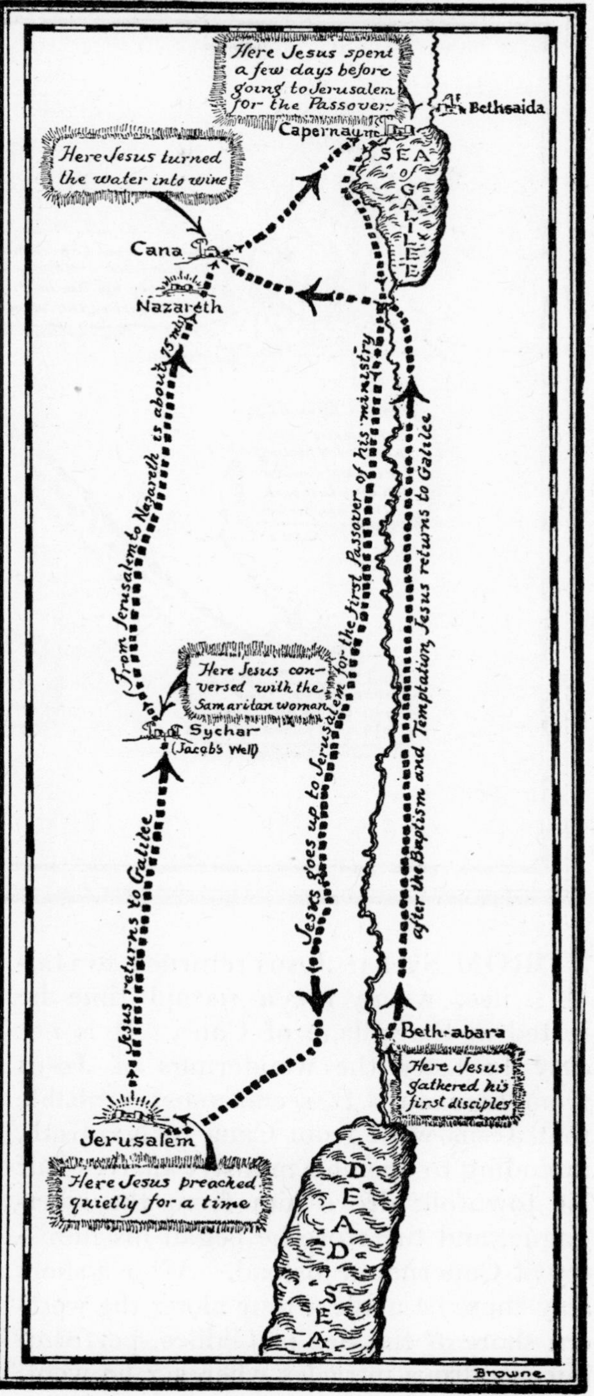

Now it came to pass that about this time John the Baptist, who had never ceased to carry on his prophetic work at Beth-Abara, was flung into prison by Herod Antipas because he dared to denounce the king for his sins. When Jesus learned of this he made haste to leave Judea, for he realized it was not quite safe for any prophet to remain there just then. Together with his followers he set out at once to return to Galilee by way of Samaria, which was the shortest route. On the way he stopped to rest by the side of a well in Sychar, the ancient Shechem; and seeing a Samaritan woman go by with her pitcher on her head, he begged her for a little water to drink. Now the Samaritans were despised by the Jews, for they were considered to be a half-breed race, and therefore the woman was astounded that Jesus, who obviously was a Jew, should lower himself to ask for water from her pitcher. Whereupon Jesus revealed to her that he was the Messiah, and she hurriedly went to the city and told them what manner of a man she had met. Then the people of Sychar welcomed Jesus, and he tarried with them two whole days, during which period many others besides that woman became assured he was none other than the Savior.

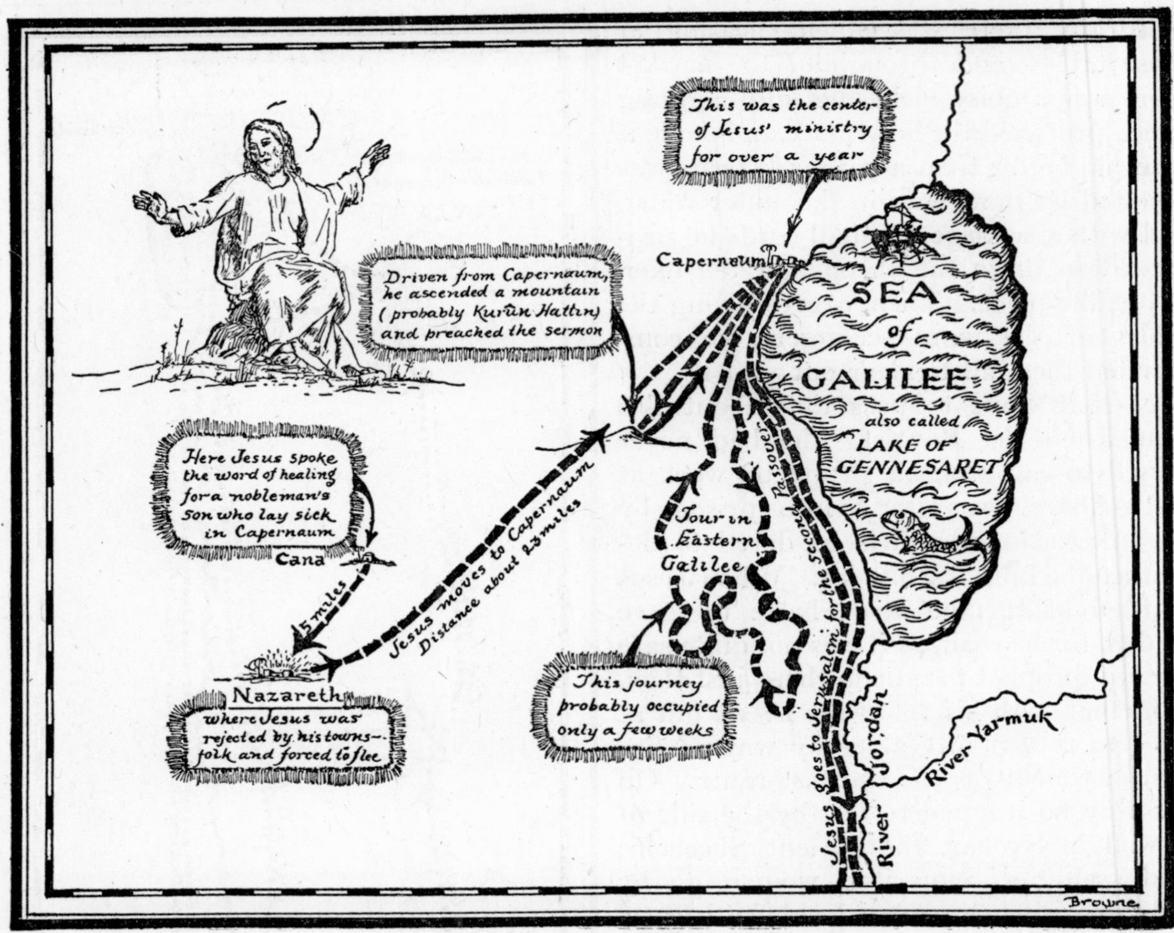

FROM Sychar Jesus returned to Galilee, where for a second time he rested in the village of Cana. It is not easy to trace the wanderings of Jesus from here on. It seems most probable that Jesus went from Cana to Nazareth, intending to open his ministry there. But his townfolk drove him from the synagogue, and therefore he began his ministry at Capernaum instead. After a short stay there he made a tour along the western shore of the Sea of Galilee, performing wondrous miracles wherever he went. Then, according to the Gospel of John, he went up a second time to Jerusalem for the Passover. But on his return to Capernaum he found enemies plotting against him there, and therefore he left the city and went up with his followers into the hills. Jesus realized it was not good for him to continue wandering about alone, and decided to surround himself with a band of loyal supporters. After a night spent on a mountain top in solemn meditation, he formally appointed twelve disciples, giving them their instructions in that great homily which we call the "Sermon on the Mount."

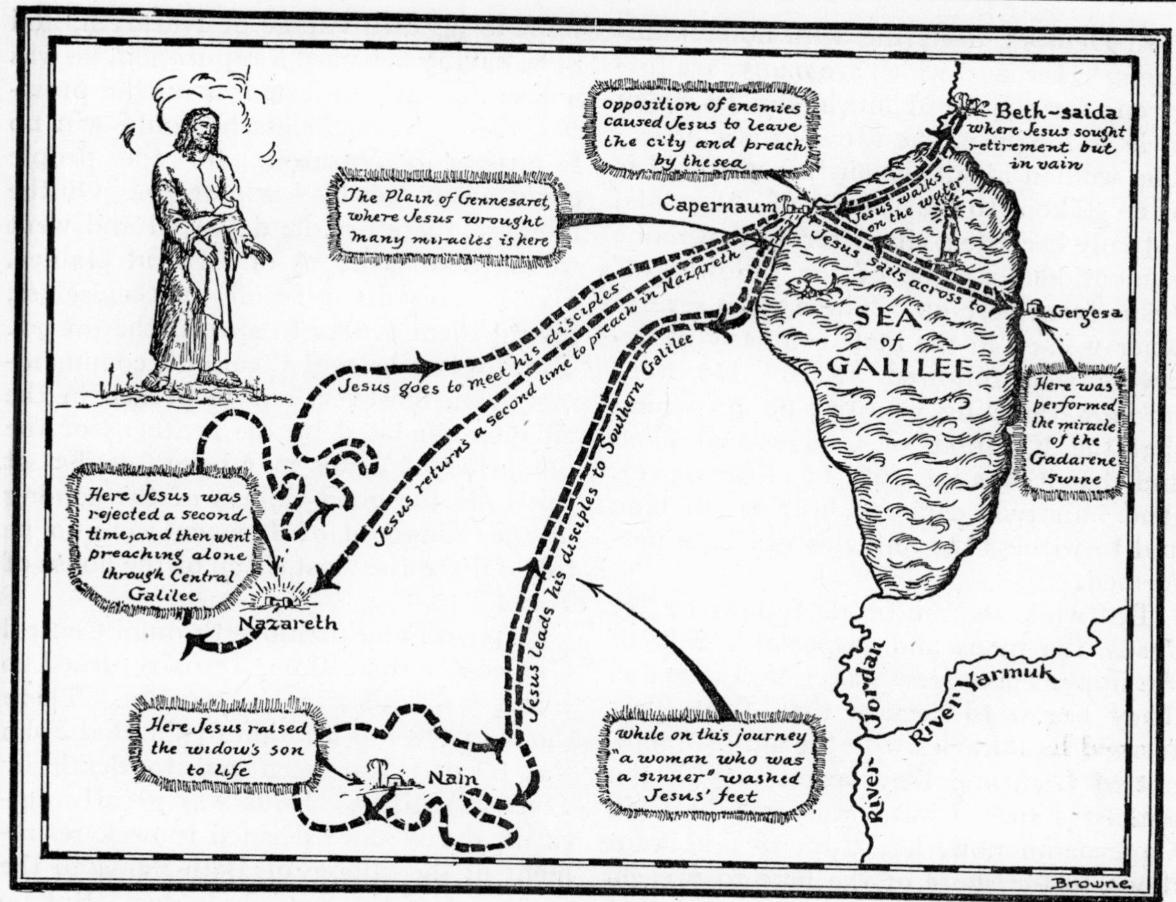

WHEN Jesus had finished preaching the Sermon on the Mount, he returned with his disciples to Capernaum, where he healed the slave of a friendly Roman officer. He remained, however, only one day in Capernaum, for he saw that he could best spread his teaching by going out and preaching through the countryside. Together with his followers he went up into Central Galilee, preaching and performing miracles along the way. At the village of Nain, Jesus raised a widow's son from the dead. Perhaps at this same time and place he received certain messengers from John the Baptist, who was anxious to learn whether Jesus was indeed the long-awaited Messiah.

Another memorable incident on this journey was the meeting with the scarlet woman. Jesus had been invited to eat in the house of a Pharisee named Simon, and there he was approached by a strange woman who anointed him with a costly unguent and washed his feet and dried them with her flowing locks. Now this woman was obviously a "sinner," and the host, who was a very strict man, marveled that Jesus would permit such a creature to approach him. But Jesus explained his conduct with the simple parable of the

Two Debtors, declaring with noble kindliness, "Her sins, which are many, are forgiven; for she loved much: but to whom little is forgiven, the same loveth little." The woman about whom this was said is often taken to be Mary of Magdala, but only because a character by that name is mentioned as one of the followers of Jesus from here on. There were several other women in the little company of believers who followed Jesus. He went through the hilly countryside preaching that the Kingdom of God was at hand and that it was the duty of all to repent. And hundreds came to hearken to him, and to witness the miracles which he performed.

But while the multitude followed after Jesus, the pious and respectable folk of the upper class grew increasingly hostile. They began to declare that Jesus performed his miracles with the aid of Satan, not of God, and they began to plot evil against him. Jesus, who was back in Capernaum now, left the city and went down to the shore of the lake to preach. And so tremendous was the crowd that came out to hear him that he had to go out in a fishing vessel and preach while floating there at the water's edge. That same evening Jesus and his disciples rowed across the lake to the eastern shore, stilling a tempest on the way. They landed near a village called Gerasa, and there Jesus performed the miracle of healing a madman, sending his many evil spirits into a herd of swine. This miracle, while it helped the madman, incensed the people who owned the swine, and they as much as ordered Jesus to leave the country. So Jesus returned to the western side of the lake. For a second time he went to his own village of Nazareth, and now, having achieved a reputation, he was not so abruptly rejected as on the previous visit. Nevertheless he could win no followers in Nazareth, for the people could not forget his lowly origin. On the morrow, therefore, he departed and went to the other villages of Central Galilee. He sent his disciples off by themselves, giving them orders to spread the gospel. Two by two he sent them out, commanding them, however, not to preach in the villages inhabited by the heathens or the Samaritans. Jesus may have felt that at this time the good tidings of the coming of the Kingdom of Heaven were to be told only to the "lost sheep of the house of Israel."

After wandering alone through Central Galilee for some time, Jesus returned to join his disciples in Capernaum. There the sad news was brought to him that John the Baptist had been put to death by Herod Antipas. Jesus was greatly agitated and at once decided to seek retirement in the village of Beth-Saida to the northeast of the Sea of Galilee. But no sooner had he reached this place than he found a great multitude awaiting him, and once more he had to preach and perform miracles. With five barley loaves and two small fishes he fed a multitude of five thousand. Whereupon the people were so impressed that they wished to take Jesus by force and make him their king. The incident is significant. Evidently most of those to whom Jesus ministered could not begin to understand what manner of a person he was. They imagined him to be one who would lead them in a great war against Rome. But what Jesus desired to preach was not war against Rome but peace with God, and therefore he hastily withdrew from the excited mob. He ordered his disciples to take ship and cross the lake again, he himself walking on the water that very night. They landed at the Plain of Gennesaret, just south of Capernaum, and there Jesus performed more miracles. Thence they returned to Capernaum, where Jesus completed his Galilean ministry by preaching in the synagogue the famous discourse on the "bread of life" which is to be found in John 6:25-57.

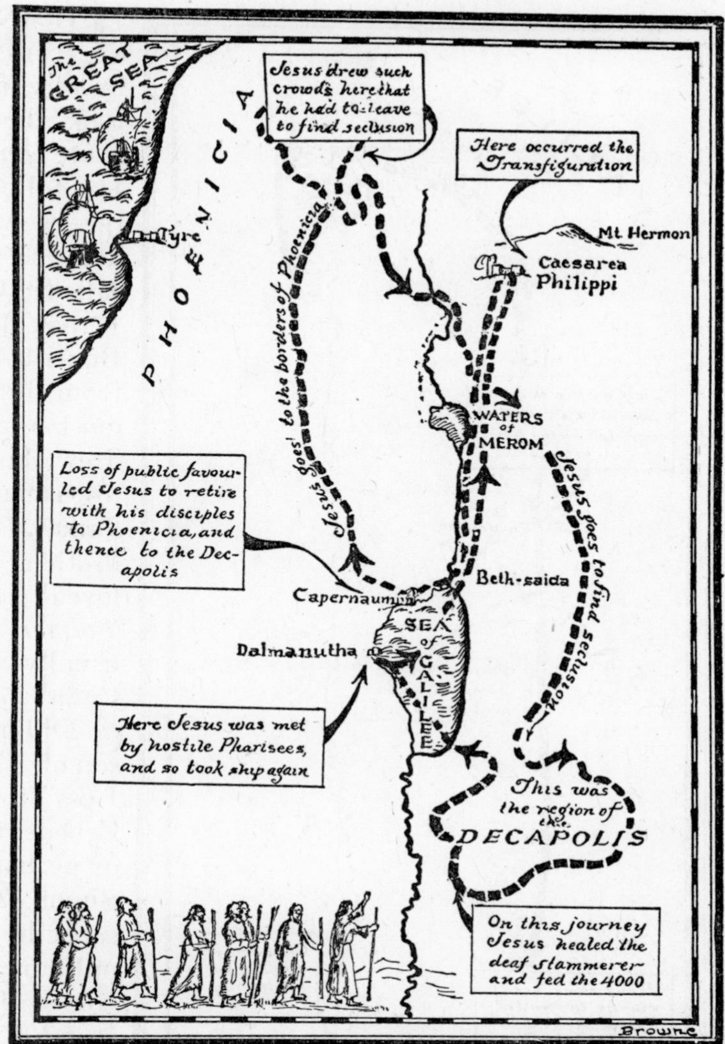

But that discourse offended many of Jesus' own followers, and only the twelve disciples retained their faith in him. So together with them Jesus fled toward Phoenicia, which was heathen territory. But even here people continued to seek him out because of his miraculous powers, and finally he was compelled to cross Galilee once more and seek seclusion in the Decapolis, which was also inhabited by Gentiles. But here again the people came to him for healing. After a while, therefore, he sailed back across the Sea of Galilee to the city of Dalmanutha, and thence almost at once to the village of Beth-Saida. From here he pushed northward to the city of Cæsarea Philippi, where he remained several days. It was during this stay that Peter openly declared to Jesus: "Thou art the Christ, the son of the living God." And thereupon, Jesus foretold how he would have to go up to Jerusalem, suffer death, and after three days rise again. With three of the disciples he then went up into one of the numerous mountain ranges in the neighborhood and there was miraculously transfigured.

The little company then returned to Capernaum and after dwelling there quietly for some time, they turned their faces southward and went up to Jerusalem.

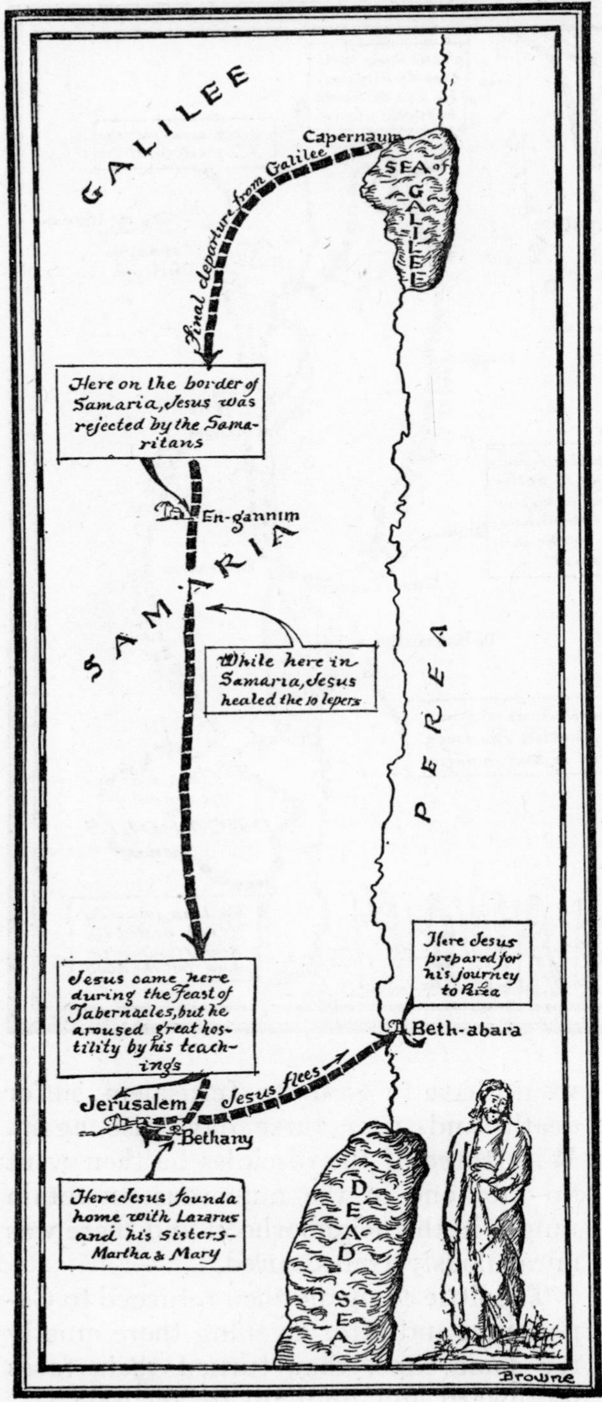

JESUS did not follow the usual caravan route which went to Jerusalem by way of the Jordan Valley. Instead he took the shorter but far more difficult route across the mountains of Samaria. His followers were few, chief among them the twelve disciples. It might be well to name them here: (1) Simon, who was also called Cephas ("stone") or Peter ("rock"), a former disciple of John the Baptist, and a native of Beth-Saida, who from first to last seems to have been the most important of the disciples; (2) Andrew, his brother; (3) Philip, a fellow-townsman of Simon and Andrew; (4) James, the son of Zebedee; (5) his brother, John, "the disciple whom Jesus loved"; (6) Bartholomew (that is, *Bar-Tolmai* "the son of Tolmai"), who is usually identified with Nathanael from Cana; (7) Matthew or Levi; (8) Thomas or Didymus ("a twin"); (9) James, the son of Alpheus, usually referred to as "the Less" to distinguish him from the son of Zebedee; (10) Judas Thaddeus, a brother or perhaps a son of James the Less; (11) Simon Zelotes, so named probably because he had belonged to the Zealots, the militant rebels against Rome, before he joined Jesus; (12) Judas Iscariot (that is, *Ish-Kerioth,* "a man of Kerioth," which was a little village in Judea). With these disciples and a handful of other followers, probably most of them women, Jesus made his way to the village of Bethany, near Jerusalem, where he found shelter in the house of Lazarus and his sisters, Martha and Mary. Thence he made an excursion to the Temple, but aroused so much opposition by his preaching there that he was compelled to flee at once to Beth-Abara across the Jordan.

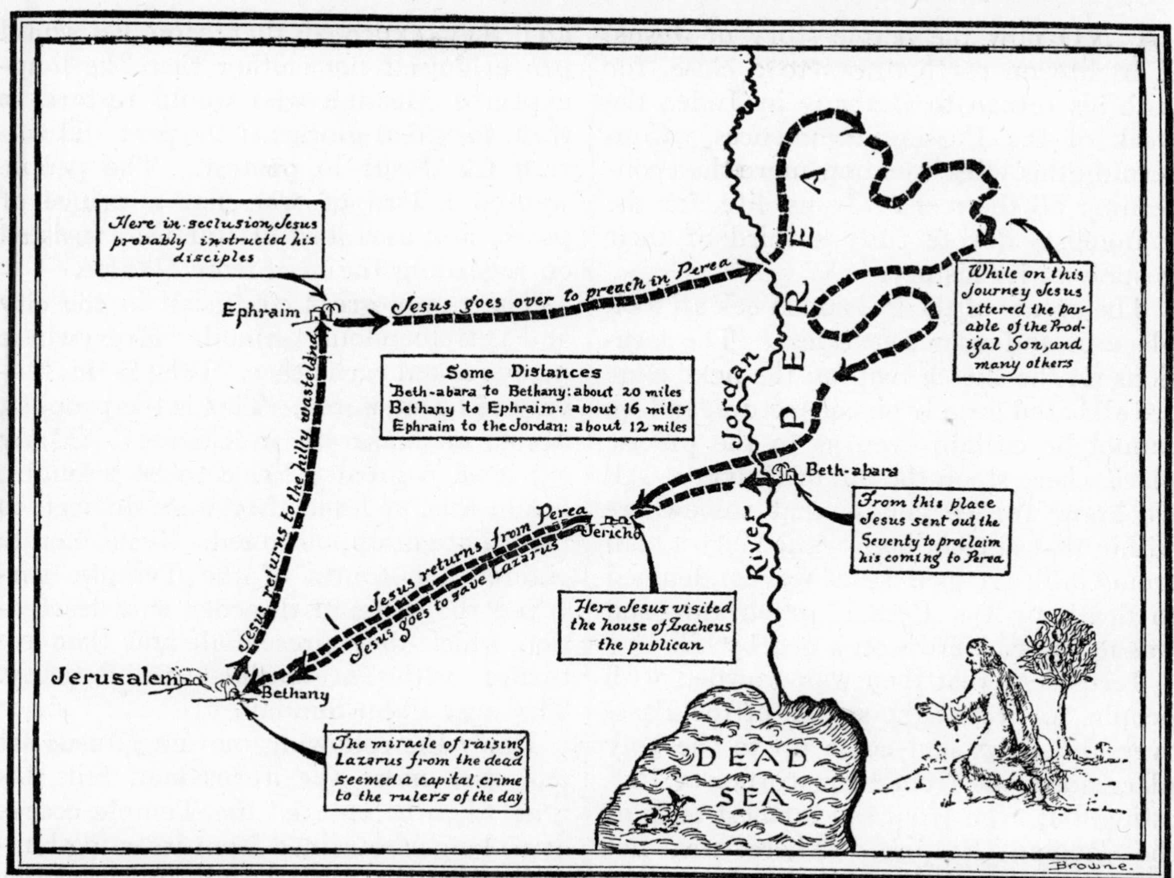

JESUS saw that Judea was not yet ready for his gospel, and he determined to preach for a while in the villages of Perea, on the east of the Jordan. But before he could set out on this journey he heard that Lazarus was desperately ill in Bethany, and he hastened to his rescue. By the time, however, that Jesus reached Bethany, Lazarus was already dead, and there was nothing left save to raise him to life again. This Jesus did, and the miracle aroused so much excitement among the populace that the elders of the Jews were terrified. They feared the Roman officials might take the excitement to be the prelude to a new uprising, and might immediately begin a reign of terror. In self-defense, therefore, the Sanhedrin, the court of the Jews, resolved to put Jesus out of the way. But Jesus was forewarned of this decision, and straightway went across the hills to Ephraim, a village in southern Samaria. Here he and his disciples remained in quiet until, after several weeks, they felt it safe to cross over the Jordan into the province of Perea. There Jesus ministered for some time, performing few miracles but preaching many of his most beautiful parables. And finally, feeling the time was ripe, he girded his loins and made ready to return to Judea.

AND now the heroic story of Jesus' life on earth draws to a close, for with his return to Bethany in Judea the week of the Passion commences. Concerning this week we know more than concerning all the rest of Jesus' life, for the evangelists devote fully a third of their gospels to its history.

The events of the Passion Week all took place in and near Jerusalem. The locations on the sketch map on the next page are all based largely on conjecture, and we cannot be certain even as to the precise place where stood the hill of Calvary. All we know for certain is that somewhere within that ancient high-walled city a man from Galilee named Jesus was condemned to death by the Roman procurator and was nailed to a cross on a nearby hill.

Jerusalem just then was crowded with people, for it was the season of the Passover and Jews had come up to the holy place not alone from every corner of Palestine, but even from the farthest ends of the Roman Empire. There was not nearly room enough within the city for the great multitude, and hundreds of the pilgrims were quartered in the villages nearby.

Jesus and his followers stopped in Bethany, which was less than an hour's walk from the capital. Every day for three days Jesus made the journey to Jerusalem from Lazarus' house where he lodged. On the first day he entered in great triumph, for the populace knew of his coming and hailed him with hosannas. To them he was a great military hero whom they looked to as their deliverer from the hated Roman, and they strewed his path with palm leaves. They called him their Messiah and the Son of David, and they expected that soon he would prove himself none other than the long-expected Messiah who would restore to them the great glories of the past. It was vain for Jesus to protest. The people wanted a lord of war, not a prince of peace, and as a lord of war they insisted on regarding the man from Galilee.

There was great confusion in the city and a tremendous turmoil. Everywhere people asked each other, "Who is this?"—only to be answered, "This is the prophet, Jesus, of Nazareth in Galilee." Many expected a great miracle to be wrought, but in this, at least, they were doomed to immediate disappointment. Jesus merely entered the courts of the Temple, surveyed the scene of disorder and desecration which they presented, and then returned with his disciples to Bethany. That was Palm Sunday.

Early the following morning Jesus set out once more for Jerusalem, but this time when he entered the Temple courts he no longer refrained from asserting himself. For the second time in his career he drove the merchants and the money-changers out of the Temple, declaring with righteous wrath that God's house was not for thievish traffic but for prayer and praise.

On the third day he returned again to Jerusalem, this time occupying himself with preaching to the people. The officials both of the priests and the rabbis came to him with many questions, striving to trip him into some statement which would prove him either a blasphemer against God or a rebel against Rome. Toward the close of the day Jesus retired with his disciples to the Mount of Olives which overlooks the city. There he sat

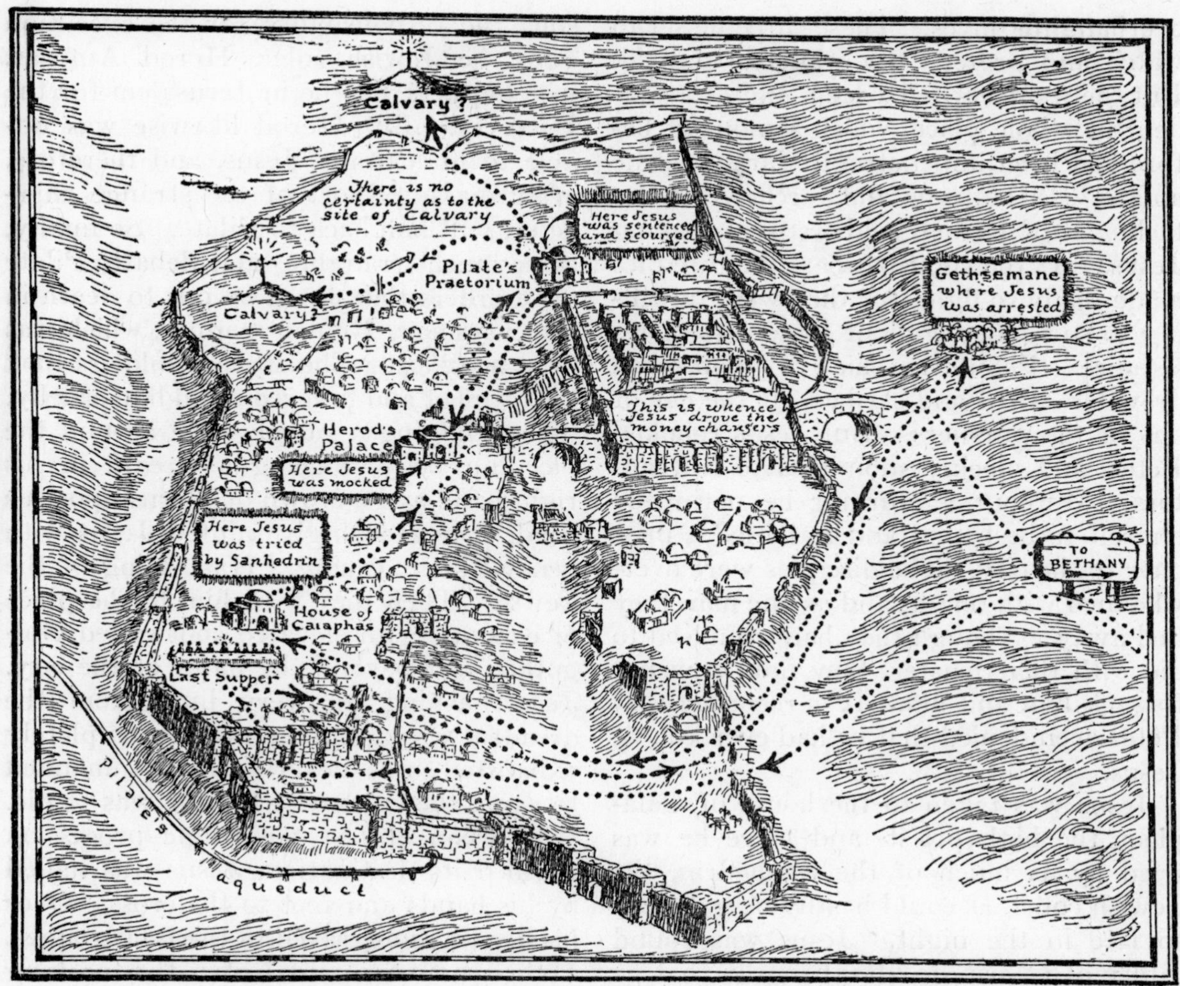

and prophesied the things which were soon to come to pass.

It is probable that the next day Jesus remained in Bethany, for we have no record of any event that transpired on it. On the evening of the fourth day, however, Jesus and his disciples came once more to Jerusalem. They gathered in a room which tradition claims to have been in a house on Mount Zion, and there ate what was destined to be the Last Supper; and there they listened to the last words of their leader. Jesus knew that the end of his earthly days had come. Near midnight he left the supper room and went with his disciples across the valley to a secluded spot called Gethsemane, east of the city. It was a place where olive trees grew in abundance, and where one might be safe from pursuit. He left the greater number of his disciples on the outskirts of the wooded spot and took only three of his closest followers with him when he advanced farther into the shadow of the overhanging olives. These three he set to watch and protect him while he prayed. But the watchers fell asleep, and of a sudden the whole place, which a moment before had been impenetrably dark, became ablaze with lanterns and torches. A detachment of Roman soldiers were seeking Jesus. At the sight of them the disciples made ready to fight, for they were unwilling to surrender without some sort of resistance. Peter, the chief of them, even drew his sword and slashed off the ear of one of the pursuers. But Jesus rebuked Peter, and meekly submitted to his captors. Without a murmur he permitted himself to be bound and to be led a prisoner to the city. The disciples were overwhelmed with terror, and as one man they fled away. Though they had promised to die with their master, they now cravenly forsook him and hid. It is recorded that Peter even denied that he had ever known Jesus.

Jesus was taken to the house of Caiaphas, the high priest, and there he was tried by as much of the Sanhedrin, the Jewish court, as could hastily be gathered so late in the night. Jesus was found guilty of uttering a blasphemy in that he dared to proclaim himself the Messiah, the Son of God. In Israel in that day such a claim was counted a capital crime, and Jesus was sentenced by the priests.

But it was impossible for the Jews to administer capital punishment, for the right had been taken from them when their land became a Roman province. Accordingly Jesus was taken over to the house where Pilate, the Roman procurator, was living just then. Pilate questioned Jesus, but, unable to make out just what the Galilean stood for, he tried to shift the responsibility for the execution onto the Jewish ruler, Herod Antipas, who happened to be in Jerusalem for the Passover. But Herod likewise was unable to understand Jesus, and therefore, after making sport of the strange character, sent him back to Pilate. So finally, after much wrangling and debate, Pilate gave orders that Jesus be put to death in the customary Roman manner, which was by crucifixion. The Roman soldiers took the prophet and first scourged him cruelly. Then, flinging a purple robe around the bleeding body, placing a wreath in his right hand and a crown of thorns upon his head, they mockingly saluted Jesus with bended knee, crying, "Hail, King of the Jews." Then they took him to the place of execution, an elevated spot called Golgotha, just beyond the gates of the city. Jesus, aching in every limb from the dreadful scourging, and almost completely exhausted, was nevertheless commanded to carry the cross on which he was to die. And when at last the tragic procession reached its destination, Jesus was nailed by his hands and feet to the cross. Over his head was engraved in three languages, Hebrew, Greek, and Latin, the mocking phrase: "This is Jesus, the Nazarene, King of the Jews." To embitter his last moments still further, the Romans crucified two thieves with him; but Jesus was not moved to wrath. "Father, forgive them," was his only prayer, "for they know not what they do."

Until eventide he hung there thus, and then, too broken to withstand the torment any longer, Jesus cried out: ***Eloi, Eloi, Lama Sabachthani?*** ("My God, my God, why hast thou forsaken me?") And then "he gave up the ghost."

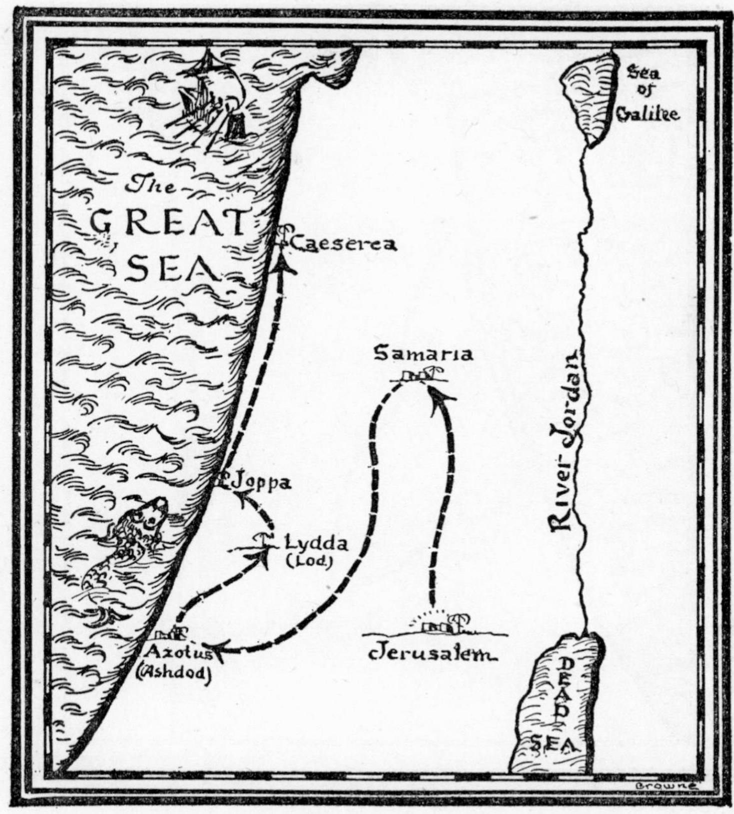

BUT that was not the end of Jesus; in a profound sense it was rather the beginning. The Bible tells us how after three days Jesus arose again from the dead, and his resurrected body was seen in one place after another by certain of those who had followed him on earth. The first recorded appearance was that seen by Mary Magdalene at Jerusalem on the morning of the Resurrection Day. That afternoon Jesus appeared also to Peter, and to two disciples who may have been in hiding at a village called Emmaus, not far from Jerusalem. That same evening ten of the disciples were visited by the spirit, and a week later all eleven disciples saw the resurrected Jesus. (The twelfth disciple, Judas Iscariot, had betrayed Jesus to the Romans when they came to arrest him at Gethsemane, and had afterwards hanged himself in shame.) During forty days these various appearances occurred in Jerusalem and in Galilee, and at the end of that time Jesus ascended into heaven with the solemn promise that soon he would return once more to the earth.

And then a new sect of Judaism gradually arose in Jerusalem and Galilee. It was not yet a new religion, for its followers were strict and pious Jews who differed from their co-religionists only in that they believed the Messiah had already come. They had no idea of preaching their beliefs to the Gentiles, for they firmly believed that the only door into their brotherhood was through the profession of Judaism and through the rite of circumcision. The members of this sect were probably for the most part Galileans, and were certainly simple people of humble station. But after a while they began to gather to their company a number of Jews who had come in contact with the great outside world, and were not so narrow as the Palestinians. But they were earnest, pious folk nevertheless, and they were won over to the sect of the Nazarenes because of the tremendous enthusiasm of its members. The converts, old and new, lived together as in one family. No doubt they were all very poor, and they shared in common the little which

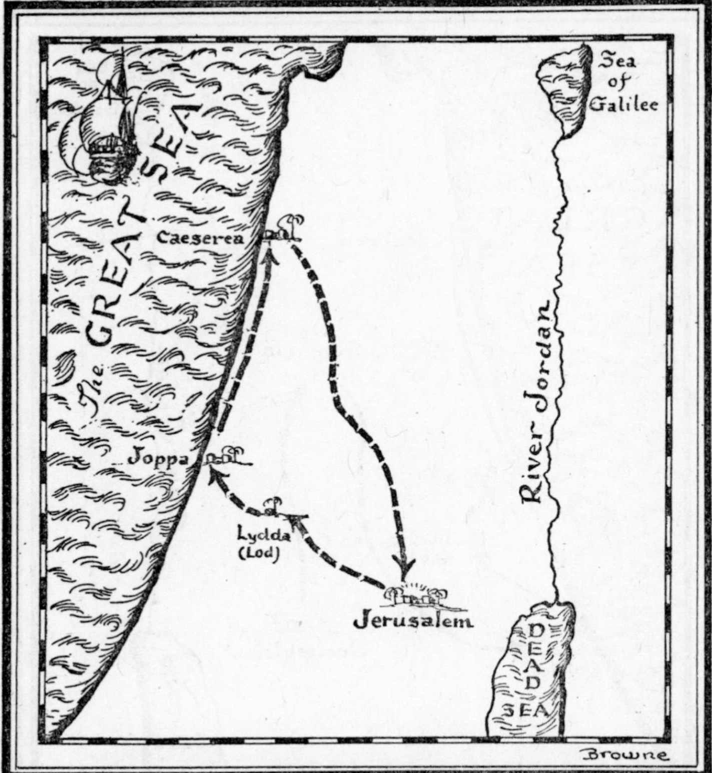

they possessed. They were firmly convinced that in but a little while their Savior would return, and the Kingdom of Heaven be established on earth, and for that reason they would not concern themselves much about earthly things. Their only desire was to win as many souls as possible to the belief in the risen Jesus, for they felt it their duty to prepare as many people as possible for his second coming. But in the beginning they carried on their missionary activity only among their fellow Jews. Not until the Hellenized members in the sect became more numerous than the provincial Palestinians was any attempt made to preach the good tidings even among the half-Jews dwelling in Samaria.

The first missionary to preach to people outside the fold of Jewry was a man named Philip, himself one of the Hellenized Jews. Driven from Jerusalem by persecutors of the sect, he went up and down the countryside, spreading the tidings that the Messiah had already come and was now waiting to come a second time. The path he followed is traced on the map on the preceding page. He halted in Cæsarea, and there he remained some twenty years, no doubt continuing to spread the gospel all the time.

A second missionary to dare to accept Gentiles into the fellowship of the Nazarenes was none other than Peter, who had been chief of the disciples. After the death of Jesus he became virtually the head of the little sect in Jerusalem, and he seems at first to have been opposed to the idea of preaching the gospel to non-Jews. But after some years he went forth to visit the little churches which Philip had established, and on this journey he was completely converted to the policy of the Hellenists. At Cæsarea he formally accepted into the sect a Roman centurion named Cornelius, baptizing him in the name of Jesus, without first requiring the man to become circumcised. The act did not pass unnoticed, however. When Peter returned to Jerusalem he had to justify his action to the strict Jews in the sect. He was not deposed from his position at the head of the Jerusalem brotherhood; but many of the members remained bitterly opposed to the new tendency.

BUT the greatest of all the missionaries was a certain Jew named Saul, or Paul, a native of Tarsus in Asia Minor. He had first come to Jerusalem to study under the rabbis there, for though he was from a Hellenized city, and though his father was a citizen of the Roman Empire, Saul was a strict Pharisee. When first he came to Jerusalem he bitterly opposed the little group of Jews who believed that the Messiah had already come in the person of Jesus, and he joined in the riot against them which ended in the death of one of their chief men, Stephen, and in the flight of many of the others. Even more, he set out in pursuit of a number of the fugitives when he learnt they were spreading their heresy in Damascus. But on the way to that city he saw a vision of Jesus and became himself suddenly converted to the new faith. When he reached Damascus he joined the fugitives and there began to preach their own doctrine of the risen Christ. For a while he wandered in what is described as "Arabia," but what was probably the desert region to the south of Damascus. From there he returned to Damascus and thence to Jerusalem, where he was accepted into the mother church. Then he returned to Tarsus, his birthplace, and lived in retirement for several years.

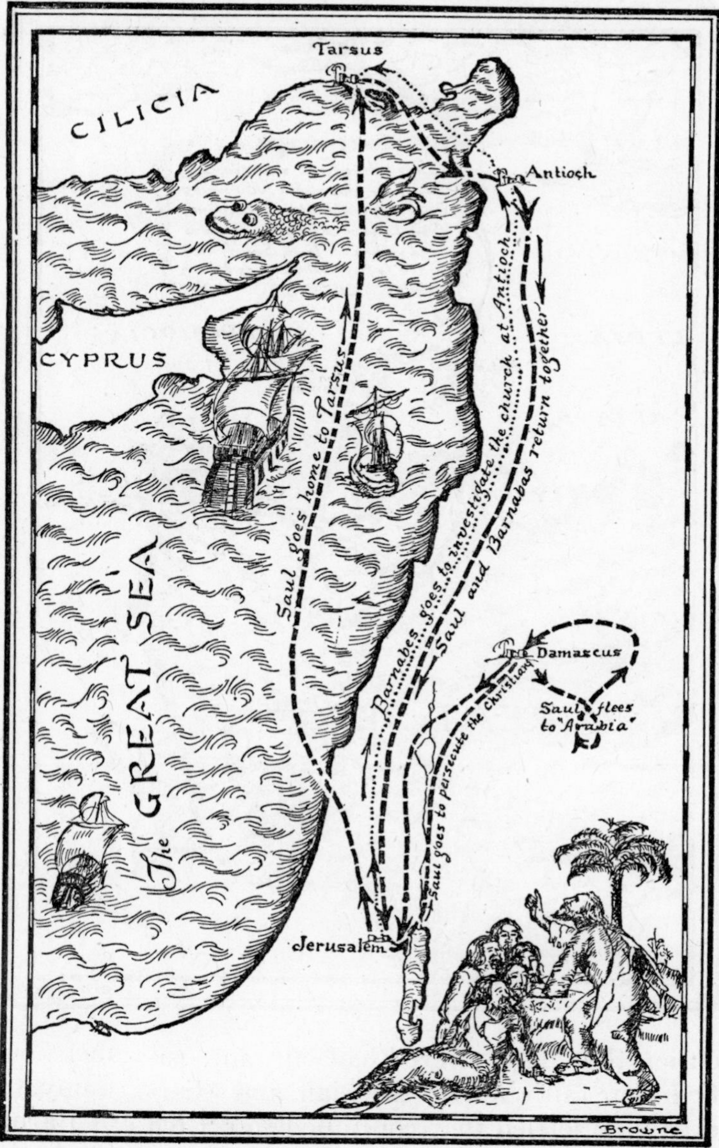

Now after the first great riot against the Nazarenes in Jerusalem, the Hellenized element in the sect was scattered far and wide. Some of its members, as we already know, sought refuge in Damascus; others, like Philip, took to Cæsarea; still others found a resting place in the important Syrian city of Antioch. The perse-

cution they had suffered had only intensified their faith in their Messiah, and wherever they settled they continued to preach the gospel of his second coming. At first they preached in the synagogues and only to the Jews, but later they began to preach also to the Gentiles. Especially in Antioch did they preach to the non-Jews, and there before anywhere else the movement actually broke from the synagogue and became a religion of its own. The members here were drawn in increasing numbers from the pagan population, and were freely baptized without being required to accept the Holy Law of the Jews. They called themselves "Christians," a name derived from the Greek word *Christos,* which is the equivalent of the Hebrew *Messiah,* and means "Anointed One."

When news of this radical development reached Jerusalem there was much concern, for the believers left behind in Jerusalem were all strict Jews. Accordingly they sent one of their number, Barnabas, to investigate the situation in Antioch. Barnabas was completely won over by what he saw, and instead of returning to Jerusalem with complaints he remained in Antioch to direct the work. In a little while he felt the need for a co-worker, and therefore went over to Tarsus, which was not far away, to persuade Paul to join him. Paul agreed, and from then on for some years the two men worked together in great harmony.

Barnabas and Paul labored together at Antioch for a year, and the organization they developed there became one of the most important in the early history of Christianity. They interrupted their ministry to go down to Jerusalem with a gift from Antioch to the poor disciples in Jerusalem. Having delivered this gift they returned to Antioch and remained there until they were ready to undertake their first great missionary journey together.

Paul and Barnabas took with them on this first long journey a relative of the latter whose name was Mark. The three men took ship from Seleucia, about sixteen miles from Antioch, and sailed to the island of Cyprus about sixty miles from the coast. Their first stopping place was at Salamis, where they preached in the synagogue. Then they crossed the island, preaching on the way, until they came to Paphos. Thence they set sail for Attalia in Asia Minor, a distance of about one hundred and seventy miles. Without halting they moved on to Perga, a Greek city about eight miles from the sea, but here their young assistant, Mark, deserted them. So now Paul and Barnabas traveled alone. They went to Antioch in the province of Pisidia, where Paul preached at length in the synagogue and was able to make a few converts. But before the work could get well under way there, the elders of the synagogue drove the two agitators out of the city and they fled to Iconium, some eighty miles away. Here again they aroused bitter opposition, so they pushed on to Lystra. Here, too, they suffered persecution, and Paul was even stoned. They went on to Derbe, where for a change they were allowed to labor in peace. Thence they might have been able to make their way across the mountains to Tarsus without much difficulty; but they refused. Despite the obvious danger involved, they turned in their tracks and went back to each of the cities they had just visited. And thus they made their way home to Antioch.

The second missionary journey began with an unfortunate disagreement between Paul and Barnabas, and the two men parted company. Barnabas went with Mark to Cyprus, and Paul, taking with him a young man named Silas, or Sylvanus, set out for Asia Minor. Unfortunately the New Testament has almost no record of the work which Barnabas did. We are informed only of the adventures of Paul, and therefore we are able to follow none other. Starting from Antioch over land, Paul visited the churches of Syria and then pushed on into Asia Minor. He revisited Derbe, Lystra, and the other cities where he and Barnabas had founded little churches on the first journey. Paul's path is traced on the map on the following page, but only with approximate accuracy, for we are not told the names of the new cities which he visited. All we know is that, after wandering for a time in Galatia, Paul and Silas together with a third companion, Timothy, who had joined them at Lystra, got as far as Troas, the ancient city of Troy. Here they were joined by a fourth missionary, Luke, who later wrote the Third Gospel and the Book of Acts.

From Troas the little company crossed over to Europe, and at the ancient town of Philippi they won their first European convert. But there again the missionaries encountered opposition. Paul and Silas were scourged and imprisoned, and were set free only by a miracle. They moved on to Amphipolis, but finding no synagogue or Jewish population there, the missionaries moved on by way of Apollonia to Thessalonica. Here there was a large Jewish population and a synagogue in which Paul preached during three Sabbaths. He succeeded in found-

ing a church mostly of Gentiles, and by this act so enraged the Jews that he and his companions were compelled to flee the city by night.

The missionaries then moved to Berea, where they were so well received that to this day "Bereans" is the name given to eager students of the Bible. Thence Paul moved to the great old city of Athens, where he was given an opportunity to lecture before the philosophers. But he failed to impress them, and therefore he moved on to Corinth, where he had better success. Here he remained for a year and a half, supporting himself by his trade, which was that of a tentmaker. He lived in the home of two earnest converts, Aquila and Priscilla, and spent all his free time spreading the gospel either by word of mouth in Corinth or by letters written to other cities.

When he finally left Corinth, Paul set sail for Asia Minor, taking with him his friends, Aquila and Priscilla. These he left in Ephesus to try to create a church there, while he himself went on to Jerusalem to deliver a sum of money for the relief of the poorer members of the brotherhood there. This money had been gathered from among Paul's converts in Asia Minor and Greece. It demonstrated the fine spirit of those Gentile Christians, and no doubt greatly influenced the attitude of the strict Jewish brethren in the mother church at Jerusalem. Once he had delivered the gift, Paul saw no reason for remaining longer in Jerusalem, and immediately returned to Antioch.

THE third missionary journey lasted almost four years. Following his previous course over land, Paul revisited the churches of Asia Minor, going as far as Ephesus, where Aquila and Priscilla had been laboring for some time. Here Paul found a small community of Jews who belonged to a sect which still maintained that John the Baptist had been the Messiah. He won them over to his own belief, and for three months waged an aggressive campaign among the rest of the Jews and also the inquiring Gentiles. But fierce opposition arose on the part of the elders of the synagogue, and Paul was driven to take a most serious step: he actually called the believers in Christ right out of the Jewish communion. And thus was the Christian church formally brought into being.

Paul remained in Ephesus two years. Then he went north to Troas, and thence over the water to Philippi. He revisited the various churches he had created on his second journey, making a circuit through all of Thessaly, Greece, and Macedonia. Then he returned to Troas, walked over land to Assos, and then set sail for Tyre in Phoenicia. Here he found a church already existent, and he preached in it all during one week. He preached also to the Christian brotherhood which he found already established at Ptolemais, the next port at which his vessel called. Then, though gravely warned against it, he proceeded to Jerusalem.

As we already know, many of the brethren in Jerusalem had all along looked with disfavor upon Paul's missionary labors among the Gentiles, and by now they had grown almost dangerously antagonistic. So when Paul arrived in the Holy City his friends urged him to go with some of his converts to the Temple and thus prove that he had not forsworn his ancestral faith. Paul agreed, but his conduct was misunderstood. He was recognized by certain of the orthodox Jews, and when they saw his companions they leaped to the conclusion that Paul was trying to desecrate the holy shrine by bringing Gentiles into the Inner Court. A mob fell upon him and would have beaten him to death there and then had not the Roman sentries interfered. To save him from the mob Paul was taken in chains to the fortress of Antipatris in Samaria, and thence to Cæsarea. Here he languished in prison for two years, until at last, despairing of ever receiving justice at the hands of the local rulers, he exercised his right as a citizen of the empire and appealed to the supreme court at Rome. After a stormy and perilous voyage, he finally reached Rome, where he was kept a prisoner two years more. What occurred then we do not know. A very ancient tradition tells us that Paul, after being acquitted, continued his missionary work for a time. But later he was re-arrested and was executed just outside the city of Rome.

Pontus
Euxinus
THRACIA
BITHYNIA
MYSIA
PHRYGIA
Pergamos
Thyatira
LYDIA
Sardis
Smyrna
Philadelphia
Ephesus
Laodicea
CARIA
PISIDIA
LYCIA
Mare
Lycium
Browne

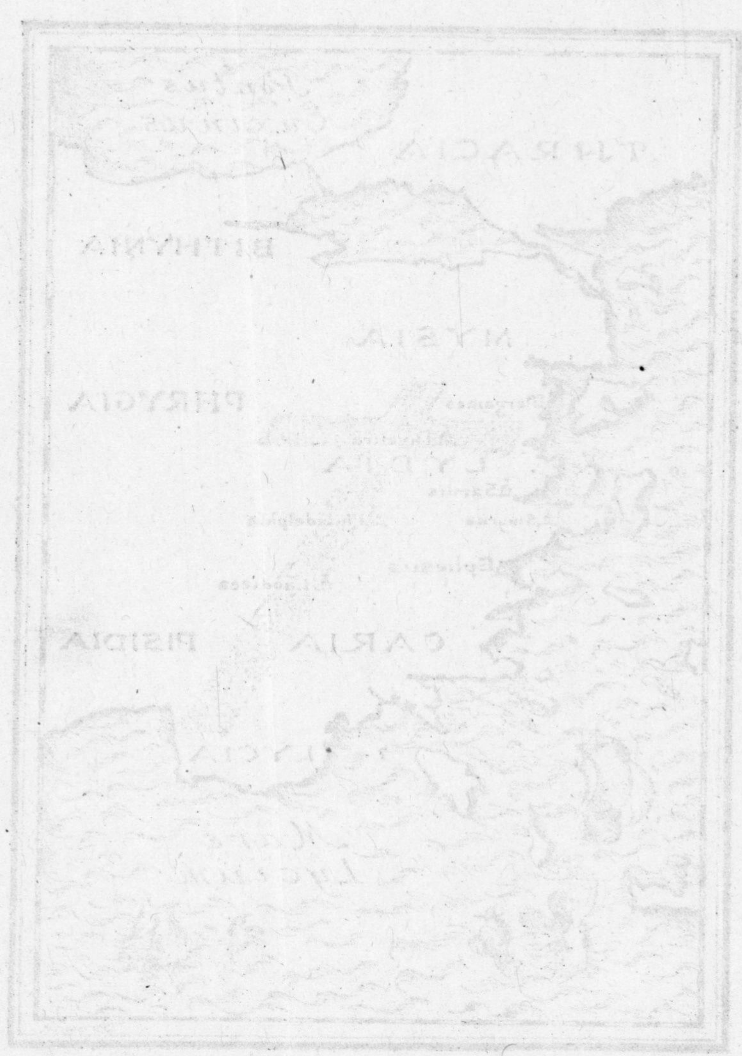

SUMMARY OF THE BOOKS OF THE CHRISTIAN SCRIPTURES

SUMMARY OF THE BOOKS OF THE CHRISTIAN SCRIPTURES

THE Gospels are four in number, each describing the life and words of Jesus from an individual point of view, and each seemingly intended for a particular group of readers.

(1) *St. Matthew* is interested chiefly in the past, and writes primarily to show the Jews how the life of Jesus fulfilled all the ancient prophecies concerning the coming of the Messiah.

(2) *St. Mark,* on the other hand, lives in the present, and seems to be writing for a Roman public, for his ever-present desire is to give a picture not of a mythical hero, but of a living man.

(3) *St. Luke* has his eyes fixed on the future, and his direct purpose seems to be that of showing his own countrymen, the Greeks, how Jesus was fitted to be the savior of all nations in every age.

(4) *St. John* writes for the instruction of the early Christian church, and considers the philosophic mysteries involved in the whole idea of the incarnate Word of God.

(5) *The Acts of the Apostles.* This book, as its opening verse implies, is the "second part" of the Gospel written by St. Luke. It is a continuation of the story of Jesus, revealing how his spirit guided the early destinies of the church founded in his name. The book opens with the story of the Ascension and then tells of the first gathering of the believers on Pentecost day in Jerusalem. From Jerusalem the scene of the story widens and we learn how the gospel was spread abroad first in Judea, then to Samaria, and finally to the Gentiles throughout the Roman world. Most of the book is concerned with the missionary journeys of Paul, probably because the author, Luke, was Paul's companion on some of these journeys. The book closes abruptly with Paul's imprisonment at Rome.

The Epistles of St. Paul. The ministry of the great "Apostle of the Gentiles" lasted about thirty years. During this time he had occasion to write numerous letters either to encourage those in far places whom he had organized into churches, or to defend himself from his detractors. All the letters extant today belong to the latter half of Paul's ministry. The approximate dating for the various Epistles is as follows:

I & II Thessalonians	A.D. 52-53
I & II Corinthians, Galatians and Romans	A.D. 57-58
Philippians, Colossians, Ephesians, Philemon	A.D. 62-63
Titus, I & II Timothy	A.D. 66-67?

The order in which the Epistles are here individually described is that of our modern versions of the New Testament.

(6) *The Epistle to the Romans* was written by Paul from Corinth just before he went on his final visit to Jerusalem. Paul intended to visit Rome soon, and he wrote this letter partly to prepare the church there to receive him. It gives an account of the doctrines to which he had finally arrived after his long contest with the strict Jews who were in control of the mother church at Jerusalem.

(7) *The First Epistle to the Corinthians* deals with a number of problems which seem to have arisen in the Corinthian church and concerning which the apostle's advice had been asked. The first of these was the question of insubordination which threatened the unity of the church and his own authority. The second problem was that of chastity and marriage. Paul says that those who cannot live the lives of celibates should marry—but forever. There should be no remarriage after separation. Paul maintains, however, it is better not to marry at all, for connubial life tends to hinder complete Christian service. Various other matters are discussed, some of practical importance and others of doctrinal character.

(8) *The Second Epistle to the Corinthians* was written after Paul learnt how his first had been received. The apostle is thankful that his advice was accepted, but he confesses that there is a root of evil still remaining among the Corinthian brethren, and he warns them that those who have tried to undermine his work will not be forgotten when he returns to Corinth.

(9) *The Epistle to the Galatians* was written by Paul after he heard the sad news that the converts he had won in Galatia had forsaken his gospel and were in danger of returning to strict adherence to the Jewish law.

(10) *The Epistle to the Ephesians* seems to have been addressed not to one particular church but to have been a sort of circular letter carried around by its bearer from church to church in Asia Minor. It is in part a theological treatise discussing the place of the church in relation to the whole council of God.

(11) *The Epistle to the Philippians* was written by Paul while he was in chains at Rome. Its main purpose is to express his gratitude to the Philippians for their kindness in sending one of their number to minister to him while a prisoner. Incidentally Paul takes the opportunity to warn them against false teachings and to exhort them to unity, to humility, and to a vigorous striving after holiness.

(12) *The Epistle to the Colossians* was written to a church with which Paul was not personally acquainted. A messenger had brought report of the bewilderment in the church at Colossae because of certain strange theological problems which had been raised there; and the apostle strives to solve these problems.

(13) *The First Epistle to the Thessalonians* was written from Corinth during Paul's first visit to Europe. Paul had founded a church in the important city of Thessalonica, but had been driven from the town before he had been able to establish his work. Once and again he had made plans to return, but in vain. However, he had been able to send his loyal companion, Timothy, to bring cheer to the believers in Thessalonica, and this first Epistle tells of Paul's happiness at the fine report which Timothy had brought back to him.

(14) *The Second Epistle to the Thessalonians,* written soon after the first, was elicited by Paul's concern because in the interim the believers in Thessalonica had suffered persecution, and in their distress had taken refuge in hysterical hopefulness. They had become convinced that the second advent of Christ was almost on them, and in consequence had become improvident and idle. And, much to his chagrin, Paul had heard that his first letter was being used to fan this unhealthy excitement. Accordingly Paul wrote this Second Epistle, seeking to make his doctrine clearer and to guard against further misrepresentation. He tried to sober the Thessalonians by assuring them that the time was far from ripe for the second coming.

(15) *The First Epistle to Timothy* is said to have been written after Paul had been released from his first imprisonment in Rome. Apparently the apostle had revisited Ephesus and had left Timothy there to check the growth of certain wrong ideas to which the Ephesians were attracted. The letter gives advice to Timothy concerning these ideas.

(16) *The Second Epistle to Timothy* was written from Rome at the time of the second imprisonment of Paul. The apostle's life was in jeopardy and some even of his trusted friends had deserted him. The letter begs his "darling son," Timothy, to come to him at once, and to bring Mark with him. Paul does not know whether Timothy will be able to reach him in time, for the sword of the executioner is already hanging over his head. And in that last moment the apostle throws off all restraint and gives full expression to his great love for the younger man who had been his faithful companion during many years.

(17) *The Epistle to Titus* was written before those to Timothy. It is addressed by Paul to one of his young co-workers whom he had left behind in Crete to look after the church there. It gives Titus instructions as to how to manage the difficult task of holding the disorganized church together.

(18) *The Epistle to Philemon* was written by Paul to a Christian whose runaway slave, Onesimus, had been converted and was ready to return in penitence. Paul begs Philemon to be merciful to the repentent wretch and to receive him back in the spirit of true Christian brotherhood.

(19) *The Epistle to the Hebrews* was written to the little brotherhood of Nazarenes in Palestine. We do not know who was its author. Its phraseology, its elaborate symmetry and polished rhetoric, distinguish it markedly from the epistles of Paul. It attempts to bring cheer to the believers, many of whom were deserting the new faith because the promise of the speedy return of Christ had failed so long to materialize.

(20) *The Epistle of St. James* was written probably by the brother of Jesus who became the head of the church at Jerusalem about 62 A.D. It has no theological content but is a fine moral preachment offered to the "faithful" ones scattered throughout the world.

(21) *The First Epistle of St. Peter* was written apparently from Rome and was addressed to the Christians in Asia Minor. It strives to encourage the scattered communities so that they might be able to bear the persecutions which just then had begun to grow increasingly fierce.

(22) *The Second Epistle of St. Peter* was written to the same churches and largely with the same purpose as the first. Among other things it endeavors to rekindle the hope in the promised second coming.

(23) *The Epistles of St. John* are three in number and are concerned with various theological matters.

(24) *The Epistle of St. Jude* was written by a brother of James, and therefore one of the brethren of Jesus. It is addressed to certain Christians who had misinterpreted the teachings of the missionaries and had sunk into all manner of pagan immoralities, claiming that the new-found grace of God granted them the right to indulge themselves as they pleased.

(25) *The Revelation of St. John the Divine,* the closing book of the Bible, is an apocalyptic work—that is, a book which in mysterious symbolism presents the vision of what must happen when the Awful Day at last dawns on the earth, and the Kingdom of Heaven is ushered in.

INDEX TO TEXT AND MAPS

INDEX TO TEXT AND MAPS

N
W
E
S
CAPPADOCIA
CILICIA
Tarsus
Antioch
ASSYRIA
or
GOZAN
PADAN-ARAM
Where Abraham lived and Jacob married
CHITTIM
or
CYPRUS
ARAM now called SYRIA
This is the great
Here many of the Israelites were driven into exile in 722 B.C.
THE GREAT SEA
which is now called
THE MEDITERRANEAN
Phoenicians
Damascus
CANAAN
Jerusalem
Philistines
MOAB
EDOM
THE GREAT DES
A vast dry waste
swarming with ferocious c
of Bedouins
This is
EGYPT
The Wilderness
of the Wanderings
Here lay the
LAND of GOSHEN
where the Hebrews
were held slaves
This is where
THE RED SEA
was crossed by
the Hebrews
This is the great River Nile
Mt. Sinai
This is the
RED SEA
The An
Holy